Better Life and Business: Cell, Brain, Mind and Sex Universal Laws

Authored By

Branko Souček

IRIS, Integrated Reasoning Informing and Serving
Italy

CONTENTS

FOREWORD

The title of the eBook is "Better life and business: cell, brain, mind and sex universal laws". The eBook integrates the computer, brain and behaviour sciences with the medicine, business and life. New Universal Laws are similar in the cell and genetics, in the brain and mind, in the business and society. These massively parallel laws are hidden in the natural intelligence processes and in the computerized experiments, and mathematical equations and models.

This eBook opens the Universal Laws towards the prolongation of the healthy life and business spans and towards the bright future. The eBook links the fifty years of Prof. Souček's research in world leading institutes and universities. For several decades the world has been using his discoveries and many of his books, published in New York and translated into Russian, Japanese, and Croatian. I was one of his students and colleagues on the international projects and at the conferences where he was an invited speaker. He has organized the world leading scientists into the IRIS Group for brain and computer research. In this eBook Prof. Souček integrates his and IRIS vast experience with his latest discoveries.

This eBook can serve as a reference for the practicing scientists, engineers and medical doctors as well as a textbook for the students for new undergraduate and graduate courses.

Borko Furht

Department of Computer & Electrical Engineering and Computer Science
Florida Atlantic University
Boca Raton
USA

PREFACE

Learning, generalization, seeing and recognition are the major features of natural intelligence. Each of these features has been also investigated by science, medicine, business and technology. The ultimate solutions are man-made systems that integrate all these features into: Learning, generalization, seeing, recognition hybrids. These features are inseparable in living organisms. For this reason it is not easy to make computer systems or models for brain and behavior.

The eBook describes in details the **Cell, Brain, Mind and Sex Universal Laws**, discovered through my research. This has involved several decades of computerized experiments. My findings, theory and computer models have passed through the hurdle of peer review by world's recognized journals. This eBook presents, for the first time, all my findings linked together.

The eBook offers a new explanation of the Self Organization of Intelligence in the brain and world: space; time; quantum; chaos; random and controllable measurement and processes; deterministic and fuzzy predictability. For this research I have spent fifty years in Institute Ruder Boskovic; University of Zagreb; Brookhaven National Laboratory N.Y.; SUNY; U of AZ. I acknowledge excellent working condition and the stimulating atmosphere.

This eBook defines the new brain, life, business computer inter-discipline: Cell, Brain, Mind and Sex UNIVERSAL LAWS. These laws explain in a new way the natural selection and reproductive success in the cell, brain, mind, sex; as well as in the local and global society and business. The world summits, governments, leaders and scientists are now desperately trying to find the way out from the world business crunch, with little results so far.

This eBook proposes an entirely new way out: BETTER LIFE AND BUSINESS based on the cell, brain, mind, sex Universal laws. These laws lead to the intelligent business; bio technology and bio medicine, bright future; long and happy life; without the world business crunch, unemployment and the climate change. Yet strictly related to the Nature, Biology, Medicine, Science and Applications.

The eBook has been written as a textbook for students, as well as a reference for practicing scientists, medical doctors, engineers, businessmen. This eBook leads to the conflicts of interests and to inevitable changes. This eBook is generating new classes of experts and leaders; of teachers and professors. This eBook is spreading the ideas for new original research, development and projects.

Treatment is kept as straightforward as possible, with emphases on experiments, models, functions, systems and applications. A moderate background, like that offered to undergraduates, is assumed. The eBook can be used to teach these **new courses:**

Brain like computers, networks and clusters, based on the Cell Brain Mind Sex Universal Laws.

Neurobiology, behavior and medicine, based on the Cell Brain Mind Sex Universal Laws.

Neurobiology, behavior and medicine, based on the brain like computers, networks and clusters.

CONTENT and SUMMARY pages, outline the chapters 1 to 10.

I express my thanks to my wife Snjeska, for her valuable comments on my manuscript; she inspires me all the time with her poetry: http//sites.google.com/site/snjeskaSoučekpoetessa/

Our children Amalia and Branko encourage us constantly to live and work with joy and optimism.

ACKNOWLEDGEMENT

"I am grateful to PERIODICUM BIOLOGORUM for allowing me to reprint my paper previously published in this journal".

CONFLICT OF INTEREST

The author(s) confirm that this chapter content has no conflict of interest.

Branko Souček

IRIS, Integrated Reasoning Informing and Serving
Italy
E-mail: branko.soucek@libero.it

Send Orders of Reprints at reprints@benthamscience.net

CHAPTER 1

LIFEBIZ MANIFESTO: Cell, Brain, Mind; Anesthesia and Operation of the World

Abstract: The LIFEBIZ theory and practice follow the natural life processes of intelligence. **LIFEBIZ is related to the Brain sciences**. By adjusting the rate of triggering and the internal time constants, brain generates various brain event trains: Poisson; almost Poisson; uniform distribution; almost periodic. Many event trains are active simultaneously in the brain and mind tissue. The time intervals of trains cover a broad range from 0 to 1225 ms, with the peaks in 3,6; 25; 175 and 1225 ms. These event trains support the links between the brain agents. The links and the agents support the brain functions in the Self Organization SO of Understanding U, Consciousness C, Emotions E and Knowledge K. This is a nested, fractal, dynamic, fuzzy loop of the trains and signs. The brain signs are the pieces of mosaic used to build the mind. The same concept is used to build the LIFEBIZ. **By treating biological, economic and technological systems alike, LIFEBIZ both advances and opens new job profiles and business**. To be attractive for the market, consumer goods and industrial hardware of all kinds must be wrapped into LIFEBIZ package which includes: natural interface to the users based on non-restrictive dialogue, speech and image; features of adaptability, learning, sensing the environment; human like behavior offering the users a new sensation of mind and body, new experiences happenings and pleasures. These require qualities and status associations. **The same equations and laws explain the Cell, Brain, Mind as well as the life. Road to the bright LIFEBIZ future is open**.

Keywords: Anesthesia, operation, health, cell, DNA code, genetic intelligence organization, gene, gene link, base, LIFEBIZ laws, SOUČEK laws, courtship, mimicry, send and receive windows, brain, mind, life, consciousness, business, market, bank, money, computer, neural net.

INTRODUCTION

Commercialization of LIFEBIZ products, networks, technologies and concurrent systems and intelligent real time systems will grow rapidly, including: new products, applications, chips, systems, training, consulting, and research that focuses on neural, concurrent or intelligent systems. Government funding organizations should support the biologically based computing. Investments, capital from banks and venture capital should flow into the LIFEBIZ. LIFEBIZ grows from the following research seeds: brain, biology, Bio; computer, software, Soft. The goal is: better life and business in accordance with the nature. See a long list of references, with minute details [1-33].

LIFEBIZ MANIFESTO

This is a declaration, aim, invitation and explanation, how to develop beautiful life in accordance with the laws of nature. This is a summary, a feasibility study.

Civilization and nature are living together; sometimes in cooperation; another time in fight. Civilization proved to be a winner in some periods and locations. Yet the ultimate winner has been, and it will be, the nature. LIFEBIZ follows the natural life laws, with the aim: more of cooperation; less of fight. This is possible only if civilization understands the laws of nature. It is relatively easy to understand the external, visible laws of nature. It is difficult to discover and to understand the internal, invisible laws of the intelligent nature. These laws strictly follow the concrete experimental data, computer models and the new theory. They cover the cell, brain, mind and sex; animal and human life.

LIFEBIZ MANIFESTO Grows Gradually Through the Time, Following the Cell and Brain Laws

1. The nucleus of each cell keeps the genetic code. In genetic code a gene keeps the information necessary to produce one single protein. There are about 100.000 genes; each composed of 20 coding words (amino acids); each composed of 3 out of 4 coding elements (A, C, G, U).

2. The assemblage of Genetic Signs is a crop of the signs developed through evolution and stored in DNA. Formation of genetic signs goes through the cycle of variation, selection and reduplication of selected. New signs are continually cropping up, but as there is a DNA limit, many signs gradually become extinct. In short, favored signs survive the natural selection.

3. The assemblage of Learned Signs is a crop of personal and of learned experience stored in the long term memory: in neuron – synapse connections.

4. Finally in the brain, the genetic and learned signs are stored in the dispersed neural networks: in 25 billion of neurons; some of which with thousands of synapses; hence with many thousands of billions interconnections; with large associative neural networks.

Dendritic growth and spine production of the large, layer III, pyramidal, neurons corresponds with the intensive cognitive development during early childhood. They play a dominant role in preserving cognitive functions.

5. The theory explains and proves the existence of the BET and SIGNS, from the level of the neurons – synapses, all the way to the level of the evoked potentials and of the behavior.

6. Psychological experiments suggest the information flow of trillions bits per second for human sensory input, but only about 10 bits per second for the input into short term memory. It is clear that enormous data compression, clustering, quantizing takes place.

7. Brain mind nested, fractal, TISS clusters are capable of solving problems of seemingly arbitrary complexity. Yet the learning procedures follow simple principle: brain event trains, BET and SO laws.

8. The brain and mind attractions, BRAMA, merge and compress the strong desires. The burning, passionate, unrestrained, excessive desires come from the concurrent, nested, fractal, selfish, TISS agents and unit**s.**

9. The brain and mind follow two different avenues, logical/programming, L/P; and transformation/mapping, T/M. L/P is based upon algorithms, procedures and rules. T/M is based on learning and on building associations. These two types of information processing are conceptually compatible. In other words, it is becoming clear that it may often be impossible to satisfactorily describe the operation of transformation in terms of an algorithm, and *vice versa*. For example, brain action, based on T/M, may provide useful solution to important application area, without allowing us to discover the fundamental ideas used in the solution. The solution is based on the SO laws**.**

10. The mind is a traffic of the electrochemical brain event trains, BET in TISS.

11. The quantity and complexity of TISS clusters and SO laws strongly distinguishes the human brain, language, consciousness and abstraction, from the animal brains. The quantity is in proportion with the number of nerve cells: in human brain, billions of cells, complex UCEK functions; in octopus brain, 520 millions of cells, simple UCEK functions; in insect brain, over 1 million of cells, elementary UCEK functions. In each brain the UCEK functions are in relation with its environment and life complexity.

12. There is an enormous degree of the modularized, nested and repetitive human TISS clusters. They follow the SO laws and the signs BILO, COMET, SAVA. The signs are present in the cerebral cortex, cerebellum, brain stem and spinal cord: in the pyramidal, stellate, Martinotti and granuli cells. Within and between the neural networks, the signs participate in the internal, multilevel, complex, pattern recognition and generalization. The signs merge: time, information and sets; continuous and discrete; selection of specific and overlap; rules and associations.

13. Multilevel, parallel and sequential loops perform the pattern recognition, associative reasoning, speech and thinking.

14. The brain signs are the pieces of mosaic used to build the mind.

15. The brain networks are using the assembled signs to cooperate and to fight, until the winner takes all. Again and again. Here and there all over the brain.

16. Large parts of the neural interconnections within the human neo cortex are related to the complex associations and to the language. The unique human language grows out of the internal signs BILO, COMET, SAVA.

17. The word finding increases the activity in dorso lateral prefrontal cortex and decreases the activity in posterior cortical regions. This is because the prefrontal TISS units act to gate, and select the posterior TISS units.

18. The State of Mind. SO of UCEK creates the State of Mind. There is no central executive. It is SO that leads the tracks of thoughts. SO explains the active forms of encoding and retrieval, which depend on the lateral frontal cortex; and the more passive forms of encoding and retrieval, which result when incoming or recalled stimuli automatically trigger stored representation. High or low levels of UCEK states select the mind tracks in a fraction of a second. The mixture of high and low levels slows the decision process.

19. Time Event Train TET

Brain Event Train, **BET**. Equation:

$$g(x) = \lambda\tau_2\exp\{-\lambda\,\tau_2[\ln 1 - \ln(1 - x)]/a\} / a\,(1 - x)$$

Cell Event Train, **CET**. Equation is the same with the specific cell parameters. Life Event Train, **LET**. Equation is the same with the specific life parameters. The same equations and laws explain the Cell, Brain, Mind as well as the life. **Road to the bright LIFEBIZ future is open.**

20. Quantum pile-up, QPU, explains the quantum transmitter release: pile up of discrete attributes (vehicles) generates the continuous amplitude: QPU is a discrete to continuous; molecule to process link. QPU equation:

$$f(s)=e^{-m}\cdot g_0(s)/0! + e^{-m}\cdot m^1\cdot g_1(s)/1! +\ldots+ e^{-m}\cdot m^k\cdot g_k(s)/k!$$

The same QPU law and equation explain the cell, brain, mind and life; yet with the specific cell, brain, mind and life parameters. In the **cell** QPU explains the End Plate potential amplitude distribution. In the **brain** QPU explains the quantum mind, built from the random brain attribute processes. In the **life** QPU explains the collective decision, built from the human and business attribute decision pieces.

21. Decision, Action: Holistic Self Organization SO of UCEK. Certainty grows from the unconscious decision, to the conscious will, to the illusion and action:

Tdec = 2 MA – AMA = 341ms

Twill = MA+AMA = 204ms

Till = 3MA + 3BRA = 86ms

Until now each law presents a specific bio electrical, bio chemical process: with the equation, curve, data. Each law is supported by the animal and human experimental data and by the theoretical model. Data and models are in excellent agreement. Each law is related to the process, rather than to the status. It is a piece. Complex, massively parallel actions of various pieces, form the life intelligence functions.

22. LIFE follows the cell, brain, mind laws:

- from discrete bio event trains; to continuous time; **TET**

- from discrete attributes, molecules, quantum; to continuous

QPU amplitude

- from BRA, AMA, MA to the brain mind attraction **BRAMA**

- life grows through the merger of the chemical logic and the Bio processes, laws.

LIFE = chemical logic + bio processes: cell, brain mind laws.

These explain the memory and learning: Self Organization of Understanding, Consciousness, Emotions and Knowledge.

23. LIFEBIZ merges the life and business; following the above life laws.

FUTURE = LIFEBIZ

The experimental findings and the evoked potentials indicate that the verbal chaos is structured, nested and synchronized. This arrangement is regulated both in the time and in the space. Behind the verbal chaos, there is the BRAMA fractal protocol and the Quantum Mind barrier. REASON is based on the Continuous, Quantizing, Discrete process. The Elements or pieces of Consciousness CON, explain the innate and learned **Bio** assemblage. They can be used as a guide to build the CON Software **Soft**: **Selective courting.** The CON system gradually narrows the windows. The goal is to detect/select the right partner and to avoid the risk of courting the wrong partner. Bio: brain windows before mating. Soft: low risk credit scoring.

Mimicry. The CON system gradually widens the windows. The goal is to attract/select as many partners as possible. Bio: brain windows for feeding. Soft: help desk for marketing.

Context Switching. Sudden change in CON behavior, based on the past history, recalled experience and on environmental conditions. Bio: brain windows after mating. Soft: EDI-switch for adaptive purchasing.

Aggression. One subsystem tends to take control of the whole CON system. Bio: time coding in insect chirping. Soft: competition networks.

Alternation. Two [or several] subsystems are taking control of the CON system in alternation. Bio: time coding in insects; leader/follower chirping. Soft: travelling salesman, genetic programming.

Solo. One subsystem is in control of the whole CON system. Bio: time coding in insects; leader chirping. Soft: winner takes all.

Transmitting. Exchange of conscious messages among subsystems. Bio: quantum transmitter release on neural terminals. Soft: conscious message packages.

Bio to Soft. Millions of the pieces will be developed through years. They will be used to build the new, beautiful life and complex, massively parallel business: **Innovative, ground breaking, revolutionary LIFEBIZ.**

Anesthesia and operation of the world. Environment factors are key determinants of the human health. Exposure to pollutants and chemicals could elevate the risk of cardiovascular and other diseases. Lead poison enters human body from the old water pipes, canned beverages, cars. Dangerous fine particles enter from the air; *etc.* Cut the world in order to remove and repair a diseased or damaged parts. Transplant SOUČEK LAWS from the Cell, Brain, Mind, to the new LIFEBIZ: "first, time is life; then, time is money". New York publisher, Wiley Inc., is spreading the Souček LIFEBIZ books around the world, calling them "innovative, ground breaking, revolutionary". Learning by working, new feasibility studies and applications asks for cooperation; lectures; seminars; constant consulting; projects; right now, short and long terms. An original CD offers the details, theory, experiments, curves, equations, international experience, bio to soft pieces. Some pieces have been already developed in the evergreen books and laws listed in Appendix. Also the related activities and the concrete International projects are described in the Appendix.

APPENDIX

BACKGROUND: LIFEBIZ strongly merges the brain and the computer research. Souček has developed the LIFEBIZ seeds through the following activities.

FOUNDER OF THE COMPUTER SCIENCE AND CYBERNETICS

From 1955–1959 Souček has designed the first digital computer in Croatia, and has published the first computer paper: 256 channel analyzer, memory, logic, programs, Elektrotehnika 4, 1959. He founded the first laboratory, of Cybernetics. He extended his computer into an on-line, real-time, associative analyzer. **This was the brain-like computer, first in the world science; it has increased the neural and nuclear spectrometry by a factor of 1000 times**. See Fig. **1**.

Souček has been an invited speaker on the Annual National Conference in Washington 1965, and on many other International conferences. Scientists from USA, Europe, China, Russia and Japan have come to Souček for specialization. Souček founded the first University course "Digital Computers"; He founded in 1966 the first Electronic Scientific Computer Center ERCE, and in 1973 he leaded the extension of ERCE into the University Computer Center SRCE. He founded in 1969 the International Conference DATA PROCESSING, then 3-day MICRO-Seminars; and in 1968 has organized the extension of his MICRO Seminar to MIPRO Conferences.

FOUNDER OF THE INTERNATIONAL IRIS GROUP:

The Group comes from world renowned projects, laboratories and universities involved in research, development and application of Integrated Reasoning Informing and Serving Systems. IRIS includes real-time, neural, fuzzy and parallel computing and bio experiments and models.

SIXTH GENERATION COMPUTER TECHNOLOGY PROJECTS:

Brain, Computer

Souček and IRIS are the authors and editors of ten books presenting the Sixth Generation Projects results; published in New York and translated into Croatian, Japanese and Russian in over 100.000 copies: Minicomputers [first choice award 1973]; Microprocessors [first choice award 1976]; Computers in Neurobiology 1976; Neural and Massively Parallel Computers 1988; Neural and Concurrent Real-time Systems 1989; Dynamic, Genetic and Chaotic Programming 1992; Fuzzy, Holographic and Parallel Intelligence 1992…… He is the author of a book in Split: Quantum Mind Networks 1997.

SOUČEK 2012: Better Life and Business

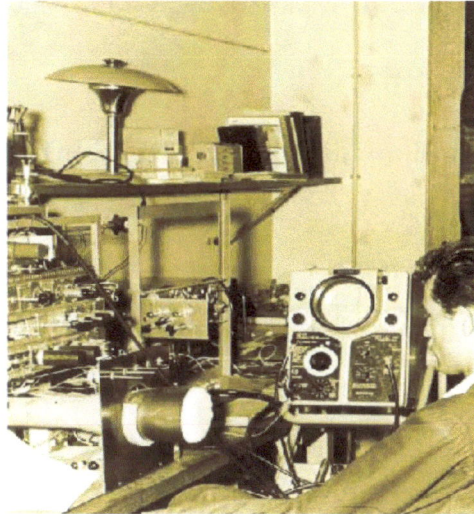

SOUČEK 1959 is building the real-time Brain-like digital computer

Figure 1: Branko Souček, from the first brain – like computer, to the better life and business e-book.

DISCOVERER OF SOUČEK LAWS: CELL, BRAIN, MIND, SEX

Souček has performed the research, experiments and models: from the end-plate potential quantum transmitter release processes, to the complex neural event trains. He has discovered the new Cell, Brain, Mind,Sex laws: Brain Internal Language Organization BILO; Brain Event Trains BET; Brain Tissue TISS; Brain Compressor and Meter COMET; Brain Mind Attractions BRAMA; Brain

Windows; Brain Genetic Intelligence Organization GENIO; Explosion of Self Organization SO BANG. Quantum Pile Up QPU; Quantum Biology UNIVERSAL LAWS and Universal Natural Constants: BRA=3.6 ms, AMA= 25 ms, MA = 175 ms; BRAMA=1225 ms. Note: bio quantum is far from the physical sub atomic quantum units, such as the Planck constant, h.

ACKNOWLEDGEMENT

I have spent fifty years working out the Self Organization of life intelligence: in Institute Ruder Boskovic; U of Zagreb; Brookhaven National Laboratory N.Y.; SUNY; U of AZ. I acknowledge the stimulating atmosphere and excellent working conditions. I am learning a lot from my children Branko, Amalia and Marina. BRA, AMA, MA= BRAMA Law and Constants.

DISCLOSURE

"The content of this chapter has been previously published in *Periodicum Biologorum Vol. 112, No. 4, 479-482, 2010*".

ABBREVIATIONS

SO   = Self Organization

U   = Understanding

C   = Consciousness

E   = Emotions

K   = Knowledge

Brain, mind, self-organization laws:

BRAMA   = Brain and mind attraction, 1225 ms

BRA   = Brand the features, 3.6 ms

AMA   = Amass the chunks, 25 ms

MA   = Master the associations, 175 ms

BILO   = Brain internal language organization

COMET   = Compressor, meter

SAVA   = Selective audio video association

bC   = Brain Consciousness

fbC   = Frequency of brain Consciousness= 5.7 cycles per 1000 ms

BET   = Brain event train

TISS   = Time, information, sign, set

Cell, genetic, self-organization laws:

GENIO   = Genetic intelligence organization, 1250 nm

BRAG   = Brand the features, 3,64 nm

AMAG   = Amass the chunks, 25.5 nm

MAG   = Master the associations, 178.5 nm

CILO   = Cell internal language organization

CEMET   = Cell meter

CELA   = Cell association

cC   = Cell Consciousness

fcC   = Frequency of cell Consciousness= 5.6 cycles per 1000 nm

CET   = Cell event train

LISS   = Link, information, sign, set

REFERENCES

[1]   SOUČEK B. Mono stable Systems Triggered at Random. *Nuclear Instruments Methods 1964; 29:* 109–114

[2]   SOUČEK B. Application of pile-up distortion calculation. *Rev Scientific Instruments 1965; 36:* 1582–1587

[3]   SOUČEK B. Influence of the Latency Fluctuations and the Quantum Process of Transmitter Release on the End-Plate Potentials' Amplitude Distribution. *Biophysical Journal 1971; 11:* 127–139

[4]   SOUČEK B. Complete Model for the Statistical Composition of the End-Plate Potential. *J Theoretical Biology 1971; 30:* 631–648

[5]   SOUČEK B. Applications of computers and mathematical models to the study of neuronal systems, Nuclear and neuronal pulse spectrometry. *Computer Physics Communications 1973;5:* 115– 122

[6]   CARLSON AD, SOUČEK B. Computer simulation of firefly flash sequence. *Journal of Theoretical Biology 1975; 55:* 353–370

[7]   SOUČEK B. Model of Alternating and Aggressive Communication with the Example of Katydid Chirping. *J Theoretical Biology1975; 52:*399–417

[8]   SOUČEK B, VENCL F. Bird Communication Study Using Digital Computer. *J Theoretical Biology 1975; 49:* 147–172

[9]   VENCL F, SOUČEK B. Structure and Control of Duet Singing in the White-Crested Jay Thrush. *Behavior 1976; 57:* 20–33

[10] SOUČEK B, CARLSON AD. Brain Windows in Firefly Communication. *J Theoretical Biology 1986 119:* 47–65

[11] SOUČEK B, CARLSON AD. Brain Window Language in Firefly. *J Theoretic Biology 1987; 125:* 93–103

[12] SOUČEK B, CARLSON AD. Computers in Neurobiology and Behavior. Wiley New York 1976.

[13] SOUČEK B, SOUČEK M. Neural and Massively Parallel Computers. Wiley New York 1988.

[14] SOUČEK B. Neural and Concurrent Real-Time Systems. Wiley New York 1989

[15] SOUČEK B and the IRIS Group. Neural and Intelligent Systems Integration. Wiley New York 1991.

[16] SOUČEK B and the IRIS Group. Fast Learning and Invariant Object Recognition. Wiley New York 1992.

[17] SOUČEK B and the IRIS Group. Fuzzy, Holographic and Parallel Intelligence. Wiley New York 1992.

[18] SOUČEK B and the IRIS Group. Dynamic, Genetic and Chaotic Programming. Wiley New York 1992

[19] PLANTAMURA VL, SOUČEK B, VISAGGIO G. Frontier Decision Support Concepts. Wiley New York 1994

[20] SOUČEK B. Quantum Mind – Evoked Potential Link. *Per Biol1998;100(2):* 129–140

[21] SOUČEK B. Quantum Mind Emerges from the Prefrontal Cortex Nested, Fractal Chaos. *Per biol1999; 101(2):* 109–119

[22] SOUČEK B. Quantum Mind Compresses the Verbal Stories. *Per biol1999; 101(3):* 193–201

[23] SOUČEK B. Quantum Mind Measures the Verbal Stories. *Per biol2000:102(4):* 331–342

[24] SOUČEK B. Universal Brain Theory: The Self Organization of Understanding, Consciousness, Emotions and Knowledge. *Per biol2001; 103(3):* 219–228

[25] SOUČEK B. The Brain Agents Universe. *Per biol2002; 104(3):*353–369

[26] SOUČEK B. The Brain and Mind Tissue, TISS: node, group, flock, pool. *Per biol2002; 104(3):* 345–352

[27] SOUČEK B. The Brain and Mind Attractions, BRAMA, the Brain Internal Language Organization, BILO, the Consciousness. *Per biol20O3; 105(3):* 207–214

[28] SOUČEK B. The genetic and learned brain and mind event trains BET and signs: BILO,COMET, SAVA, CON. *Per biol2004; (106)3:*265–278

[29] SOUČEK B. The DNA code, the brain event trains BET and the self-organization SO make a single entity: life and consciousness. *Per biol2004; 106(4):* 443–444

[30] SOUČEK B. Genetic Intelligence Organization GENIO. *Per biol2005; 107(4):* 385–39

[31] SOUČEK B. Genetic Intelligence Universe GENIUS+; Cell internal language organization CILO; Origin of life and consciousness. *Per biol2007; 109(2):* 89–99

[32] SOUČEK B. Self organization of understanding, consciousness, emotions and knowledge: Cell, Brain, Mind, Sex. *Per biol2008; 110 (1):* 3-10

[33] SOUČEK B. Better life and business based on the Cell, Brain, Mind, Sex, Laws: LIFEBIZ. *Per biol*2009;111(1): 137–143

Send Orders of Reprints at reprints@benthamscience.net

CHAPTER 2

Better Life and Business Based on the Cell, Brain, Mind, Sex Laws: LIFEBIZ

Abstract:

Background and Purpose: Explosion of intelligence due to the human interventions leads to prosperity, but also to the strange attractions and dangerous chaos (like a big bang). The way out is presented: the LIFEBIZ theory and practice. It follows the natural life intelligence processes.

Materials and Methods: The life intelligence processes, data and computer models, are described. They come from the experiments with the animals and human.

Results: The map of life intelligence processes is formed. The map presents the figures, curves and data for major processes: aggression, mimicry, chaos, trains, pile up, attractions, courting, mating….emotion, reasoning, consciousness.

Conclusions: The life grows above the bio chemical logic. The business grows above the market logic. Described LIFEBIZ (theory and practice) explains the life intelligence elementary processes: major basic functions, 30 laws and 100 equations. Through interaction, elementary processes form millions of complex processes: from the cell, brain, mind and sex to the local and global life and business. LIFEBIZ follows the natural life SOUČEK LAWS: Self Organization of the Understanding, Consciousness, Emotions and Knowledge; cell, brain, mind, sex. Joy in the world, for the next generation, for us. Time is life, rather than time is money. Searching for the new LIFEBIZ solutions will require the new research and development. LIFEBIZ will stop the unemployment and the climate change. Strictly related to the Biological sciences.

Keywords: Cell, DNA code, genetic intelligence organization, gene, gene link, base, LIFEBIZ laws, SOUČEK laws, courtship, mimicry, send and receive windows, brain, mind, life, consciousness, business, market, bank, money, computer, neural net.

INTRODUCTION

Leader makes the forecast. His worldwide contacts with bankers, multinational fund managers, and important public officials enable him to make bold forecasts–based on information from those who are in a position to see and profit from major financial trends. His forecasts are based on his thorough understanding of geopolitical forces combined with his personal contacts with the high-powered decision makers in the world of International finance.

Branko Souček

The world business CRUNCH is now here. The World summits, governments, leaders and sciences are desperately trying to find the way out, with little results so far: Lenders make only totally-safe, no-risk loans. Investors will invest only in sure things. It was 1954 before the DOW Jones Industrial Average reached the level it had attained in the boom of the 1920s. I am proposing an entirely new way out: follow the cell, brain, mind, sex laws [1-32]. They also explain the World life and business.

The bio names become the Business symbols. **Living organisms**, say: insect, bird, mouse, human. **Business organizations**, say: workshop, factory, company, bank. Following sections describe the newly discovered life processes. Section MARKETBIZ presents the current developments. Section LIFEBIZ shows the new research, development and theory.

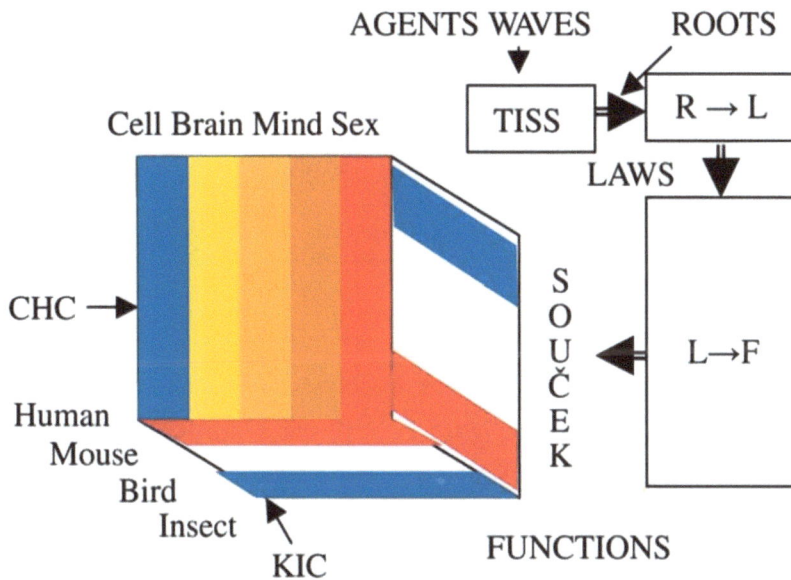

Figure 1: SO BOW over the LIFEBIZ self-organization. Point Associations: R-›L, Roots to Laws; L-›F, Laws to Functions. Red: Long. Violet: short. Point KIC, Knowledge in Insect Cell. CHC, Consciousness in Human Cell.

CHAOTIC AGGRESSION; LEARNING; CONSCIOUSNESS

Human Brain, Mind and behavior are composed of communicating agents. Three classes of duets have been identified. **The chaotic duet** is a dynamic structure.

Duet trajectories concentrate into a narrow attractor space. This is a case of massive self-organization. **The courting / mimicry duets** are based on symbol-signal processing and are capable of discovering the hidden information by observing sample behavior and comparing it with the past learned experience. **The pattern duet** is capable to recognize inexact, incomplete patterns. Through many duet loops, the human brain agents called katydids, fireflies and birds learn about the partner, and adapt answers and behavior. Symbol-signal processing is responsible for mental states and for consciousness. The genetic, sensation and mental vehicles in all layers of the Barrier, combine the born-with knowledge, with learning. The layers are unconscious of the underlying vehicle traffic regulations. Yet each layer of the Barrier recognizes the intentions and the meaning of quantum messages within its duet domain. The duets are involved in the Universal Brain and Mind self-organization and in perception. The dynamic nodes, groups, flocks and pools form the brain-mind tissue TISS: time, information, sign, set.

COURTING AND MATING; MIMICRY AND EATING

Abbreviations and Table **1** show the Animal and Human Cell Brain Mind and Language. First, the language story is measured by the speaker's innate story meter Request. Second, the story formation is confronted with the accumulated emotions based on the speaker's past experience. Past experience has been measured by the emotion meters: Fight, Feed, Flight, Court *etc.*

Quantum Mind meters relate the stories and emotions, and the supporting circuits in the prefrontal cortex and in amygdala.

The chaotic DUETS search for a solution: minimal risk and pain; maximal benefit and pleasure. The search is directed back and forth between the cortical columns, thalamus, basal ganglia and amygdala, generating a chain of thoughts. The speaker is conscious of this chain of thoughts. The Principal story and emotion meters keep reducing the search space in every step, in a fast and approximate way. This compression emerges from the dynamic interactions between flocks of selfish neural agents. Universal selfish agents are present all over the animal and the human world. These selfish agents do not have representations of the environment, stories and emotions. They respond to the present state of their neighborhood and to the accumulated past history of stimulation. The behavior and the rule set of a selfish agent are controlled by its oscillators and memories. The self-organization of the agents space leads to the dominant modes, binding the underlying oscillators, which leave the trace in the human evoked potential. In this way the Mind Brain Body Link is closed. The building bricks and the self-organization is the Link of the Mind-Brain-Body holistic structure.

MOSAIC. Short time local processes, are the pieces of mosaic needed to explain the brain and mind. The pieces form the long time complex processes, in the neural networks, prefrontal cortex, temporal, parietal and occipital cortex as well as in the sub cortical structures. The same laws explain the cell, brain, mind; as well as the local and global life and business processes. The Key processes are: courting and mating; mimicry and eating. These are the dominant forces for the third Millennium business.

THE BRAMA PRINCIPLE: STRONG ATTRACTIONS AND PASSIONATE DESIRES

For a long time the brain and the mind are considered to be federations of distinct modules or sub functions. I consider the brain and mind as a single nested, fractal, dispersed entity that uses the strong attractions or desires, BRAMA. BRAMA is the bursting, passionate, unrestrained, excessive desire. Presented theory is supported by experimental findings, and computer models. I compare the dynamics of the brain and mind with the dynamics of the flock of birds. The flock of birds, the colony of ants, the school of fish, have no leader, and no control mind. It is the individual members following certain simple laws that make the group respond the way it does. In other words, the behaviour is built from the bottom-up and is governed by the cooperative action of many small Brain Mind agents. The BM agents include primitives or components of intelligence, communication and attractions. Resulting decisions, behavior or organizations are based on: distributed decision making; collaborative reasoning; distributed control; community coordination; cooperation; groupware, attractions.

Table 1: Courting and mating, or mimicry and eating

	Cell Internal Language Organization CILO	Brain Internal Language Organization BILO	Mind, Language Bank and Trust	Natural and Financial Sex Behaviour
Patrolling, Courting and Mimicry Signs	Cell send and receive windows and bursts	Brain send and receive windows and bursts	Mental, sensation and genetic windows/vehicles and bursts	Body send and receive windows/vehicles and flashes
Stimulus and Response Bursts	Chemical vehicles, Cell Event Trains CET	Family of short Brain Event Trains BET	Cooperation of short Brain Event Trains BET	Light flashes
Box of parallel mating messages	Right DNA codes of membrane proteins, short pieces, RNA	Right brain event trains and associations	Right patterns, mental elements, symbols, concepts and stories	Right male sperm genome and female sex cell genome
Mating actions and products	New proteins	New features, chunks, associations	Vertical thinking, **reasoning, pattern recognition, decision**	Mating process
Box of parallel Eating messages	Wrong DNA codes of membrane proteins, short pieces, RNA	Wrong brain event trains and associations	Wrong patterns, mental elements, symbols, concepts and stories	Wrong partner's body
Eating actions and products	Box is broken into pieces that serve as food and energy	Box is broken into pieces that serve to form new features, chunks, associations	Box is broken into pieces that serve for **mind wandering lateral thinking, ideas**	Body is broken into pieces that serve as food and energy

MARKETBIZ: SUCCEEDING THROUGH CHANGE; "MORE FOR YOUR MONEY"

MARKETBIZ changes are always present: new customer service and decision support are leading areas of revenue growth of companies. Computing is moving into desktop, hand and pocket calculators. Decisions support systems proliferate in cars and houses. A large percentage of them will have to deal with fuzzy and inexact data. Long decisions cycles must give way to very quick decisions based on available information: in education, medicine and ecology; in food and power systems. Users will expect systems capable of learning from experience and building personal memory based on associations maps. Personal assistant and decision support systems for managements and manufacturing will dominate the market over the years; until the CRUNCH.

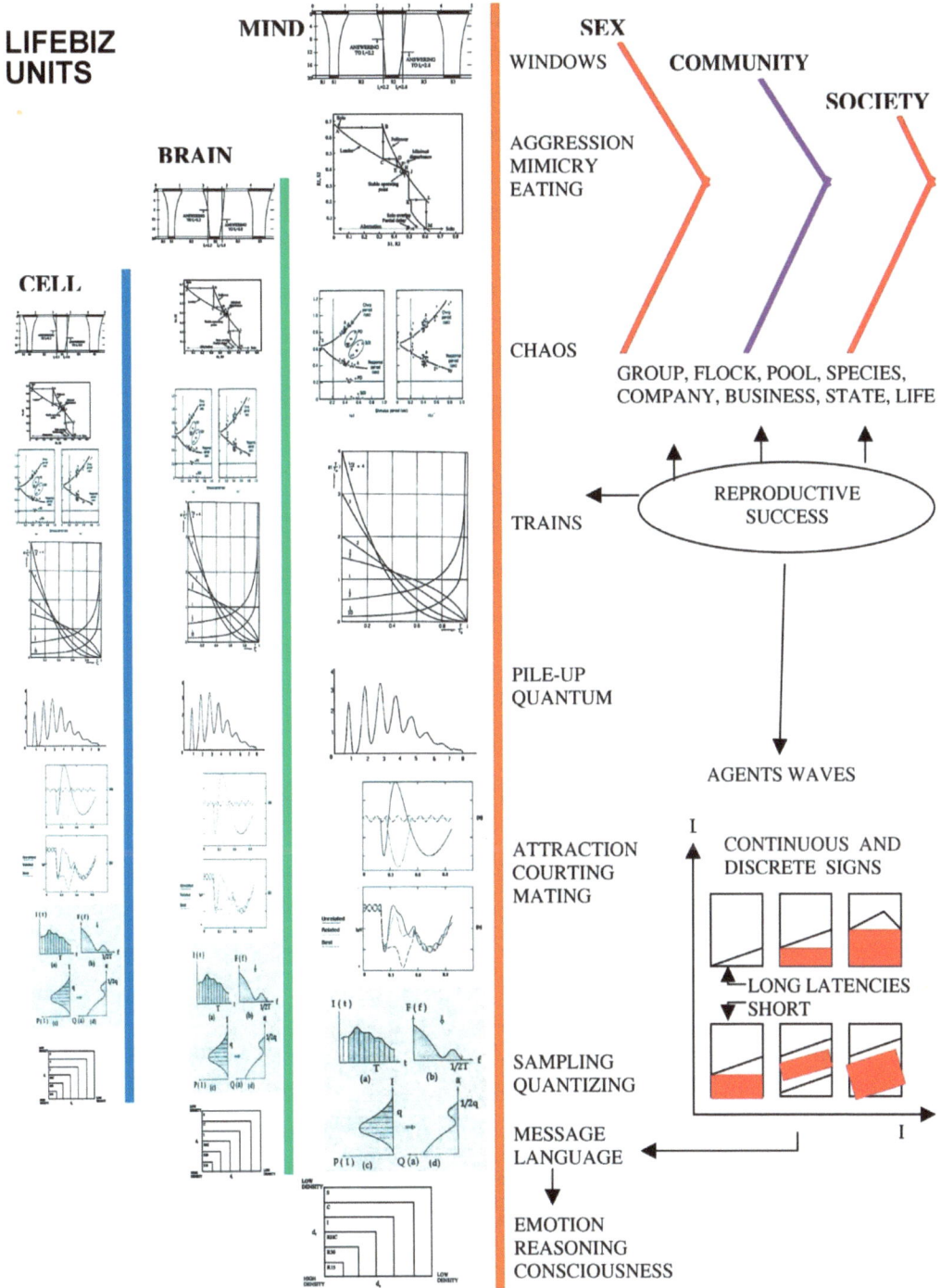

Figure 2: SOUČEK Laws over the LIFEBIZ UNITS: CELL, BRAIN, MIND, SEX.

LIFEBIZ FOLLOWS THE LIFE PROCESSES: "JOY TO THE WORLD"

LIFEBIZ is a major, dominant change: from the market processes to the natural life processes. The related life processes and models are described in minute details in the evergreen books [12-19]; as well as in [1-31]. For the summary of life intelligence processes see [32]. In [32] each process is presented in his specific figure. The curves and numbers strictly follow my experimental data. Now, for easy transition from the life processes to the LIFEBIZ, I am using in both cases the same figures and symbols, in the following way.

- Living organisms: insect, bird, mouse, human.

- LIFEBIZ organizations: workshop, factory, company, bank.

- Laboratory, department, university, ministry.

- Living organisms units: cell, brain, mind, sex.

- LIFEBIZ organizations units: cell, brain, mind, money/data interchange.

Current business disease reaches epidemic proportions. It is the time to search for internal hidden triggers in the business cell, brain, mind and sex. The triggers combine the internal signals and create entirely new meaning and specific internal languages: cell, CILO; brain, BILO; mind, animal/human languages. The complex, massively parallel internal associations matrixes combine the signals into roots; into processes; into laws; into functions.

Fig. **1** presents the self-organization bow over the LIFEBIZ intelligence. Fig. **2** presents the map of the LIFEBIZ intelligence processes: windows, aggression, mimicry......... emotion, reasoning, consciousness. **Example 1**: LIFEBIZ mind aggression is related to many smaller LIFEBIZ brain aggressions; to many, many small LIFEBIZ cell aggressions. **Example 2**: the train processes are the mixtures of Poisson and periodic components. Again LIFEBIZ mind train grows above many LIFEBIZ brain trains; above many, many LIFEBIZ cell trains. **Example 3**: Pile up process combines the random times with the convolution of Gauss amplitudes. Large mind pile up grows above many small brain pile ups; above very large number of miniature cell pile ups. In both: LIFE and LIFEBIZ. In general, variety of complex LIFEBIZ processes and systems are growing above the multiple interactions between elementary processes.

The above concrete processes, curves, data and figures, present the base for the original, scientific, professional analysis of LIFEBIZ processes. This is an entirely new way to the new life and business; to the future.

The cell, brain, mind and computer links and discoveries [1-32] should be extended and applied in LIFEBIZ economy, science, medicine, education, technology,…

Brain like computers and business systems include: adaptive and learning systems, artificial and neural systems, neural computers, adaptive goal directed expert systems based on genetic mutation algorithms, event train computers, transformation and mapping systems, associative memories and processes, fuzzy and pseudo associative systems, hyper cubes, array processors, programmable connections machines, concurrent systems and computer and systems that follow neurons biology and behavior. By treating biological, economical and technological systems alike, LIFEBIZ both advances and opens new job profiles and business. To be attractive for the market, consumer goods and industrial hardware of all kinds must be wrapped into LIFEBIZ package which includes: natural interface to the users based on non-restrictive dialogue, speech and image; features of adaptability, learning, sensing the environment; human like behavior offering the users a new sensation of mind and body, new experiences happenings and pleasures. These require qualities and status associations. Commercialization of LIFEBIZ products, networks, technologies and concurrent systems and intelligent real time systems will grow rapidly, including: new products, applications, chips, systems, training, consulting, and research that focuses on neural, concurrent or intelligent systems. Government funding organizations should support the biologically based computing. Investments and capital funding from banks and venture capital should flow into the LIFEBIZ. The application areas include: pattern recognition in business, signals and images; speech, vision, robotic, industrial and financial process control; knowledge data bases, online simulation and decision making, intelligent artificial organs, psychology software and services. **Productivity and quality through research and development in LIFEBIZ systems enhances competitiveness in the world market and in the new way of living.**

The bible is speaking of 7 good years and of 7 bad years. The stock market cycle is about 49 years. The agriculture and the Morava man appear about 13000 and 26000 years ago. The above data as well as the cell and brain data are used to form Fig. **3**. Fig. **3** shows the SO BANG, CRUNCH and the WAY OUT. SO BANG grows from the fast human interventions. It will change the predator, pray cycles and their amplitudes and speeds. Human community and society must learn from the nature. No investment team is complete these days without the SO learned from cell and brain. The ultimate strategy is **succeeding through change**, where only the best intelligent agents survive in a **self-modifying** system.

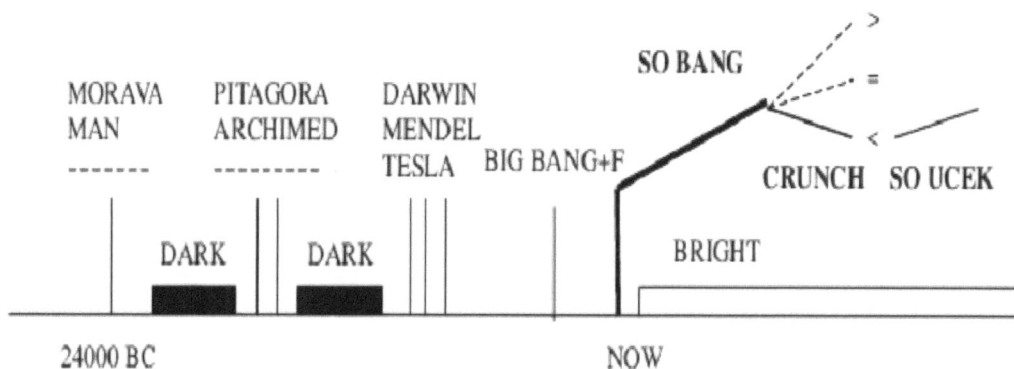

Figure 3: SO BANG, CRUNCH and the way out. From the special bright BRAINS; over very long dark ages; to the financial deregulation BIG BANG+F, to the intelligence SO explosion, named SO BANG; and to the bright future. Line >: natural resources > population needs; SO BANG grows. Line =: natural resources = population needs; SO BANG is stable. Line <: natural resources < population needs; SO BANG becomes CRUNCH: a difficult moment at which important decisions must be made. When it comes to the crunch, you reach the point where to act and decide. You, company, country, world. CRUNCH might lead to: paradise reduced to the local and global oases; warm planet, epidemic; time machine; strange attractions and dangerous chaos; modified population needs. Solution is the UNIVERSAL Law of Life: SO UCEK: Self Organization of UNIVERSAL Consciousness, Emotions and Knowledge. This law governs the whole cell; the whole brain; and the whole earth communities and societies life and business. This law leads to the intelligent business, bio technology and medicine, long and happy life.

CONCLUSION: FUTURE=LIFEBIZ

The World Forums, January 2009 to 2013, have concluded: "The raw unregulated market business doesn't work. Ask the experts what to do, and the most honest reply is: I don't know".

My reply is: "we should do the LIFEBIZ"

LIFEBIZ follows the natural life SOUČEK LAWS: Self-Organization of the Understanding, Consciousness, Emotions and Knowledge; cell, brain, mind, sex. Joy in the world, for the next generation, for us. Time is life, rather than time is money. Searching for the new LIFEBIZ solutions will require the new research and development. LIFEBIZ will stop the unemployment and the climate change. Far from "The Modern Utopia" and from "The Big Brother that is watching us". Strictly related to the Biological sciences.

For equations, data files, figures, tables and instructions see [1-32], with long lists of references describing my concrete models experiments and results.

Your life and business are the specific pieces of the World life and business. **Find your massively parallel links; and use the right combination of the SOUČEK laws: they explain the cell, brain, mind and sex; as well as the local and global life and business.**

EXIT FROM THE WORLD CRISIS

Self-Organization of Understanding, Consciousness, Emotions and Knowledge

SOUČEK-LIFEBIZ

MARKETBIZ is growing through the application of advanced technology in the market and finance. The back propagation has been used in the long range of marketing and political forecasting. Rule based systems assume that when an event perturbs the systems, it will revert to equilibrium after a short time. Neural networks, Genetic and Fuzzy algorithms solve problems by evolving solutions as nature does. All these systems correctly predict market direction when the moves are small, but they are wrong on almost every large move. The result might be the CRUNCH, see Fig. **3**.

LIFEBIZ follows the SOUČEK laws: Cell, Brain, Mind, Sex [1-32]. The first important step of nature is the pre-processing of signals and data. Before performing any useful forecasting, SOUČEK laws extract leading indicators from the time series. This is the most critical part of constructing a good decision: in the live cell, brain, mind and sex; as well as in business. Second important step of nature is the conversion of input data into the fuzzy representation for collection of membership functions. Within each class, the membership measures the degree of adherence to the particular attribute of a class. A group of fuzzy rules forms a fuzzy associative memory. When a set of inputs arrives, each rule or law that has any truth in its premise, will be fired. See Figs. **1** and **2**. Many life decisions are the result of pain taking trial and error: the life rules and laws are hidden. These is why it took 50 years to discover SOUČEK laws [1-32].

Now these laws explain the life in a new way, with the functions, equations and numbers; hence above the verbal descriptions. Now we can use these laws to analyze the life in a more precise way.

Understanding SOUČEK laws is necessary to have an inside view in the life and in the business. With this **SEMINAR** you will became the LIFEBIZ expert and leader. You will create a new life and business; science and technology; physiology and medicine. You will stop the world crisis, unemployment, climate change. You will became the **SOUČEK-LIFEBIZ WINNER IN YOUR FIELD**.

NOTE 1: Upon receiving your E-mail request, I will E-mail to you: SOUČEK LAWS (10 publications = 10 files = 100 pages)

NOTE 2: For details of experiments and models developed through time see the evergreen books [12-19].

When I receive your request for seminar, together we shall fix date and place.

ACKNOWLEDGEMENT

I have spent fifty years working out the Self Organization of life intelligence: in Institute Ruder Boskovic; U of Zagreb; Brookhaven National Laboratory N.Y.; SUNY; U of AZ. I acknowledge the stimulating atmosphere and excellent working conditions.

DISCLOSURE

"The content of this chapter has been previously published in *Periodicum Biologorum, Vol. 111, No. 1, 137-143,2009*".

REFERENCES

[1]   SOUČEK B. Mono stable Systems Triggered at Random. *Nuclear Instruments Methods 1964; 29:* 109–114

[2]   SOUČEK B. Application of pile-up distortion calculation. *Rev Scientific Instruments 1965; 36:* 1582–1587

[3]   SOUČEK B. Influence of the Latency Fluctuations and the Quantum Process of Transmitter Release on the End-Plate Potentials' Amplitude Distribution. *Biophysical Journal 1971; 11:* 127–139

[4]   SOUČEK B. Complete Model for the Statistical Composition of the End-Plate Potential. *J Theoretical Biology 1971; 30:* 631–648

[5]   SOUČEK B. Applications of computers and mathematical models to the study of neuronal systems, Nuclear and neuronal pulse spectrometry. *Computer Physics Communications 1973;5:* 115– 122

[6]   CARLSON AD, SOUČEK B. Computer simulation of firefly flash sequence. *Journal of Theoretical Biology 1975; 55:* 353–370

[7]   SOUČEK B. Model of Alternating and Aggressive Communication with the Example of Katydid Chirping. *J Theoretical Biology1975; 52:*399–417

[8]   SOUČEK B, VENCL F. Bird Communication Study Using Digital Computer. *J Theoretical Biology 1975; 49:* 147–172

[9]   VENCL F, SOUČEK B. Structure and Control of Duet Singing in the White-Crested Jay Thrush. *Behavior 1976; 57:* 20–33

[10]   SOUČEK B, CARLSON AD. Brain Windows in Firefly Communication. *J Theoretical Biology 1986 119:* 47–65

[11]   SOUČEK B, CARLSON AD. Brain Window Language in Firefly. *J Theoretic Biology 1987; 125:* 93–103

[12]   SOUČEK B, CARLSON AD. Computers in Neurobiology and Behavior. Wiley New York 1976.

[13]   SOUČEK B, SOUČEK M. Neural and Massively Parallel Computers. Wiley New York 1988.

[14]   SOUČEK B. Neural and Concurrent Real-Time Systems. Wiley New York 1989

[15]   SOUČEK B and the IRIS Group. Neural and Intelligent Systems Integration. Wiley New York 1991.

[16]   SOUČEK B and the IRIS Group. Fast Learning and Invariant Object Recognition. Wiley New York 1992.

[17]   SOUČEK B and the IRIS Group. Fuzzy, Holographic and Parallel Intelligence. Wiley New York 1992.

[18]   SOUČEK B and the IRIS Group. Dynamic, Genetic and Chaotic Programming. Wiley New York 1992

[19]   PLANTAMURA VL, SOUČEK B, VISAGGIO G. Frontier Decision Support Concepts. Wiley New York 1994

[20]   SOUČEK B. Quantum Mind – Evoked Potential Link. *Per Biol1998;100(2):* 129–140

[21]   SOUČEK B. Quantum Mind Emerges from the Prefrontal Cortex Nested, Fractal Chaos. *Per biol1999; 101(2):* 109–119

[22]   SOUČEK B. Quantum Mind Compresses the Verbal Stories. *Per biol1999; 101(3):* 193–201

[23]   SOUČEK B. Quantum Mind Measures the Verbal Stories. *Per biol2000:102(4):* 331–342

[24]   SOUČEK B. Universal Brain Theory: The Self Organization of Understanding, Consciousness, Emotions and Knowledge. *Per biol2001; 103(3):* 219–228

[25]   SOUČEK B. The Brain Agents Universe. *Per biol2002; 104(3):*353–369

[26]   SOUČEK B. The Brain and Mind Tissue, TISS: node, group, flock, pool. *Per biol2002; 104(3):* 345–352

[27]   SOUČEK B. The Brain and Mind Attractions, BRAMA, the Brain Internal Language Organization, BILO, the Consciousness. *Per biol20O3; 105(3):* 207–214

[28]   SOUČEK B. The genetic and learned brain and mind event trains BET and signs: BILO,COMET, SAVA, CON. *Per biol2004; (106)3:*265–278

[29]   SOUČEK B. The DNA code, the brain event trains BET and the self-organization SO make a single entity: life and consciousness. *Per biol2004; 106(4):* 443–444

[30]   SOUČEK B. Genetic Intelligence Organization GENIO. *Per biol2005; 107(4):* 385–39

[31]   SOUČEK B. Genetic Intelligence Universe GENIUS+; Cell internal language organization CILO; Origin of life and consciousness. *Per biol2007; 109(2):* 89–99

[32]   SOUČEK B. Self-organization of understanding, consciousness, emotions and knowledge: Cell, Brain, Mind, Sex. *Per biol2008; 110 (1):* 3-10

Send Orders of Reprints at reprints@benthamscience.net

CHAPTER 3

Self-Organization of Understanding, Consciousness, Emotions and Knowledge: Cell, Brain, Mind, Sex, Life

Abstract:

Background and Purpose: This work develops the new intelligence Self Organization, SO; theory and practice.

Materials and Methods: The experimental data and the theoretical results come from the animal and human cell, brain, mind and sex: firefly, katydid, frog, bird, rodent, human prefrontal cortex.

Results: SO is a never ending, chaotic process that grows from the bottom up, without the leader or central control. It combines the inherited instructions and rules into complex processes and functions. SO laws cover the cell, brain, mind, sex, community and society. Hence they are universal. SO is composed of several basic functions, 30 laws and 100 equations. The data are measured in a short time scale from 0 to 2000 ms. The presented theoretical curves are strongly related to the experimental data.

Keywords: Cell, DNA code, genetic intelligence organization, cell internal language organization, consciousness, brain, mind, sex, life, SOUČEK laws, courtship, mimicry, send and receive windows, information compressing and packaging.

INTRODUCTION

The Self Organization SO deals with the concrete pieces: the cell and brain event trains and agents. Internal male and female agents are the internal parents. Their internal offspring is a hybrid of their particular characteristics.

SOUČEK, new theory and practice, based on a set of SO roots, laws and functions; set of numerical equations, numbers and patterns; SO programs supported by SO agents.

SO PHYSIOLOGY, new study of the cell, brain and behavior, based on the SO theory and practice.

SO MEDICINE, new methods that use SO, to explain and treat illness and damage to the cell, brain and behavior.

SO JOBS – new research and clinical methods based on the SOUČEK links. Data banks and related drug testing. Mind, business, computer interfaces. Thinking machines. Long and happy life.

SO BANG – explosion of intelligence due to the human interventions; prosperity, but also the strange attractions and dangerous chaos (like a big bang).

EXPERIMENTAL AND THEORETICAL RESULTS

This work unifies my experimental and theoretical findings. For details and equations see [1-31]. The work explains the life intelligence with the universal laws, SO.

1. **The roots of intelligence SO** grow from the organic mutation, variety, adaptation and evolution.

2. **The cell event trains and agents universe** is my extension and complement to the genetic code theory. The agents intelligence is organized in the nested, fractal sequences composed of **links**. The links are compared with the mapped genes on the chromosomes of Drosophila fruit fly. **The Cell Internal Language Organization, CILO**, senses the neighboring cells and the cell internal clock. CILO, new chemical signals, meters and associations constantly trigger and organize the neighboring genes, within the link information sign set. These links grow in many different ways, **beyond the genome limits**, and do quite different things, say, in fruit fly, mouse and human. The frequency of **cell consciousness** is 5.6 cycles per 1000 nm.

3. **The living cells** grow from organic molecules according to the cell intelligence SO laws; including the Cell Event Trains CET and the cell cooperation flows. In other words, the cell grows above the chemical logic. **Cell is intelligent**. The cell internal male agents and the female agents are sending and receiving the message signs, through the windows. The messages change one or several bases at a given site on a pre-existing RNA molecule. This new RNA molecule although slightly differing from the original, would direct the

synthesis of a protein molecule differing slightly but significantly from that previously produced by the cell. This explains the multiple gene to protein associations.

4. **The Brain Event Trains and Agents Universe** is a result of my long work: computerized experiments and models. To the newly discovered agents I have given the name of animal used in experiments: **FIREFLY; KATYDID; BIRD**. With the same agents I explain in a new way the human Prefrontal Cortex, Thalamus, Basal ganglion loops. The major brain event **trains** come from my experiments and models with the frogs and human. I show that the brain adjusts the rates of triggering and the internal time constants. In this way the brain generates various event trains: **Poisson; almost Poisson; uniform distribution; almost periodic**. **The Brain Internal Language Organization BILO** supports the agent and train links. The frequency of **brain consciousness** is 5.7 cycles per 1000 ms.

5. **The conscious brains** grow from the living cells according to the brain intelligence SO laws; including the Brain Event Trains BET and the brain cooperation flows. Many event trains are active simultaneously in the brain and mind tissue. The time intervals of trains cover a broad range from 0 to 1225 ms, with the peaks in 3,6; 25; 175 and 1225 ms. These event trains support the links between the brain agents. The links and the agents support the brain functions in the Self Organization SO of Understanding U, Consciousness C, Emotions E and Knowledge K. This is a nested, fractal, dynamic, fuzzy loop of the trains and signs. The brain signs are the pieces of mosaic used to build the mind. **The mind grows** from the brain, according to the mind intelligence SO laws, including the language, reasoning, compressing and measuring laws.

6. **The sex** male/female message box is related to the intelligence mating in: cell, CILO; brain, BILO; mind, language; sex. **Courting and mating; mimicry and eating** are present in: cell, brain, mind and sex.

The male emits strings of bursts. The female responds after each male burst. After mating, the female converts to predatory behavior and will no longer respond to her own male's bursts. Instead, she responds to the bursts patterns of other males, capturing and eating them.

7. **Internal male and female agents** are the internal parents. Their internal offspring is a hybrid of their particular characteristics. The trait of one parent is dominant over the trait of the other parent. The results are the **dominance, segregation and independent assortment**, which are present in four levels: cell, brain, mind and sex.

8. **The latency** L is a continuous function of stimulus and a discrete function of the context stored in the memory. In this way, the latency and answer can be switched from one window to another, although the windows are far away. **Window languages and signs** are present in: cell, CILO; brain, BILO; mind, language; and sex behavior.

9. **The Self Organization SO** deals with the concrete pieces: the cell and brain event trains and agents. SO takes the pieces and generates the functions. SO is composed of many laws and of more than **100 equations**. SO explains in a new way the **origin of life**, as well as the animal and human **brain, behavior and mind**.

10. **SO opens a new interdisciplinary science**: from the smart human head, to even smarter, technical nets, computers, devices, where only the most effective intelligent agents, ideas and structures survive in a self-modifying system. The winners are used as the dominant force in the Science, Technology, BIO Medicine; Clinic; Education.

SO BOW; FUNCTIONS; LAWS

SO BOW, spectrum of intelligence cycles Fig. **1**: from very short in cell, to very long in society (like a rainbow; from violet to red); short wave Cell; Brain; Mind; long wave SEX; **SPECIES**: short genome Insect; Bird; Mouse; long genome Human. Fig. **1** indicates the common links between SO Functions of bio units and of animals. This is due to the continuous descent of bio units and of animals. SO Functions have all sorts of details in different points. Yet every Function contains the same plan. The basic pattern is the same. The single plan testifies to common ancestry, with evolutionary divergence occurring as details become modified to fit each point to its particular way of life.

SOUČEK: short learned Understanding; Consciousness; Emotions; long innate Knowledge. Each of these functions is a different mixture of SO LAWS. See the Laws to Functions L -› F Association. The functions grow from the complex associations. They are not always precisely identifiable because they overlap. The same is true for the Laws. Each law is a different mixture of the Roots. See the Roots to Laws R -› L Association.

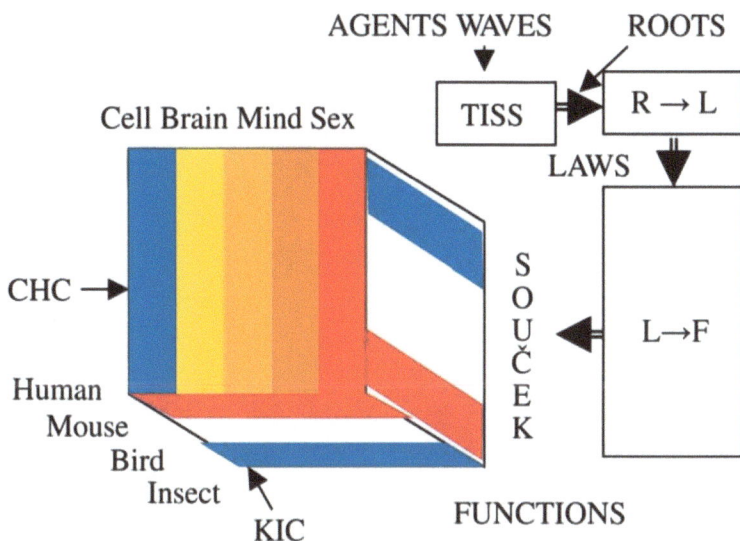

Figure 1: SO BOW over the LIFEBIZ self-organization. Point Associations: R-›L, Roots to Laws; L-›F, Laws to Functions. Red: Long. Violet: short. Point KIC, Knowledge in Insect Cell. CHC, Consciousness in Human Cell.

SO LAWS: are common to all, but details vary between the concrete cell, brain, mind and sex; and between animals. See Fig. **2**.

WINDOWS Internal Language Organization

AGGRESSION in leader, follower chirps

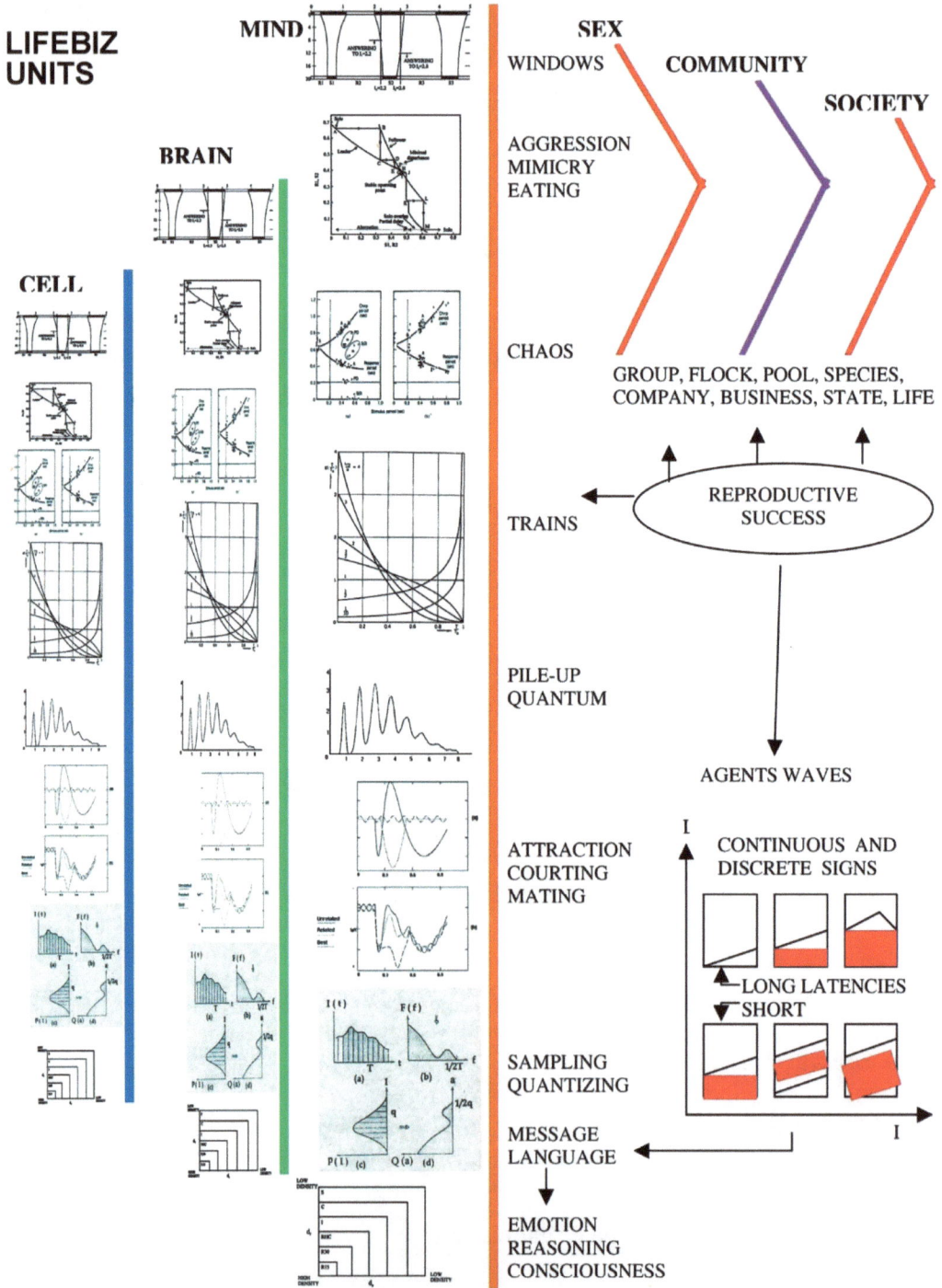

Figure 2: SOUČEK LAWS over the LIFEBIZ UNITS: CELL, BRAIN, MIND, SEX.

CHAOS in agent singing, bursts; **TRAINS** of internal events; **QUANTUM** transmitter release; **ATTRACTION**, strong desire; **SAMPLING** of information; **QUANTIZING** of continuous signal; **CONSCIOUSNESS** in cell, brain, mind and sex. Other laws:

PILE – UP; CQD; BIRD agent; **KATYDID** agent. **FIREFLY** agent; neural computing; message **QUANTUM**; mind **BARRIER**; **BRAMA**; brain **CHAOS**; **COMPRESSOR**; **REASON**; **METER**; **ASSOCIATION**; **TISS**; **BET**; brain mind **SIGN**; **BILO**; **COMET**; **SAVA**; **SON**; **CON**; **LISS**; **CILO**; **GENIO**; **GENIUS+**.

SO SENSATION IN MOLLUSK

SO NEURAL NETWORKS define the basic behavior of the system. Thus, models for complex animal and human behavioral features should account for electrophysiological details and complexity of the single neuron as well as the connectivity and architecture of neural networks.

Neurons form the nodes. To test the context of a neural network involved in the control of complex behavior, the rhythmic feeding activity observed in Pleurobranchaea is presented. This carnivorous mollusk will initiate a rhythmic protraction and retraction of its proboscis when presented with food stimuli, culminating in bites and swallowing of the food. The neural elements responsible for the animal's behavior are distributed between the cerebral and buccal ganglia. Individual elements in the model are composed of functionally equivalent neurons in the animal, and many of the connections in the network have long delays, indicating that they are polysynaptic.

1. The rhythmic behavior, once initiated, can persist even if food stimulus is taken away. **2.** The feeding behavior is harder to initiate or is suppressed completely when the animal is satiated. **3.** The animal exhibits choice behavior between feeding and withdrawal due to a noxious stimulus. When both types of stimuli are present, it chooses one or the other, depending on the stimulus strengths. **4.** The animal exhibits the rudimentary functions of the Understanding U, Consciousness C, Emotions E and Knowledge K. These functions are present in the Self

Organized loop. **5.** The loop links the cerebral ganglion node and the buccal ganglion node. **6.** Nodes are linked into a group.

SO REASONING

Within the brain the evolution has created the specific sets of links: for low and high level information traffic; for short and long distances; for small and high information volumes. These are node, group, flock and pool links. In this way the architecture has a general connectivity within the group and slightly restricted between groups, flocks and pools. Very large sets of fuzzy associations may be enfolded within the same set of nodes. Stimulus-response associations are both learned and expressed in one non-iterative transformation. The neural process ideally embodies the concept of **content addressable memory**. Multiple pattern associations, at nearly arbitrary levels of complexity, may be enfolded onto a neural node. Encoded responses or "outputs" may subsequently be generated or accessed from the node *via* content of input. Input fields may be representative of addressing schemes or "syntax," and are transformed in an inherently parallel manner through all of the contents enfolded within the node. In response to a stimulus signal, the node regenerates the associated output data field, indicating also the degree of confidence in that output association.

The node network is capable of enfolding associations in the sense that input of one pattern prototype will induce the issuance of the second, thus subsequently inducing the issuance of a third, and so on.

Patterns generated within a recurrent data flow may express a linear sequence of associations, each pattern association connected through its encoding within one temporal frame (*i.e.* associations are linked by their proximity in time). This process of linear association may be considered to be a base to the associative reasoning processes where a thought train may be expressed through a sequence of associations initially learned over time. For example, the image of a fork may invoke the impression of plate, subsequently invoking an impression response in association to a kitchen table or food, for instance. In this manner, the node, group, flock and pool systems course through a sequence of sensory impressions, each of which has been formed by associations temporally connected.

SO HUMAN PREFRONTAL CORTEX

This region lies below the sulcus principalis, occupying the inferior frontal convexity, and comprises architectonic areas 47/12,45, and the ventral most part of area 46 that lies below the sulcus principalis. In the human brain, the ventrolateral frontal cortical region largely occupies the inferior frontal gyrus. The Posterior region is inhabited by the Posterior flocks, pool, groups and nodes. Each of these Posterior units is involved in its **Self-Organization**. All units together cooperate in the Posterior Self Organization. The posterior cortical association areas, where recently processed information is temporarily held while it is being integrated with incoming and recalled information, are connected with the ventrolateral frontal cortical region.

Table 1: Human prefrontal cortex in mnemonic processing

Unit	Short Term Patterns in FFF	Long Term Patterns in Associations	Language Areas
N	Feature	Frequent features, words	Neural networks in cortical columns
G	Chunk	Frequent chunks, phrases	Cortical columns
F	Association	Frequent, cognitive or semantic associations, stories	Temporal Lobe association area
P	Task	Frequent tasks, contexts	Anterior cingulate cortex Thalamus Basal ganglia

The functional interaction between the ventrolateral frontal region and the posterior association cortex is critical for the expression within memory of various executive processes, such as active selection, comparison, and judgment of stimuli held in short-term and long-term memory. This interaction, Cooperation and Self Organization involve two nested, fractal, brain-mind tissues: Frontal and Posterior. This type of interaction is necessary for active (explicit) encoding and retrieval of information, that is, processes initiated under conscious effort by the subject and guided by the subject's plans and intentions. These active forms of encoding and retrieval depend on the lateral frontal cortex. The more passive forms of encoding and retrieval result when incoming or recalled stimuli automatically trigger stored representations (*e.g.*, on the basis of strong preexisting associations or matching to stored representations).

Table 2: Human prefrontal cortex in pattern recognition

Time T	ms	Information I	SET S	Size of Pattern x	Number of Patterns y	Number of Units z
BRA	3,6	Feature	N	10^5	10^5	7·7·7
AMA=7·BRA	25	Chunk	G	10^6	10^4	7·7
MA=7·AMA	125	association	F	10^7	10^3	7
BRAMA=7·MA	1225	Task	P	10^8	10^2	1

These latter aspects of mnemonic processing do not critically depend on the lateral frontal cortex, and, this accounts for the normal performance of the brain.

The Self Organization of the Frontal and of the Posterior regions coordinate, interpret, and elaborate the information in consciousness to provide the hippocampal--associative-memory system with the appropriate encoding information and retrieval cues that it takes as its input. Comparable processes are involved in evaluating the hippocampal system's output and placing those retrieved memories in a proper spatiotemporal context.

Nodes, groups, flocks and pools are "conscious" of the various processes involved in each unit's internal memory search. They are not conscious of the operations of the hippocampal-associative system, or of the operations of the strategic frontal system that occupy consciousness. The unit is aware of the questions it delivers to other units, the answers it gets from them, and the evaluation of the answers, but it is not aware of the external operations and of the hippocampus itself. On the other hand, the complete region is involved in engram formation and reactivation in the neo cortex, priming, procedural memory, manipulations of strategies, and in cognitive resources (see Table **1**).

TISS, tissue of intelligence: Time, Information, Sign and Set. **Time T**: BRA, AMA, MA. **Information I**: feature, chunk, association. **Sign Sg**: BILO, COMET, SAVA: **Set S**: node, group, flock. These are four different, but related and precisely defined **component** classes of intelligence tissue TISS.

HUMAN BRAIN intelligence flow is presented in Table **2**. This is an estimation of TISS optimal parameters, related to the BRAMA period of 1225 ms. In this period TISS could deal with: 1 task; 7 associations; $7 \cdot 7$ chunks and $7 \cdot 7 \cdot 7$ features. In the extreme case TISS could deal with the P, F, G, N units in the same ratio: 1; 7; $7 \cdot 7$; $7 \cdot 7 \cdot 7$. The N unit supports the short distance, strong flow. Large number of N units, $z = 343$ supports the fast learning and the pattern object recognition. In other words, each N unit overlaps y patterns; of moderate size x. The situation gradually changes through G, F and P units.

Intelligence flow involves s discrete codes: words, phrases, numbers, s! combinations. They are stored in the content addressable, **specific memories s**:

$$s = \Sigma \cdot z = [1+7+7 \cdot 7+7 \cdot 7 \cdot 7] = 400 \tag{1}$$

Each of s codes is associated with its xy general pattern g

$$g = x \cdot y = 10^{10} \tag{2}$$

For the human sensory input, in a single BRAMA period of 1225 ms, the BRAIN intelligence flow INFLOW in bits is about

$$INFLOW = s \cdot g = 400 \cdot 10^{10} = 4 \cdot 10^{12} \tag{3}$$

Through fractions of INFLOW, the node, group, flock and pool systems course through a sequence of sensory impressions. The brain dynamic, fuzzy and discrete combinations, flow through the internal, innate "neural and massively parallel computers" [13]. As a result, only the human brain is able to construct unlimited set of discrete expressions starting from the limited set of words. This involves the SOUČEK bow, functions and laws [1-31].

SO BRAIN EVENT TRAINS

Accurate understanding of the mechanics of individual neurons and their interactions in specific brain areas has been achieved in a broad range such as: mollusk, rodents, human prefrontal cortex, frontal cortex for mnemonic processing, neural computing. The goal is to reveal how brain operates. In this work and in [1-31] I present an entirely new explanation, SO of intelligence. Animal life grows above the chemical logic. The life involves also the SO of intelligence. SO is composed of many oscillators and of the massively parallel random event trains.

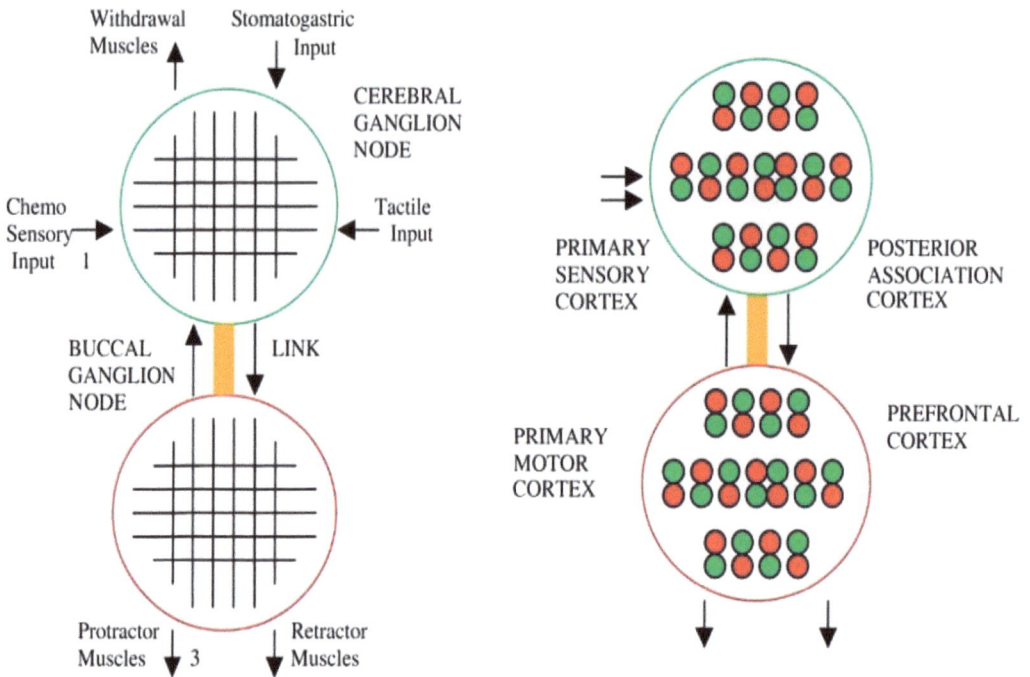

Figure 3: Left: SO of intelligence in the mollusk Pleurobranchala. Learning and memory loop. Right: SO of intelligence in the Brain, Mind. Many learning and memory loops.

Fig. **3** left presents the SO in the mollusk Pleurobranchala: The Cerebral Ganglion Node and the Buccal Ganglion Node. The neural networks are presented as single neurons. The two nodes are linked into a group. Here are rhythmic feeding behaviors of neurons produced when food stimulus is presented to neuron 1:

LLLLLLLLLLLLLLLLL   Neuron 1

LLLLLLL LLLLLL LLLLL   Neuron 3

The protractor and retractor neurons fire in alternating trends of action potentials, and the feeding activity, once initiated, persists even when food stimulus is removed. The node response combines the train of action potentials with the bursting and oscillations. The synaptic efficiency is influenced by the width of presynaptic action potential, postsynaptic time constant, learning and memory. When the Cerebral ganglion senses the environment, it creates the transcription BET. BET switches the Buccal ganglion, that creates BET'. Through the link,

BET, BET' form the **learning** loop. The loop is active even after the stimulation. This is a **memory** of the past environmental condition.

Fig. **3** right presents the **brain-mind** activity composed of processes. A process starts, performs actions and finishes. Many processes are active at the same time, and processes can send messages to one another. Several communicating processes could run on several nodes, or concurrently on the same node. The same is true for groups, flocks and pools.

Many laboratories through years have collected thousands of experimental data files. Yet it was difficult to explain the neural processes. Now, the random neural processes are explained by equation 4:

$$g(x) = \lambda\tau_2\,(1 - x)\,/\,a = \lambda\tau_2\,(1 - T/T_0)\,/\,a \tag{4}$$

The life is a set of chemical and of intelligence processes, and of equilibrium. Equations in [1 to 30] explain the cell and brain intelligence processes. Known organisms share a similar bio SO, and an almost identical set of SO processes, laws and functions. See Figs. **1**, **2** and **3**.

Life = DNA logic and SO intelligence $\qquad\qquad\qquad\qquad$ (5)

A link unit connects the process on a point to point basis. It operates with the continuous and discrete information (CQD), as well as with the information trains. Hence the link behaves as:

1) **neural network;**

2) **holographic network;**

3) **discrete, fuzzy processors with local memory**. This is very different from computer channels which only carry discrete data and messages. Links are polite, aggressive or patient. The polite link will wait until the process is supplied. Equally, an output will not be sent until the receiver is ready. The aggressive link will interrupt the process. Each TISS unit has its Local Primary Oscillators, Timers and BRAMA-like Protocols.

TISS Self-Organization Includes

1) **Synchronization;**

2) **Merging** towards the set of attractors in parallel chaotic activities;

3) **Temporary reconfiguration** of the topology. TISS runs through a lot of temporary topologies;

4) **Slight local changes** in the case of inherited, instinct, born with actions;

5) **Some local changes** in the case of learning, adaptation and conditional reflexes;

6) **Distance temporary changes** in the case of creative thinking and of mind wandering. The brain-mind tissue is composed of many TISS that form the dynamic never repeating active sets. These active sets operate in parallel, sequential or overlapping modes. TISS is composed of the dynamic, fuzzy, nested, fractal clouds. Many associations can be **distributed** one over another in the same cloud. Hence they **overlap**. This is combined with the **partial selection**. Dynamic, nested, fractal **TISS cancels the border between the brain and the mind. There is only one brain-mind tissue, TISS**. TISS generates fuzzy overlapped functions, such as Understanding, Consciousness, Emotions and Knowledge. Instinct inherited knowledge or predisposition is located in fixed areas. Learning from the environment and reflexes are dispersed around these fixed areas. Creative thinking, thought wondering, imagination come from the active areas all around the brain-mind structure. Each unit and agent has: The response function responsible for the inherent built in program; transfer function which deals with the input-output relations; continuous and discrete long term and short term working memories. Hence the unit and agent have the representation of the local world and to some extent are free from the environmental dependency. The units and agents communicate using the Brain Internal Language

Organization BILO. The firefly **understands**, **U**, the courting message through the receive windows. The mollusk is **conscious**, **C**, of the presence of the food and enters into a rhythmic feeding behavior. The firefly after mating changes her **emotions**, **E**. She is not interested anymore for a courting partner. She is now inviting a visitor that she could eat. The bird inherits the **knowledge**, **K**. This includes the song that the young bird inherits from the parents, and then improves through learning. Katydid **associates**, **A**, the chirping call with the potential courting partner and with its location on the tree. In short, each animal as well as each TISS unit and its agent performs the local Self Organization of the local U, C, E, K and A. All units and agents together Cooperate in the overall TISS Self Organization. TISS involves the context switching as observed in fireflies; chaotic attractions as observed in katydids; continuous and discrete messages as observed in birds. The FFF information transmission and mixture combines the neural impulse trains, with the fast acting transmitters: inhibitory GABA; excitatory glutamate; and modulatory dopamine, serotonin and acetylcholine.

CONCLUSIONS

GENETIC and BIOLOGY Theories: Animal cells grow and operate following the fixed, genetic, DNA, logic and programs (or mutations). Animal and human innate, instinct behavior follow the fixed programs. Cells and animals are not supported by languages.

SOUČEK Theory: The fixed genetic and instinct logic and programs are supported by the parallel internal languages, CILO, BILO: with the continuous signs and with the discrete codes; with the fuzzy, adaptive coded windows. These are internal simple words and phrases; and the context switching. In this way animal cells, as well as the animals, are able to learn and understand. The same is true for the animal and human brain mind internal units: nodes, groups, flocks and pools. Cells, units and animals are intelligent, within their specific domains. **Hence the animal life grows above the chemical logic. The life is intelligence. The origin of life and consciousness is in the genetic intelligence universe**

GENIUS+, developed by chance. This involves the SOUČEK bow, functions, laws and processes [1 to 30].

DNA logic involves the slow adaptation and preadaptation by chance. SO intelligence combines in a new way the already available preadaptation. In this way **SO intelligence creates the fast evolution**. This is a "cultural " development within the cell and brain, based on the internal SO processes and languages CILO, BILO [1 to 30].

SO processes are active in the cells and neurons. They explain the learning (growth of synapses) as well as the memory (new synapses), see [1 to 4]. SO processes in the inter spaces and extra spaces extend the Genome to Proteome growth and the sensing of environment [29,30].

AGENT is a blob of matter similar to the school of fish, flock of birds or colony of ants. See Fig. **1**. The agent's behavior is built from the bottom up, involving the primary oscillator. **Primary oscillator** generates the special, link sequence. In other words, the communication features of the agent are controlled by an oscillator which defines the behavior. Hence, it can be called the primary oscillator. The primary waveform produces the sequences in cooperation with the window and answer waves. Hence, an agent is a set of oscillators; a set of waves. Agents are attracted by the internal chunky patterns: modest attraction, unconsciousness and intuition; strong attraction, consciousness and understanding.

SO explains the patterns of neuronal organization and the way they work. SO is the advanced stage of the attempt to understand the brain, which may well be the last of all the frontiers of knowledge that man can attempt to penetrate and encompass. The brain research will occupy the years of our future. Vigorous and exciting new disciplines emerge: neurochemistry, molecular neurobiology, neuron genetics, neuropharmacology. But also: **brain communications, brain networks, brain computers and brain theories**.

ACKNOWLEDGEMENT

I have spent fifty years working out the Self Organization of life intelligence: in Institute Ruder Boskovic; U of Zagreb; Brookhaven National Laboratory N.Y.;

SUNY; U of AZ. I acknowledge the stimulating atmosphere and excellent working conditions.

DISCLOSURE

"The content of this chapter has been previously published in *Periodicum Biologorum, Vol. 110, No. 1, 3-10,2008"*.

REFERENCES

[1]   SOUČEK B. Mono stable Systems Triggered at Random. *Nuclear Instruments Methods 1964; 29:* 109–114.

[2]   SOUČEK B. Application of pile-up distortion calculation. *Rev Scientific Instruments 1965; 36:* 1582–1587.

[3]   SOUČEK B. Influence of the Latency Fluctuations and the Quantum Process of Transmitter Release on the End-Plate Potentials' Amplitude Distribution. *Biophysical Journal 1971; 11:* 127–139.

[4]   SOUČEK B. Complete Model for the Statistical Composition of the End-Plate Potential. *J Theoretical Biology 1971; 30:* 631–648.

[5]   SOUČEK B. Applications of computers and mathematical models to the study of neuronal systems, Nuclear and neuronal pulse spectrometry. *Computer Physics Communications 1973;5:* 115– 122.

[6]   CARLSON AD, SOUČEK B. Computer simulation of firefly flash sequence. *Journal of Theoretical Biology 1975; 55:* 353–370.

[7]   SOUČEK B. Model of Alternating and Aggressive Communication with the Example of Katydid Chirping. *J Theoretical Biology1975; 52:*399–417.

[8]   SOUČEK B, VENCL F. Bird Communication Study Using Digital Computer. *J Theoretical Biology 1975; 49:* 147–172.

[9]   VENCL F, SOUČEK B. Structure and Control of Duet Singing in the White-Crested Jay Thrush. *Behavior 1976; 57:* 20–33.

[10]   SOUČEK B, CARLSON AD. Brain Windows in Firefly Communication. *J Theoretical Biology 1986 119:* 47–65.

[11]   SOUČEK B, CARLSON AD. Brain Window Language in Firefly. *J Theoretic Biology 1987; 125:* 93–103.

[12]   SOUČEK B, CARLSON AD. Computers in Neurobiology and Behavior. Wiley New York 1976.

[13]   SOUČEK B, SOUČEK M. Neural and Massively Parallel Computers. Wiley New York 1988.

[14]   SOUČEK B. Neural and Concurrent Real-Time Systems. Wiley New York 1989.

[15]   SOUČEK B and the IRIS Group. Neural and Intelligent Systems Integration. Wiley New York 1991.

[16]   SOUČEK B and the IRIS Group. Fast Learning and Invariant Object Recognition. Wiley New York 1992.

[17]   SOUČEK B and the IRIS Group. Fuzzy, Holographic and Parallel Intelligence. Wiley New York 1992.

[18]   SOUČEK B and the IRIS Group. Dynamic, Genetic and Chaotic Programming. Wiley New York 1992.

[19]   PLANTAMURA VL, SOUČEK B, VISAGGIO G. Frontier Decision Support Concepts. Wiley New York 1994.

[20]   SOUČEK B. Quantum Mind – Evoked Potential Link. *Per Biol1998;100(2):* 129–140.

[21]   SOUČEK B. Quantum Mind Emerges from the Prefrontal Cortex Nested, Fractal Chaos. *Per biol1999; 101(2):* 109–119.

[22]   SOUČEK B. Quantum Mind Compresses the Verbal Stories. *Per biol1999; 101(3):* 193–201.

[23]   SOUČEK B. Quantum Mind Measures the Verbal Stories. *Per biol2000:102(4):* 331–342.

[24]   SOUČEK B. Universal Brain Theory: The Self Organization of Understanding, Consciousness, Emotions and Knowledge. *Per biol2001; 103(3):* 219–228.

[25]   SOUČEK B. The Brain Agents Universe. *Per biol2002; 104(3):*353–369.

[26]   SOUČEK B. The Brain and Mind Tissue, TISS: node, group, flock, pool. *Per biol2002; 104(3):* 345–352.

[27]   SOUČEK B. The Brain and Mind Attractions, BRAMA, the Brain Internal Language Organization, BILO, the Consciousness. *Per biol2O03; 105(3):* 207–214.

[28]   SOUČEK B. The genetic and learned brain and mind event trains BET and signs: BILO,COMET, SAVA, CON. *Per biol2004; (106)3:*265–278.

[29]   SOUČEK B. The DNA code, the brain event trains BET and the self-organization SO make a single entity: life and consciousness. *Per biol2004; 106(4):* 443–444.

[30]   SOUČEK B. Genetic Intelligence Organization GENIO. *Per biol2005; 107(4):* 385–39.

[31]   SOUČEK B. Genetic Intelligence Universe GENIUS+; Cell internal language organization CILO; Origin of life and consciousness. *Per biol2007; 109(2):* 89–99.

Send Orders of Reprints at reprints@benthamscience.net

CHAPTER 4

The Genetic Intelligence Universe GENIUS+: Cell Internal Language Organization CILO; Origin of Life and Consciousness

Abstract:

Background and Purpose: This work develops the new genetic intelligence theory as a complement to the genetic code theory.

Material and Methods: The genetic intelligence is organized in the nested, fractal cell event trains CET. The trains are compared with the send and receive windows measured on the firefly Photuris versicolor.

Results: The new GENIUS+ theory is developed. It covers the cell, brain and behavior; hence it is universal. The cell intelligence is composed of the intelligence links; related to the length, locus, loop, distance; and to the cell working association and memory. The primary, window and answer oscillators generate the sequences of send and receive windows. They are entrained by the stimulus and they define the latency of the answer. The initial phase is determined by the contents of memories. The frequency of cell consciousness is 5,7 cycles per 1000 nm.

Conclusions: The human genes and the mouse genes are 99 per cent similar in DNA codes. Yet the human GENIUS+ intelligence links are different from the mouse GENIUS+ intelligence links. These are two different building, linking plans, producing two different lives: human and mouse. The GENIUS+ is a missing link between the genome and proteome. The cell Primary waveforms and oscillations are responsible for an inherent time, space, link program that controls the communication and the behavior of cell agents. The Primary waveform also controls the relationship between the stimulus and the response by narrowing and widening the receive and send windows. Hence the Primary waveform presents the basic, precise, and quantitative description of a part of the cell Self Organization SO. Three waveforms (primary, window, answer), lead complex segments of the cell SO. They define the Cell Internal Language Organization CILO.

Keywords: Cell, DNA code, genetic intelligence organization, gene, gene link, base, GENIUS+ laws, courtship, mimicry, send and receive windows, brain, mind, life, consciousness.

INTRODUCTION

The cell chemical feedback is responsible for the control of chemical processes. When the presence of product is high (low), the negative (positive) feedback stops (starts) the mechanism for making it. This is explained with DNA, RNA and the functions of structural, regulator and operator genes. The signaling pathway is important in determining embryonic patterning and cell fate in multiple structures of the developing embryo. Many developmental genes of the pathway continue to function in regulation of cell growth and differentiation after embryogenesis, and are involved in patterning and development of variety of organ systems.

Yet, there are more proteins in the proteome in comparison with the genes in genome. It has been estimated that the human proteome is at least an order of magnitude more complex than the human genome, since it is assessed that there might be as many million human proteins. [1-23]. This missing link I explained in [48] and here.

This work shifts from the genome mapping, sequencing and determination of genome functions, as well as from the brain structures [1-23] to the intelligence organization in the cell. It develops the cell, genetic, intelligence laws and compares them with the brain, mind, intelligence laws [24-55]. The cell is a complex association composed of many reciprocal adjustment loops. The association element is related to the sensation and action sequences, loops and links. In the living organisms many life processes involve the continuous information signals, brain windows [29, 30], the Brain Internal Language Organization BILO [45], and the Brain Event Trains BET [46]. A computer–based analysis of the brain of the firefly, explains numerous brain windows. In this work I move from the brain laws summarized in [46], to the universal, cell and brain laws. Results are: the Genetic Intelligence Universe GENIUS+; the Cell Event Train CET and the Cell Internal Language Organization CILO. The work explains the courtship and mimicry processes within the cell. The Abbreviations cover this work, as well as [48].

CELL INTERNAL LANGUAGE ORGANIZATION, CILO

Let us start from the conclusion of [48]: the human genes and the mouse genes are 99 per cent similar in DNA codes. The building materials are similar, but the building plans are very different. The plans are related to the Cell Internal Language Organization CILO. CILO is in charge of the cell Transformation Maping T/M; Logic Programming L/P; Sampling/Quantizing S/Q, different promoters and exon splicing. CILO is present in the cell discrete units, Figs. **3** and **4** in [48], as well as in dispersed fields, full of agents and of cooperation.

Cell cooperation involves intelligence encoded in the changing patterns of an energy field and molecular clouds. The model envisages a closed feedback loop: individual agents are contributing to the common field; the field in turn influences the activity of the agent. The situation is similar to that in an orchestra: each musician contributes to the total sound; the total sound is heard by each musician. The musician adjusts his or her playing on the basis of two sets of information: the melody he or she is supposed to play and which is written on the paper, and the sound received from the common field. The cooperative-action model claims that the energy and molecular fields and clouds are the carriers of memory and cognition. The patterns are stored in the field. When a stimulus is received, it produces the field, which is compared with the stored patterns. The pattern of the stimulus causes millions of cell agents to generate a similar pattern, which has been stored in the chemical structure of these agents. One way to explain the cooperative action is through resonance: A tuning fork "remembers" the frequency it is tuned at; placed in a variable sound field, the fork will produce the originally tuned pitch when it recognizes that frequency or a frequency which is merely similar (recognizing similar but not necessarily identical frequencies). One argument supporting the model is the fact that the cell is composed of millions of molecules. It is difficult to envision the cell that would connect all of these molecules on a point-to-point basis. One possible answer is a contact less communication through the field. Through the field, a large population of molecules would be able to communicate simultaneously.

Field processing involves the number of processing agents so large that it can be treated as a continuous quantity. It is clear that processing agents on this level of parallelism cannot be individually programmed; they must be controlled en masse. This leads to a model of processing based on the transformation of continuous scalar and vector fields: field processor. The field processing can be energy or molecular. The cell field processor has field storage units for holding scalar and vector fields. Some of these units hold fixed fields for controlling the processing. Others hold variable fields captured from input or as intermediate fields in recursive processes. Field transformations processes are implemented by programmed and dynamic communication between elementary field transforms. These elementary operations permit programming any useful transformation in a modest number of steps. **Field processing is the base for the cell cooperation**. The cell intelligence is enclosed in the field patterns of the cell, not in the individual agents. Calcium-dependent conformation states coupled to charge or energy could be a medium of information transfer among the nanometer subunits, with programming by genetic or environmental effects. Transduction of information signals by ATPase mechanical proteins would result in temporal and spatial control of protein mechanical functions and cellular activity. It may be coupled to action potentials or 2+ calcium ion flux. Such coupling could result in cooperative resonances, field fluctuations, and interference patterns which might comprise "conscious" awareness functions within the cell. The matrix grid of cell subunits and associated proteins resembles the computers, cellular automata, and robots. The cell cooperation involves the regulation, information processing, and cognitive processes and communication.

CET operates within the cell protein assemblies (cytoskeletal polymers, organelles, membranes, proteins, virus coats) of nanometer size scale. CET and its nano scale oscillations support the intelligence exchange within the protein assemblies and collectives. CET operates with the intelligence (link) pieces and agents adjacent or dispersed over the DNA sequences.

Intelligence link is related to the signaling pathways, length, locus, loop, distance; and to the cell working association and memory. Hence the link is multidimensional. Only one dimension, expressed in nm, is discussed. The link is related to the intelligence content.

Organelles communicate through the internal membranes. They are dynamic and they change the shape. In this way the organelles establish contracts; form the transportation vehicles; separate the vehicles that carry molecules towards the internal and external membranes. The chemical transmitter is contained in vehicles in the organelles knot and, on the arrival of the actions potential at the terminal, some of the vehicles are discharged into the cytoskeletal clef and they pile-up. The cell PILE-UP laws, similar to the brain PILE-UP equations 1 to 17 [25, 26, 27] explain the generation of excitatory and inhibitory populations. The

CET laws are similar to the BET laws [46]. This is a process of sending and receiving of molecules and of intelligence in the link scale. This process involves the window agents with the send and receive windows?

Window agent is a blob of matter similar to the school of fish, flock of birds or colony of ants. The agent's behavior is built from the bottom up, involving the primary oscillator. See Figs. **1** and **2**.

Primary oscillator generates the special, link sequence. In other words, the communication features of the agent are controlled by an oscillator which defines the basic of behavior and communication. Hence, it can be called the primary oscillator. The output of the primary oscillator is a primary waveform, P, of a sinusoidal shape. The communication between two sequences of two agents is orthogonal to their flow. Upon receiving a stimulus, the agent modifies the operation of the primary oscillator: a sinusoidal waveform of constant period is changed into a waveform with variable period (Fig. **1a**). This entrainment lasts for three or four cycles, after which time the period of oscillations is back to the original, constant period. The memory accepts the stimulus and modulates the oscillations. However, the memory is not ideal and is slowly erased. Hence, the modulatory effect of the stimulus is strong immediately after the stimulation and slowly vanishes with time: the oscillations return to normal.

The modulated primary waveform is shown in Fig. **1a**. The primary waveform is responsible for an inherent timing program that controls the communication and behavior of the agent. The primary waveform also controls the relationship between the stimulus and the response. Hence, the primary waveform presents the basic, precise, and quantitative description of a part of the agent. It could be expected that the primary waveforms can describe the cell behavior functions in other cell agents as well. In the case of the window agent, the primary waveform is responsible for the generation of the send receive window sequences. The primary waveform produces the sequences in cooperation with the window generator.

Window generator operation is similar to that of an electronic differential amplifier. It receives control signals from two sides and produces the output that

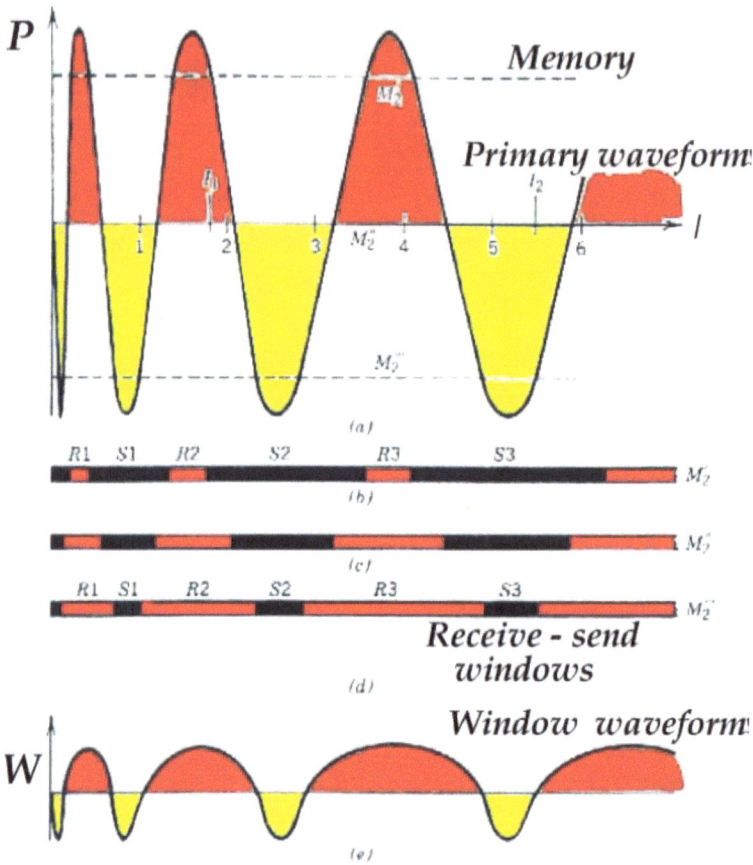

Figure 1: Primary waveform defines the basic behavior and communication: (a) primary waveform-memory interaction defines the receive-send windows: I1 and I2 represent two stimuli which arrive during different phases of the primary waveform and have different effects on memory level; (b, c, d) three window sequences corresponding to memory levels M2', M2'' and M3'''; (e) window waveform corresponding to the sequence show in (d).

is proportional to the difference between the two signals. The window generator has a memory of its own. Each stimulus received by the agent will contribute to the voltage stored in the window memory. The window memory has only a small leakage, so the voltage in the memory will keep accumulating. The discharge between stimuli is small. Two signals control the window generator: the primary waveform and the voltage form the window memory (Fig. **2**). Hence, the output W of the window generator is proportional to the difference between the primary waveform and the window memory voltage (Fig. **1e**). Positive, negative, and zero differences will produce positive, negative, and zero outputs from the window generator. In other words, the primary waveform is compared with an internal voltage or bias stored in window memory. The portion of the primary waveform above the memory produces a positive window waveform W and opens an R window.

The position of the primary waveform below the memory produces a negative window waveform and opens an S window. Fig. **1a** shows the primary waveform, P, and three window memory voltages, M2', M2'' andM2'''. Figs. **1b**, **c**, and **d** show the generated receive-send sequences for memory voltages M2', M2'', and M2''', respectively. Fig. **1e** shows the window waveform W for memory voltage M2'''. This window waveform W generates the receive-send sequence shown in Fig. **1d**. Notice the difference between the three receive-send sequences. If the memory is highly positive, such as M2' in Fig. **1**, the receive windows are narrow and the sending windows are wide open. Oppositely, if the memory is highly negative, such as M2''' in Fig. **1**, the receive windows are wide open and the sending windows are narrow. The agent keeps track of the past history of stimulation in the window memory, M2. Based on the previous flash history, the memory – in cooperation with the primary oscillator – generates the proper sequence of receive – send windows. Each stimulus contributes to the window memory. The contribution of the stimulus interval I is proportional to the value taken from the primary waveform P(I). Hence, stimulus I1 in Fig. **1a** will produce a positive contribution, and stimulus I2 will produce a negative contribution to the window memory M2. The stimulation pattern I1, I2 produces the contribution P(I1), P(I2). If P(I1)=– P(I2), the contribution to the memory is zero and memory stays unchanged during the stimulation. This is a typical situation in good courtship communication. The stimulation pattern I1, I1 will keep pushing the memory up, closing the R windows. This is typical for non-perfect courtship communication. The pattern I2, I2 will keep pushing the memory down, opening the R windows. This is typical for communication mimicry.

Answer oscillator. For each stimulation pattern, the female agent generates a flash response. The latency of the answering flash contains the message sent back to the male. If the stimulation pattern is not acceptable, the female agent does not respond at all. The generation of a flash response of fixed latency is produced by a

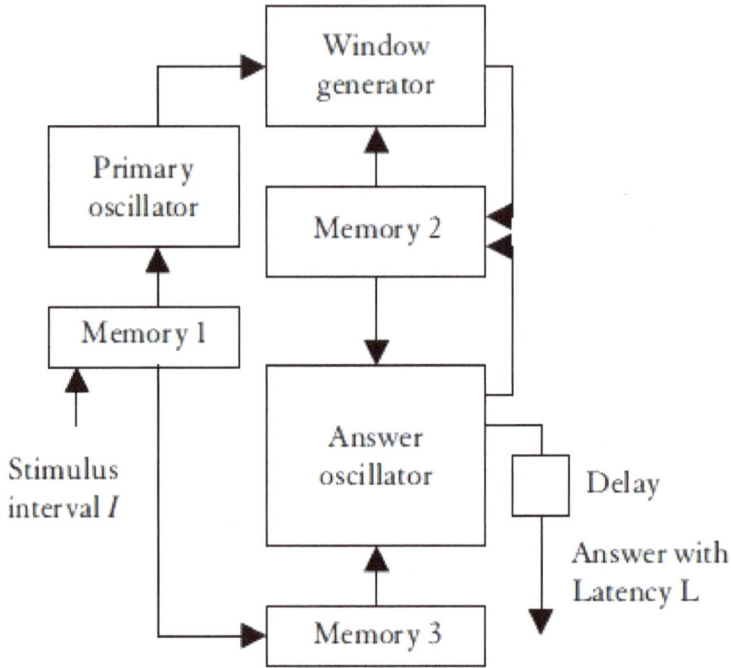

Figure 2: Model of sensory and motor control in the cell female agent, simulated on a computer. The model is divided into 3 blocks with separate memories: the primary oscillator, which is entrained by the stimulus through the memory M1; the window generator, which defines the receive-send windows through the interaction between the primary waveform and the memory M2; and the answer oscillator, which defines the latency of the answer. Its initial phase is determined by the contents of memories M2 and M3.

special oscillator. I call this oscillator the answer oscillator (Fig. **2**) and its waveform, A, the answer waveform. The answer oscillator also has a memory, M3. In addition, the window generator and the answer oscillator are mutually coupled through the common memory, M2. In this way, they entrain each other. The answer oscillator is connected to the primary oscillator's memory, M1, for the short instant when the stimulus arrives. In this way, the phase of the entrainment from the primary memory, M1, is transferred into the memoryM3 of the answer oscillator. The phase of the answer oscillator is therefore controlled by the memories M1, M2 and M3. The answering latency is not a function of the last stimulation interval only. This is due to the memories M2 and M3. As the memories are erased, the more recent stimuli produce the largest contributions to latency. The contributions of the stimuli that occurred a long time ago are slowly forgotten. The content of the memories is a weighted sum of the contributions of all stimuli. Hence, part of the latency is a function of this weighted sum. The latency is a function of the last stimulus interval, of an internal delay, of the primary cycle, and of the past history of stimulation. If two experiments are performed with the same last stimulation intervals, they might produce two different latencies. This variation in latencies was associated in the past only with random factors. In fact, this model shows that latencies are mostly deterministic and predictable. Yet the latencies depend on past history, and not on the last stimulation interval alone. This fact should also be kept in mind in models which try to explain communication behavior with one single phase.

Integrating and forgetting. Memory M2 receives information from the window generator and from the answer oscillator. The memory M2 is a coupling circuit between the window generator and the answer oscillator. Memory M2 continuously integrates (accumulates) the received information. The stored information slowly vanishes, due to forgetting. This process is described in equation 1:

$$[M_2 (I) + C_{22} P(I) - C_{23} f_1(I)] f_2 \qquad\qquad (1)$$

In equation 1, the continuous integration processes are concentrated into one instant I, where I is the stimulation interval. When the stimulus arrives, it stops the primary waveform P(I) and the primary forgetting function f1 (I). The fraction C22 P(I) is added to the window memory through the window generator. The coupling coefficient C22 defines the contribution to the memory M2, obtained through the window generator. When the stimulus arrives, the value of the primary forgetting function f1 (I) is transferred into the answer memory M3. The fraction C23 f1 (I) is added to the window memory through the answer oscillator. The coupling coefficient C23 defines the contribution to the memory M2, obtained through the answer oscillator. The forgetting process is described by f2 measured relative to the stimulus. Let us consider stimulation with the train of identical intervals I. The first stimulus contributes to the memory. The contribution still remembered when the second stimulus arrives is;

$$x = [C_{22} P(I) - C_{23} f_1(I)] f_2(I) \tag{2}$$

The contribution of the first stimulus at the time of arrival of the third stimulus is xf_2 (I). We see that contributions of n intervals form a geometrical series, with the sum:

$$sum = \left[C_{22} P(I) - C_{23} f_1(I) \sum_{n=0}^{\infty} [f_2(I)] \right]^n \tag{3}$$

$$sum = [C_{22} P(I) - C_{23} f_1(I)] [f_2(I) / (1 - f_2(I))] \tag{4}$$

Each stimulus contributes to the memory M2. As the contributions of past stimuli are slowly forgotten, the memory M2 stores the weighted sum of the past history of stimulation. The dominant effect is that of the last stimulus, because its contribution is fully remembered. The window generator produces the window waveform that is proportional to the difference between the driving signal P and the memory M2;

$$W = P - M2 \tag{5}$$

The window waveform defines the sequence of the receive-send cell windows. If the window waveform is positive, a receive R window is open. If the window waveform is negative, a send S window is open. Hence, the R-S sequence depends on the memory M2. Highly positive M2 will result in narrow R windows and in wide S windows. Oppositely, highly negative memory will result in wide R windows and narrow S windows.

CILO and Perception. A transition from continuous, fuzzy signaling to discrete coding is achieved and a communication language CILO is formed. Both receive and send windows are adaptive and also depend on the context. In the agent the response [**latency L**] is a continuous analogue function of the stimulus [**interval I**]. The basic, quantum law of cell windows is:

If there is a match between the stimulus [interval I] and one of the receive windows, and if there is a match between the internally induced response [latency

L] and one of the sending windows, **then the response [latency L] will be send out**.

Note that the cell windows define a quantum, fuzzy, symbolic presentation. The I/L transfer functions define the stimulus response relation.

Experimental data and computer model generated firefly data [29, 30] show that the latency interacts with the sensory inputs and with behavior in several ways: The latency L is a continuous [analogue] function of the stimulus interval I, and of the content of the memory. For example, stimulus I=1.5 seconds could produce the latency L in the range from 0.6 to 1 second. The latency L is also a discrete [discontinuous] function of the context stored in the memory. In this way, the latency and answer can be switched from one window to another, although the windows are far away. The latency is "labeled" by the semantic meaning of the window. Context-switching is related to the complex model of the world and to the perception. **Perception** presents a process of forming in the brain a complex model of the world, a model that is different from the sensory data stream. Based on experience, the brain compares the expected model with the received data. The main features are selected; unimportant details are neglected. The same data stream can produce two different models or conclusions, if the brain has two hypotheses. For example, the stimulus I = 1.5 sec, will produce a response through the window S1R2 for the purpose of courting but it will produce a response through the window S2R2 in the case of patrolling. What is received depends upon what is hypothesized; incorrect hypotheses lead to illusions. On the other side, the hypotheses help build the image of the world even if the data are incomplete or buried in "noise". So long as the sensory data stream can provide an occasional data point that reinforces the hypotheses, the process of understanding can proceed successfully, within the complex Brain Windows, defined by the context.

The cell consciousness cC is composed of pieces. Each piece of consciousness is a SON of the father called "Attention to the Current Task" and of the mother called "Related Experiences". Father and mother communicate by using the cell event trains and the common message clusters. The Attention presents the specific need and its non-specific general domain. The Experience responds with the born with and mutated components see Fig. **3**. The frequency of the cell consciousness (cycles in 1000 nm) [48]:

$$fcC = 1.000 / lm = 1000 / 178.5 = 5.60 \tag{6}$$

HUMAN LANGUAGE AND REASONING SKILLS

The brain is protected against intrusive chemicals by the blood-brain barrier. The blood-brain barrier keeps out any molecule that might upset the brain. It also keeps the neurotransmitters, i.e. molecules that carry messages between nerve cells, inside the brain. I introduce the mind barrier that protects the mind and keeps the knowledge-learning agents within the mind space. The Brain Mind space is formed in such a way that it supports the holistic mind-body, psycho-health balance. The mind accepts the Flow of Favorable Factors, FFF through several groups of specialized windows. The mind barrier and the windows are inherited features, in the same way as the blood-brain barrier. The windows are divided into sensation, mental and genetic windows. The windows/vehicles carry sensation, mental, and genetic elements of FFF to the mind. The sensation windows/vehicles carry signals, 4 taste elements, 7 smell elements, 30 vision elements, *etc.* The mental windows/vehicles carry the mental elements. These are more difficult to detect and define. I relate them to the behavior elements: feed, mate, fight, flight, accept, reject, search, negotiate, protect, love, like, hate, dislike, *etc.* The genetic windows/vehicles carry the genetic elements that are responsible for the unconscious behavior coded in genes. The sensation, mental and genetic elements need not be organized among themselves and in their relation to one another. The mind barrier windows help to resolve competing and conflicting demands and to establish a coherent request for the time and space resources of brain. Not everything from environment and from the brain could interact with the mind. For example, man has no sensation windows for infra-red light, for ultra-sonic calls, or for nuclear radiation. Man cannot react to these kind of events without technical devices. Human mind is well equipped with the vision related windows/vehicles. These include sensation windows/vehicles for color, orientation, edges, bars, direction of motion, angles, corners, static and dynamic features. The mental windows/vehicles include visual pattern recognition and feature extraction, vision-based navigation, vision-based feeling, vision-based reasoning, *etc.* Hence the human mind is very much oriented towards genetic, mental and sensation elements based on vision. In the same time, the human mind has no windows for dolphin-like sound elements.

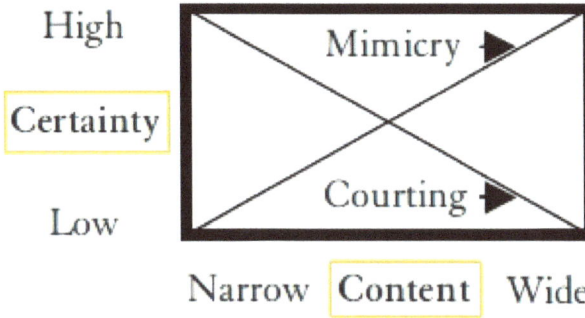

Figure 3: The genetic intelligence universe, GENIUS+. Conscious courting. Content: narrow, specific dialogue. Certainty is high, to mate the right partner. Conscious mimicry. Content: wide range of dialogues. Certainty is high, to eat the partner.

Now I come closer to the myriad of interactions within the Brain Mind collective space. The brain dynamics establishes the communication tracks in the areas of traffic. Some of the tracks exist only for an instant, other form strange attractor structures. Some of these are most probably related to the active areas AA in brain images. The images give some indication about the traffic highways and about the grouping of vehicles. The real mental contents are hidden inside of the vehicles. Some of the tracks form temporary knowledge-learning cloud. The cloud is peacefully merged with other clouds, or it produces the thunderstorm. There are tracks that live longer life as more permanent impressions. The result could be a new idea, discovery, psychological state, stress, emotions, such as love or hate. These dynamic tracks are responsible for our personality, character, talents, health and happiness. The dynamics of active areas AA suggests a feedback that connects the zones of imagination to the primary sensory zones: visual zone in case of visual imagination; acoustical zone in case of voice *etc.* That means that imagining an object is practically the same as sensing it. This involves: a) storing the data in the short term memory; b) associating it with other data presently in the memory; c) compressing or quantizing the result; d) forming a new chunk or a permanent association. Here diverse perception and imagination sequences meet and interact, through the feed-backs and the mind barrier. The windows/vehicles operate in a symbol-signal domain. Each flock is an elastic, distributed symbol. In the same time the flock carries distributed continuous signals. Symbol-signal processing is evident in CQD, DQC layers that relate continuous to discrete. The symbol-signal presentation is viewed as a collection of objects that communicate with each other through the flocks of vehicles using the mind barrier traffic procedure. The symbol-signal represents, evaluates and approximates information with some degree of fuzziness, uncertainty and incompleteness. The uncertainty or confidence factor CF can be used to refer the truth value. The truth value for "sweet" is 100, if most of symbol-signal vehicles in the "sweet" flock are activated, while it will be near 0, if only small fraction of the flock is activated. Sequences of CQD, DQC layers of the mind barrier merge genetic, sensation and mental elements into complex associations, objects and trains of thoughts. The Brain Mind barrier is a missing link between genetic and neurological structures, mind and behavior. Continuous presentation of mind and behavior is permanently related to discrete codes, including the three billion digits of the DNA-genetic code. This is the base for intuitive, inductive, and common-sense reasoning and for consciousness.

A human can store up to 10^{12} information items. The memory is organized on the principle of association; data retrieval is fairly slow (5 to 50 bits/second). Humans have strong pre-processors between the sensors and the memory, which compress and transform the sensory data into more meaningful form. The central system and the long-term memory deal only with highly pre-processed information. The main features of the brain are associative organization, self-adaptability, learning, and perception. It is estimated that long-term memory could acquire 10,000 chunks of information per year. The brain deals with sequences composed of a vast number of patterns. The brain cannot remember all these sequences and patterns, in particular if they are a part of seemingly random process that resembles the chaos. The chaos is composed of relatively simple processes: stretching, folding, repeating, symmetry, attraction, fractal self-similarity. Each of the processes can be described just with a few process-bits of information. It is enough for the brain to remember the process-bits only. This is the ultimate level of information compression or quantizing.

The Brain Mind dynamic space is composed of myriad of agents. The storage of information is not separated from learning and processing. These agents are like the stars dispersed in the Universe: they cover only a negligible part of the unlimited Understanding U, Consciousness C, Emotion E, Knowledge K, space Fig. **4**. The space is defined across two densities: df is the density of the domain specific facts and features; ds is the density of the domain specific skills for detecting tendencies and patterns. Higher densities mean more of specific, narrow domain. Lower densities mean more of general; multi domain; complexity; background knowledge; inter discipline. The agents that are relatively close (higher densities), could mate or form more easily the network related to a particular subject, or mental task. These agents form the reasoning space R, which expands with the age. Reasoning emphasizes the dominant attributes and serves when searching for expected, probable answers, vertical thinking, interpolation, case-based similarity, expertise. The agents that are far away in the space (lower densities), do not communicate or mate easily. They rarely form the subject network. If and when they do, this leads to the unexpected outcome. I call this rare outcome: intuition; spark of discovery; low density consciousness; sub consciousness. Low density space emphasizes less influential attributes and serves when looking for unexpected answers, rare discoveries, original outcomes, feeling, lateral thinking, forming and modifying the hypotheses until a pattern emerges.

Dynamic space of Fig. **4** is related to the survival fitness. Survival fitness of an individual (or of a species) is high, if he is capable to make a right choice (decision) even in a low density part of the space. The fitness is a part of natural selection's ultimate goal, reproductive success.

I use the example of medical diagnoses, to explain the Brain Mind collective space, shown in Fig. **4**.

The medical diagnoses is based on the following:

Diagnostic vector: 24 dimensional

Total number of bits: 44

In this example, possible diagnostic space is 2^{44}.

Yet the medical doctors have tried to produce the diagnoses. Obviously they were not able to correlate isolated data, lost in a huge, mostly empty diagnostic space. The diagnoses has been done on a partial analysis and on the doctor's general experience, or intuition.

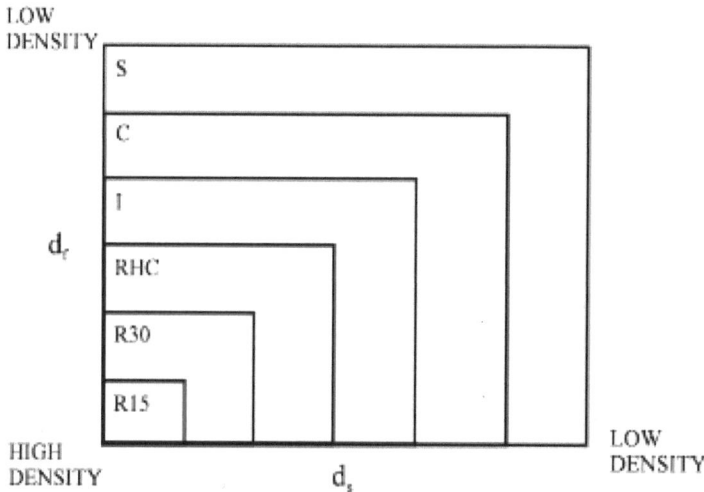

Figure 4: The Brain Mind Reasoning Spaces.: R15 -reasoning, age 15. R30 – reasoning, age 30. RHC – reasoning, human-computer. I – intuition C – low density consciousness. S – sub consciousness. The separation lines are only indicatory. The space is a continuum, with mostly low density. Higher "narrow-domain" density is found on Reasoning islands. Low and very low density defines the spaces of intuition, consciousness and sub consciousness.

Brain like computing helps to extend the reasoning space. The computer-association classifies the above diagnostic vectors into diagnostic classes, with the accuracy better than 95%. The computer-association extracts global features hidden in inaccessible or nonlinear relationships within a very long patient vector. The computer correlates the knowledge-learning pieces that are far away in the space. It increases the number of patterns and of pattern recognition skills. As a result the diagnoses is based on reasoning. I call it the Reasoning based on Human-Computer cooperation, RHC. Fig. **4** presents the operational space of the human mind, based on human related densities df and ds. If we plot the operational space of RHC into Fig. **4**, it comes out that RHC penetrates into the space of human intuition. Hence the diagnosis is based on the RHC and is not any more the result of intuition. It is very difficult or impossible to penetrate into the space of intuition, low density consciousness, sub consciousness. For thousands of years, the only possible approach was through beliefs, suggestions, meditations and hypnoses. How is that possible?

Flow of Favorable Factors, FFF, or the Flow of Field Fertility. There are myriads of "mental seeds" in the field. In one moment the field is very fertile for, say sex oriented mental seeds. This specific fertility comes from hormonal level, physical and mental inputs *etc.* of this moment. Hence the sex related mental plants grow, compete, cooperate, self-organize better than other plants. In another moment the field is very fertile for, say, the food oriented mental seeds. This specific fertility is created because the person is hungry, it smells the food *etc.* One day the person receives a very strong suggestion. The suggestion presents a dominant input into the mental fields. As a result, FFF domains related to this input become very fertile. If suggestion is given under hypnoses, the FFF domains related to the suggestion might become hyper fertile. This could be the way to modify person's FFF, which in turn modifies person's mental processes. The hyper fertile domain within FFF supports the growth, even if the domain seed density is low. As a result the mental plants grow out of seeds that are related to the seemingly long forgotten events or events that are only partially supported by knowledge. These events are stored within the spaces of low-density selective attention or sub consciousness. The hyper fertile domain might support the growth and interaction of mental plants out of proportion, changing the person's character or mental state, for bad or for good.

GENIO, GENIUS, GENIUS +

GENIO, the genetic intelligence organization [48].

GENIUS, grand rare powers of thought and imagination; very great ability (usual definition).

GENIUS +, the genetic intelligence universe; across the borders of cells and nerves; through the natural evolution and selection; survival and reproduction fitness.

GENIUS +, merges GENIO, BRAMA, SKILL and GENIUS.

GENIUS +, universal laws cover the cell, brain and behavior.

See Fig. **5**: Universal Brain Theory [42]; the Brain SO universal laws [24 – 53]; Agents Universe [43]. The Universal SO theory and Agents cover both, the cell and the brain; animals and humans.

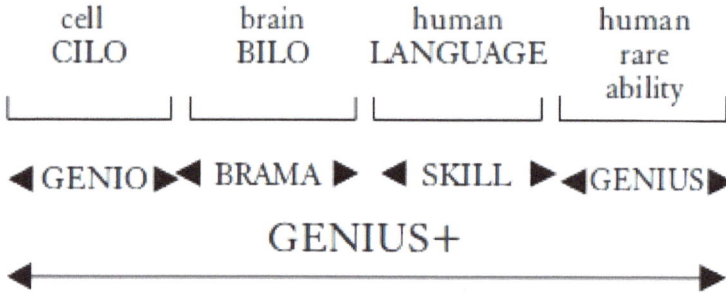

Figure 5: GENIUS+ covers the cell, brain, human intelligence and human rare abilities.

CONCLUSION

Intelligence is a mosaic that grows from pieces, linked by the common association map [48] and by the common language:

CELL intelligence; Cell Internal Language Organization CILO; Cell Event Trains CET; the molecular packages in the link scale.

BRAIN intelligence; Brain Internal Language Organization BILO; Brain Event Trains BET, carries the neural spike packages in time scale.

HUMAN intelligence; human language; learning and generalization mosaic; above BILO mosaic; above CILO mosaic.

The cell signaling pathway could be a simple one signal, one receptor, one signal transduction cascade; tightly regulated cascade; complicated functional branching where most of its components are not only involved in transduction a signal, but are also involved in other biochemical or cellular processes. Hence the protein modification is not obvious from the DNA sequence, such as isoforms and post-translations modifications. It is assessed that approximately 200 diverse types of post-translation protein modification processes occur.

Cell cooperation involves intelligence encoded in the changing patterns of an energy field and molecular clouds. The model envisages a closed feedback loop: individual agents are contributing to the common field; the field in turn influences the activity of the agent.

The cell primary waveforms and oscillations are responsible for an inherent time, space, link program that controls the communication and the behavior of the cell agents. The Primary waveform also controls the relationship between the stimulus and the response by narrowing and widening the receive and send windows. Hence the Primary waveform presents the basic, precise, and quantitative description of a part of the cell Self Organization SO. The three waveforms (primary, window, answer), lead many complex segments of the cell SO.

The organic molecules grow from inorganic molecules according to the chemical logic. The living cells grow from organic molecules according to the cell GENIUS+ laws. In other words, the living cell grows above the chemical logic. The cell is intelligent. The cell activity is capable of solving problems which, if done by human, would be considered intelligent activity.

The cell consciousness cC is related to the current awareness. The cC frequency, defined by equation 6, is 5.60 cycles per 1000 nm. The cC current content is related to the proteome. The cC certainty is related to the cC current content in Fig. **3**.

Mating/eating plans. The communication is already present in great profusion, with every agent making contact with practically all of the other agents in a local area. CILO program excites the agents. Two initially excited agents transform the communication between them from an inhibitory to excitatory state by altering chemical transmitter. Excited agents are induced to send out collateral messages toward each other, establishing communication contact. The cell internal male agents and the female agents are sending and receiving the signs, through the windows. The signs and related messages form CILO.

The male agent emits strings of bursts. The female responds after each male burst. After mating, the female converts to predatory behavior and will no longer respond to her own male's bursts. Instead, she responds to the burst patterns of other males, capturing and eating them.

An active ATP-ase (enzyme adenosine triphosphatase) releases energy for the transport of nutritional materials from membrane to membrane. These materials are then transported through the membrane and into the organelles by the activity of the ATP-ase residing directly inside the membrane. In the human genome, thousands of genes are coding for integral membrane proteins. They are related to the signaling pathways and molecular transport across membranes. The materials are needed because of a high rate of RNA production and protein synthesis within the cell. A pattern of messages is translated into an RNA molecular code. The messages change one or several bases at a given site on a pre-existing RNA molecule. This new RNA molecule although slightly differing from the original, would direct the synthesis of a protein molecule differing slightly but significantly from that previously produced by the cell. This explains the multiple gene to protein associations. It involves the serial CELL WORK that cooperates with the parallel cell GENIUS+, Fig. **6**.

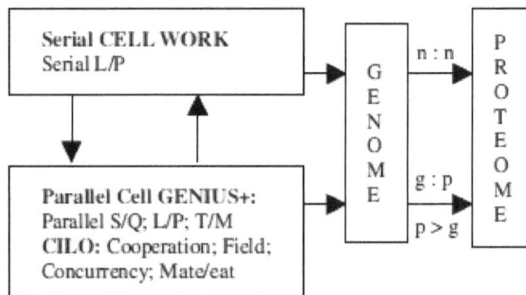

Figure 6A: Cell: Serial CELL WORK together with parallel GENIUS+.

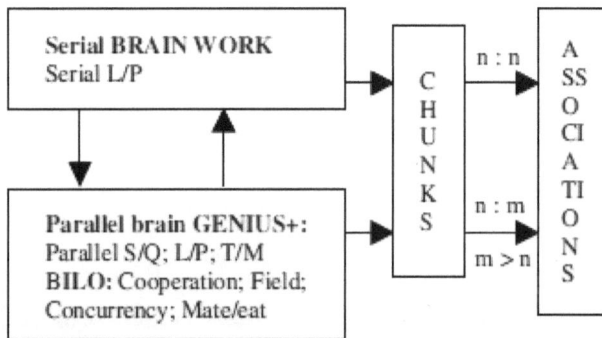

Figure 6B: Brain: Serial BRAIN WORK together with parallel GENIUS+.

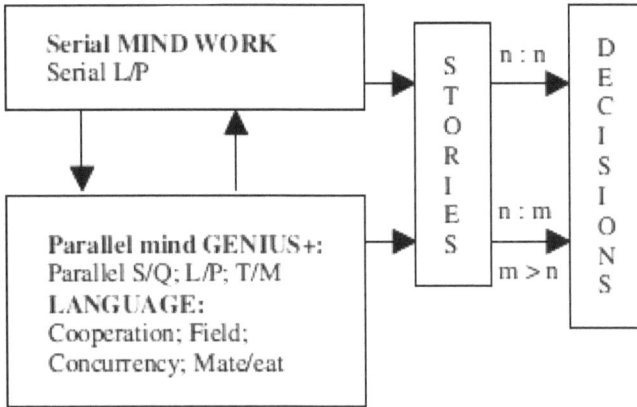

Figure 6C: Mind: Serial MIND WORK together with parallel GENIUS+.

Consciousness C in the Cell, Brain, Community mind and in the Society behavior. Specific C is explained by the specific Communication: CILO, BILO, HUMAN LANGUAGE, SEX. Behind each C is a specific window language based on equations 1 to 6 see Fig. **7**. This is the genetic intelligence universe, Genius+.

Natural selection. The bible is speaking of 7 good years and of 7 bad years. The stock market cycle is about 49 years. The agriculture and the Morava man appeared about 13000 and 26000 years ago. The above data as well as the cell and brain data are used to form Tables **1** and **2**. SO BANG grows from the fast human interventions. It will change the predator, pray cycles and their amplitudes and speeds. Human community and society must learn from the nature. No investment team is complete these days without the SO learned from cell and brain (Fig. **8**).

The origin of life and consciousness is in the genetic intelligence universe GENIUS+, developed by chance.

This involves SO of UCEK.

SO of UCEK law 1: The intelligence SO grows from the organic mutation, variety, adaptation and evolution.

SO of UCEK law 2: The living cells grow from organic molecules according to the cell intelligence SO laws; including the Cell Event Trains CET and the cell cooperation flows FFF.

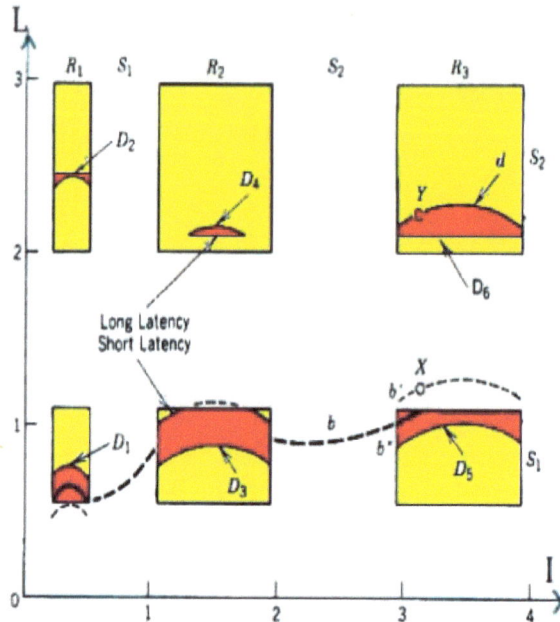

Figure 7: Window language for highly positive memory M2. The receive R windows are narow and the send S windows are wide. Belts b and d represent the vocabulary. Shaded areas represent the dialogues.

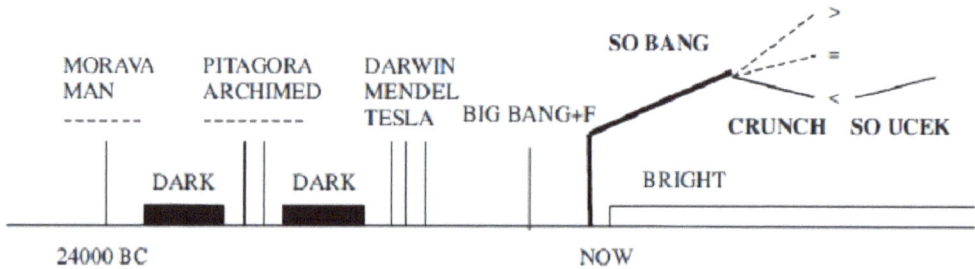

Figure 8: SO BANG, CRUNCH and the way out. From the special bright BRAINS; over very long dark ages; to the financial deregulation BIG BANG+F, to the intelligence SO explosion, named SO BANG; and to the bright future. Line >: natural resources > population needs; SO BANG grows. Line =: natural resources = population needs; SO BANG is stable. Line <: natural resources < population needs; SO BANG becomes CRUNCH: a difficult moment at which important decisions must be made. When it comes to the crunch, you reach the point where to act and decide. You, company, country, world. CRUNCH might lead to: paradise reduced to the local and global oases; warm planet, epidermis; time machine; strange attractions and dangerous chaos; modified population needs. Solution is the UNIVERSAL Law of Life: SO UCEK: Self Organization of UNIVERSAL Consciousness, Emotions and Knowledge. This law governs the whole cell; the whole brain; and the whole earth communities and societies life and business. This law leads to the intelligent business, bio technology and medicine, long and happy life.

Table 1: Frequency of consciousness

	BRA	AMA	MA	CO PERIOD	Frequency of consciousness	Frequency of consciousness
Cell nm	3,64	25,5	178,5	GENIO 1250	**7** cycles per 1250 nm	5,6 cycles per 1000 nm
Brain ms	3,6	25	175 Semantic priming	BRAMA 1225	**7** cycles per 1225 ms	5,7 cycles per 1000 ms
Community Years	1	7 Biblic 7 years	49 Market cycles	343	**7** cycles per 343 years	5,6 cycles per 275 years
Society millennium	0,25	1,8	13 agriculture	91 Sapiens sapiens	**7** cycles per 91 millennium	5,6 cycles per 72,8 millennium

Table 2: Courting and mating, or mimicry and eating

	Cell Internal Language Organization CILO	Brain Internal Language Organization BILO	Mind, Language Bank and Trust	Natural and Financial Sex Behaviour
Patrolling, Courting and Mimicry Signs	Cell send and receive windows and bursts	brain send and receive windows and bursts	mental, sensation and genetic windows/vehicles and bursts	body send and receive windows/vehicles and flashes
Stimulus and Response Bursts	Chemical vehicles, Cell Event Trains CET	Family of short Brain Event Trains BET	Cooperation of short Brain Event Trains BET	Light flashes
Box of parallel mating messages	right DNA codes of membrane proteins, short pieces, RNA	right brain event trains and associations	right patterns, mental elements, symbols, concepts and stories	right male sperm genome and female sex cell genome
Mating actions and products	New proteins	New features, chunks, associations	Vertical thinking, **reasoning, pattern recognition, decision**	Mating process
	wrong DNA codes of membrane proteins, short pieces, RNA	wrong brain event trains and associations	wrong patterns, mental elements, symbols, concepts and stories	wrong partner's body
Eating actions and products	Box is broken into pieces that serve as food and energy	Box is broken into pieces that serve to form new features, chunks, associations	Box is broken into pieces that serve for **mind wandering lateral thinking, ideas**	Body is broken into pieces that serve as food and energy

SO of UCEK law 3: The conscious brains grow from the living cells according to the brain intelligence SO laws; including the Brain Event Trains BET and the brain cooperation flows FFF [24-48, 53].

CHALLENGE

This work challenges the current four beliefs:

Computing mosaics, grid computing structures, theories and applications. Young, brilliant scientists are now making mosaics composed of the cell, brain, computer pieces. These young **intelligence jockeys**, ij, are becoming the leaders in science and applications.

An example is the computational, multi perspective recognition and visualization of patterns in genome regions [5]. This mosaic of intelligence merges the BLAST, MapDraw, multicolor DotPlot, Clustal and Sfor methods; with the Genome Sequencing Center in Saint Luis; and with the Internet Server at NIH, Bethesda. Another example is the prediction of drug utility [54]. This mosaic of intelligence merges the NIH website, MOLGEN QSPR software and Weka machine learning software. There is no limit for intelligence. GENIUS computing mosaics will grow into **an avalanche** that will change computer science, engineering, medicine, applications, business, the world.

ACKNOWLEDGEMENT

I have spent fifty years working out the Self Organization of life intelligence: in Institute Ruder Boskovic; U of Zagreb; Brookhaven National Laboratory N.Y.; SUNY; U of AZ. I acknowledge the stimulating atmosphere and excellent working conditions.

DISCLOSURE

"The content of this chapter has been previously published in *Peridicum Biologorum, Vol. 109, No. 2, 89-99, 2007*".

REFERENCES

[1]   CHIAPPA K H. 1989 Evoked Potentials in Clinical Medicine. Raven Press Ltd, New York.

[2]   CHUANG P-T, McMAHON A P 1999 Vertebrate Hedgehog signaling modulated by induction of a Hedgehog-binding protein. Nature 397: 617–621.

[3]   DEHAENE S *et al.* 1999, Sources of Mathematical Thinking Behavioral and Brain – Imaging Evidence. Science 284: 970 – 974.

[4]   DEL CASTILLO J, KATZ B. Quantum Components of the End-Plate Potential. J Physiology (London) 1950;124: 560.

[5]   DURAJLIJA ZINIC S. SitaRam: a computational approach for multi perspective visualization of higher-order and progressive patterns in highly repetitive regions of DNA. *Per bio2005;* 107: 423 – 436.

[6]   GOLDMAN-RAKIC Patricia. Architecture of the Prefrontal Cortex and the Central Executive [in Ref. (7)] 1995.

[7]   GRAFMAN J, HOLYOAK KJ, BOLLER F. Structure and Functions of the Human Prefrontal Cortex, New York Academy of Sciences, vol. 769, New York 1995.

[8]   HO R, SUTHERLAND JG, BRUHA I. Neurological Fuzzy Diagnoses: Holographic *vs.* Statistical *vs.* Neural Method [in Ref. (19)] 1994.

[9]   JIMENEZ – MONTANO MA, LUCIO – GARCIA HR, FERNANDEZ AR. Computer simulation to generate simplified proteins with stochastic grammars. *Per biol2005;* 107: 397 – 402.

[10]   KOSTOVIC I, JUDAS M, KOSTOVIC – KNEZEVIC LJ, SIMIC G, DELALLE I, CHUDY D, SAJIN B, PETANJEK Z. Zagreb Research Collection of Human Brains for Developmental Neurobiologists and Clinical Neuroscientists. International J Developmental Biol1991; 35: 215 – 230.

[11]   KRALJ M, KRALJEVIC S, SEDIC M, KURJAK A, PAVELIC K. Global approach to perinatal medicine: functional genomics and proteomics. J Perinatal Med (in press) 2004.

[12]   LEVANAT S, PAVELIC B, CRNIC I, ORESKOVIC S, MANOJLOVIC S. Involvement of PTCH gene in various no inflammatory cysts. J Molecular Med2000; 78 (3): 140–146.

[13]   LOCKHART DJ, WINZELER EA. Genomics, gene expression and DNA arrays. Nature2000; 405: 827–836.

[14]   LYON BE. Recognition and Counting Reduce Costs of Avion Cospecific Brood Parasitism. Nature2003; 422: 495 – 499.

[15]   PANDEY A, MANN M. Proteomics to study genes and genomes. Nature2000; 405: 837–846.

[16]   PETANJEK Z, ROKO RASIN M, JOVANOV N, KRSNIK Z. Magnopyramidal Neurons in the Area 9 of the Human Prefrontal Cortex. A Quantitative Rapid Golgi Stud. *Per biol1998;* 100 (2): 221 – 231.

[17]   PETRENKO O, ZAIKA AI. MOLLUM Delta Np 73 facilitates cell immortalization and cooperate with oncogenic Ras in cellular transformation *in vivo*. Molecular Cell Biol2003 23: 5540–5555.

[18]   PETRIDES M. Functional Organization of the Human Prefrontal Cortex for Mnemonic Processing [in Ref. (7)] 1995.

[19]   PLANTAMURA V L, SOUČEK B, VISAGGIO G. Frontier Decision Support Concepts. Wiley, New York 1994.

[20]   RAMACHANDRAN *VS.* The Emerging Brain. Profile Books 2003. .

[21]   RANDIC M, BALABAN AT,NOVIC M, ZALOZNIK A, PISANSKI T. A novel graphical representation of proteins. *Per biol*2005;107: 403 – 414.

[22]   SOLMS M. The Neuropsychology of Dream. Erlbaum Associates1997.

[23] SLADE N,GALETIC I, KAPITANOVIC S, PAVELIC J. The efficacy of retroviral herpes simplex virus thymidine kinase gene transfer and ganciclovir treatment on the inhibition of melanoma growth *in vitro* and *in vivo*. Arch Dermatology Res2001; 293: 484–490.

[24] SOUČEK B. Mono stable Systems Triggered at Random. *Nuclear Instruments Methods1964; 29:* 109–114 .

[25] SOUČEK B. Application of pile-up distortion calculation. *Rev Scientific Instrum1965; 36:* 1582–1587.

[26] SOUČEK B. Influence of the Latency Fluctuations and the Quantum Process of Transmitter Release on the End-Plate Potentials' Amplitude Distribution. *Biophysical Journal1971; 11:* 127–139.

[27] SOUČEK B. Complete Model for the Statistical Composition of the End-Plate Potential. *J Theoretical Biol1971; 30:* 631–648.

[28] SOUČEK B. Applications of computers and mathematical models to the study of neuronal systems, Nuclear and neuronal pulse spectrometry. *Computer Physics Communications1973; 5:* 115– 122.

[29] CARLSON AD, SOUČEK B. Computer simulation of firefly flash sequence. *Journal of Theoretical Biology1975; 55:* 353–370.

[30] SOUČEK B. Model of Alternating and Aggressive Communication with the Example of Katydid Chirping. *J Theoretical Biol1975; 52:*399–417.

[31] SOUČEK B, VENCL F. Bird Communication Study Using Digital Computer. *J Theoretical Biol1975; 49:* 147–172.

[32] VENCL F, SOUČEK B. Structure and Control of Duet Singing in the White-Crested Jay Thrush. *Behavior1976; 57:* 20–33.

[33] SOUČEK B, CARLSON AD. Brain Windows in Firefly Communication. *J Theoretical Biol1986; 119:* 47–65.

[34] SOUČEK B, CARLSON AD. Brain Window Language in Firefly. *J Theoretical Biol1987; 125:* 93–103.

[35] SOUČEK B, CARLSON AD. Computers in Neurobiology and Behavior. Wiley New York 1976.

[36] SOUČEK B, SOUČEK M. Neural and Massively Parallel Computers. Wiley New York 1988.

[37] SOUČEK B. Neural and Concurrent Real-Time Systems. Wiley New York 1989.

[38] SOUČEK B and the IRIS Group. Neural and Intelligent Systems Integration. Wiley New York 1991.

[39] SOUČEK B and the IRIS Group. Fast Learning and Invariant Object Recognition. Wiley New York 1992.

[40] SOUČEK B and the IRIS Group. Fuzzy, Holographic and Parallel Intelligence. Wiley New York 1992.

[41] SOUČEK B and the IRIS Group. Dynamic, Genetic and Chaotic Programming. Wiley New York. 1992.

[42] PLANTAMURA VL, SOUČEK B, VISAGGIO G. Frontier Decision Support Concepts. Wiley, New York 1994.

[43] SOUČEK B. Quantum Mind – Evoked Potential Link. *Per biol1998; 100(2):* 129–140.

[44] SOUČEK B. Quantum Mind Emerges from the Prefrontal Cortex Nested, Fractal Chaos. *Per biol1999; 101(2):* 109–119.

[45]   SOUČEK B. Quantum Mind Compresses the Verbal Stories. *Per biol1999; 101(3):* 193–201.

[46]   SOUČEK B. Quantum Mind Measures the Verbal Stories. *Per biol2000; 102(4):* 331–342.

[47]   SOUČEK B. Universal Brain Theory: The Self Organization of Understanding, Consciousness, Emotions and Knowledge. *Per biol2001; 103(3):* 219–228.

[48]   SOUČEK B. The Brain Agents Universe. *Per biol2002; 104(3):*353–369.

[49]   SOUČEK B. The Brain and Mind Tissue, TISS: node, group, flock, pool. *Per biol2002; 104(3):* 345–352.

[50]   SOUČEK B. The Brain and Mind Attractions, BRAMA, the Brain Internal Language Organization, BILO, the Consciousness. *Per biol2003; 105(3):* 207–214.

[51]   SOUČEK B. The genetic and learned brain and mind event trains BET and signs: BILO,COMET, SAVA, CON. *Per biol2004; (106)3:*265–278.

[52]   SOUČEK B. The DNA code, the brain event trains BET and the self-organization SO make a single entity: life and consciousness. *Per biol2004;106(4):* 443–444.

[53]   SOUČEK B. Genetic Intelligence Organization GENIO. *Per biol2005; 107(4):* 385–392.

[54]   SUPEK F, SMUC T, LUCIC B. A Prototype Structure Activity Relational Model Based on National Cancer Institute Cell Line Screening Data.*Per biol2005;107.4:451-455.*

Send Orders of Reprints at reprints@benthamscience.net

CHAPTER 5

The Genetic Intelligence Organization GENIO

Abstract:

Background and Purpose: This work develops the new genetic intelligence theory as a complement to the genetic code theory.

Material and Methods: The genetic intelligence is organized in the nested, fractal sequences composed of links. The links are compared with the mapped genes on the chromosomes of Drosophila fruit fly.

Results: The key and context links: GENIO, 1250 nm; BRAG brand the features, 3.64 nm; AMAG amass the chunks, 25.5nm; MAG master the associations 178.5 nm. Some links are related to the genes; the rest is related to the domains inside longer genes and to the signaling pathways. The frequency of cell consciousness is 5.6 cycles per 1000 nm.

Conclusions: The cell internal language organization, meters and associations constantly trigger and organize the neighboring genes, within the link information sign set LISS. These links grow in many different ways and do quite different things, say, in fruit fly, mouse and human. GENIO leads the transmission of information from DNA to the protein assembly area, that determines the fate of groups of cells and they become irreversibly specialized. In the neural cell, GENIO is within the dendrite inputs-axon output loops; it can block or start the synaptic vesicles release.

Keywords: DNA code, genetic intelligence organization, gene, gene link, codon, base, GENIO law, sampling, quantizing, information compressing and packaging, cell consciousness.

INTRODUCTION

This work shifts from the genome mapping, sequencing and determination of genome functions [1–23] to the intelligence organization in the cell. It develops the **cell, genetic, intelligence laws** and compares them with the **Brain, mind, intelligence laws** [24-50].

In the living organisms, hence in cells, many life processes involve continuous information signals as a function of continuous time. Life performs sampling and quantizing of these processes (Fig. **1**).

THE BRAIN MIND THEORY

Sampling means observing information only in points T, 2T, 3T ...... Hence the life compresses the information. Yet the life must be able to recover the information signal. This is possible because life takes more than two points per cycle of the highest significant component in a signal I (t). In other words, the frequency spectrum of I (t) is given by F (f); the sampling is correct, because it fulfils the following condition:

F (f) = 0 for f ≥ fc   **(1)**

fc = 1 / 2T   **(2)**

where fc is the turnover sampling frequency.

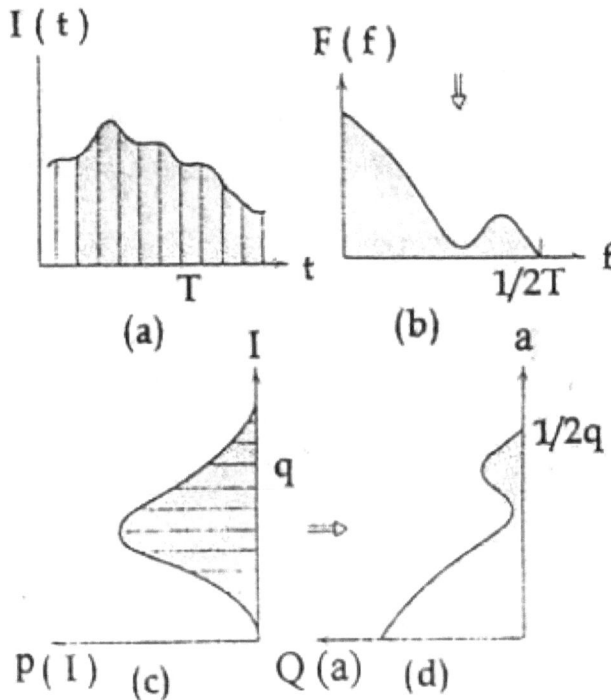

Figure 1: The Life Sampling and Quantizing. a) Information signal I (t); b) Frequency spectrum of the information signal, F (f); c) Intensity probability distribution p (I); d) Characteristic function Q (a).

Quantizing means measuring information with the quantizing step q, and expressing it as q, 2q, 3q. The information I is defined by its probability distribution function p (I). The Fourier integral of p (I) is the characteristic function Q (a).

The transformation parameter a corresponds to the frequency in the function F (f), but has no physical meaning. Like in sampling, also in quantizing, life must not lose the information. In analogy with the sampling equations 1 and 2, we can say: the characteristic function of the signal is given by Q (a); quantizing is correct, because it fulfils the following conditions:

$$Q (a) = 0 \text{ for } a \geq 1 / 2q \tag{3}$$

For most signals encountered in the life, the following rule of thumb is an adequate substitute for the quantizing equation 3: if the signal I (t) has a Gaussian intensity distribution p (I), quantizing is adequate, because the range of I (t) is at least 7 or 8 q.

The brain and mind attraction BRAMA law operates with the nested fractal information times: BRAMA, Brain and Mind Attraction, $t_l=1225$ ms; BRA, Brand the features, $t_b = 3.6$ ms; AMA, Amass the chunks, $t_a = 25$ ms; MA, Master the associations, $t_m = 175$ ms. See Fig. **2** in [42].

S/Q: sampling; quantizing. The experimentally observed, amplitude expressed evoked potentials EP waves, are the functions of time. Hence they follow the sampling law. Yet the EP is related to the sum of the brain event trains. The trains carry the information in the time scale. This time coded information follows the quantizing law. This explains the time periods:

$$BRAMA = 7 \times MA; MA = 7 \times AMA; AMA = 7 \times BRA \tag{4}$$

Fig. **2** in [52] shows a flock of MA oscillators related to the semantic Evoked Potentials. Note that the t_m is a co period, composed of two periods. In other words the period is $t_m /2$. MA oscillators are related to the selective attention or semantic consciousness. The sampling equation 2 is used to define the necessary sampling frequency of the brain consciousness (cycles in 1000 ms):

$$fbC = 1 / [2 \times (t_m / 2)] = 1 / t_m = 1000/175 = 5.714 \text{ Hz} \tag{5}$$

The brain, mind laws: The thinking intelligence complexity is related to the flocks of event trains and to their time periods. Fig. **4** in [47]: TISS, time, information, sign, set. Fig. **2** in [48]: MA master the associations, $t_m =175$ ms, indicates the flock of oscillations in the verbal Evoked Potentials. Hence the semantic **frequency of brain consciousness** is about $1000:175 = 5.714$ Hz (cycles in second). The brain consciousness is a mind intelligence function. **BRAMA** [45] **is a strong attraction**; bursting, passionate, unrestrained, excessive desire. BRAMA is the major force in the animal and human brains, on many levels. The brain mind tissue TISS operates with the dispersed, dynamic BRAMA and BRAMA protocols.

/ S: Sensation sequence /
/ A: Action sequence /

REPEAT
   GENIO:UNDERSTANDING, l_l
   S: Perception; Pattern Recognition
   A: Decision; Imagination

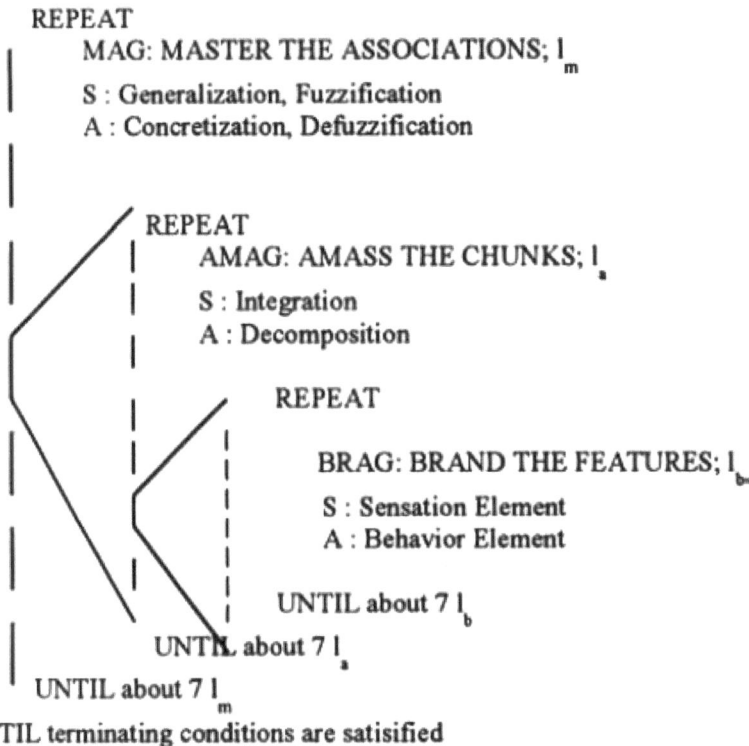

      REPEAT
         MAG: MASTER THE ASSOCIATIONS; l_m
         S : Generalization, Fuzzification
         A : Concretization, Defuzzification

            REPEAT
               AMAG: AMASS THE CHUNKS; l_a
               S : Integration
               A : Decomposition

                  REPEAT
                     BRAG: BRAND THE FEATURES; l_b
                     S : Sensation Element
                     A : Behavior Element

                  UNTIL about 7 l_b
               UNTIL about 7 l_a
            UNTIL about 7 l_m
UNTIL terminating conditions are satisified

Figure 2: GENIO fractal nested structure. The whole structure exhibits the self-similarity between the macro chaos and the micro chaos. with the **intelligence links** l_b, l_a, l_m, l_l. The result is Fig. **2** here.

THE GENIO THEORY

The genetic intelligence organization: the genes are arranged in a line along chromosomes. The recombination studies show the length of genes: from less than 10, to more than 100, to 1250 nano meters. For example, the maximum length of a gene from a fruit fly is about 1250 nm. The genes and the signaling pathways are the pieces of intelligence links. The link is related to the length, locus, loop, distance; and to the cell working associations and memory. Hence the link is multidimensional. Only one dimension, expressed in nm, is discussed. The link is related to the intelligence content. The content in a single gene in Drosophila corresponds to a family of related homologues in vertebrates. The signaling pathway is important in determining embryonic patterning and cell fate in multiple structures of the developing embryo. Many developmental genes of the pathway continue to function in regulation of cell growth and differentiation after embryogenesis, and are involved in patterning and development of variety of organ systems. Members of family of secreted signaling molecules link an enormous variety of developmental events in vertebrates and in Drosophila. GENIO operates with the intelligence (link) pieces, adjacent or dispersed over the DNA sequences. GENIO performs very efficient and precise information sampling, quantizing and using. GENIO is similar to the BRAMA law? Again see Fig. **2** in [42], but replacing **the information times**: t_b, t_a, t_m, and t_l;

Sensation sequence leads from elements to general. **Action** sequence is related to the DNA, messenger RNA, protein assembly processes; signaling pathways. **GENIO** explains the DNA structure, with the frequent intelligence (link) ratio 7x7x7: **BRAG**, brand the feature, $l_b = 3.64$ nm; **AMAG**, amass the chunks, $l_a = 25.5$ nm; **MAG**, master the association, $l_m = 178.5$ nm, **GENIO**, $l_l = 1250$ nm. The chemically expressed genome and proteome, are the functions of a link. They follow the sampling law. Yet the link is related to the information and it follows the quantizing law. This explains the links:

GENIO =7 x MAG; MAG =7 x AMAG; AMAG =7 x BRAG   **(6)**

The above theoretical results could be compared with the fruit fly experimental data: 500 genes; $l_l = 1250$ nm related to the longest gene; $l_b = 3.64$ nm related to the shortest gene.

The genetic sign is a mark that always has a particular meaning. It indicates the presence or likely future existence of something else. Each sign is a specific combination and interaction of Link L, Information I and Set S. Here I explain the genetic signs: CILO, CEMET, CELA.

CILO sign is related to simple messages and features. It belongs to the CILO, Cell Internal Language Organization. CILO is related to the computing, involved all over the cell. In CILO sign: physical forces and chemical packages carry information; there is no relation whatsoever with the subatomic quantum mechanics. **CEMET** sign deals with the chunks and simple associations. CEMET is a short name for CELL METER. CEMET group is a mixture of the compression and measure. Cell measures the stimulus and action. Cell uses a set of fuzzy clusters. Each major concept is measured with its fuzzy clusters and with the memberships to them.

CELA sign deals with the multiple complex cell associations that explain a specific genetic experience. CELA is responsible for pattern recognition and storage. CELA signs participate in the selection and overlap of the multiple genetic associations and knowledge.

The cell consciousness cC is composed of pieces. Each piece of consciousness is a SON of the father called "Attention to the Current Task" and of the mother called "Related Experiences". Father and mother communicate by using the cell event trains CET and the common message clusters, taken from CILO. The Attention presents the specific need and its non-specific general domain. The Experience responds with the born with and mutated components. Now I am using equation 5, frequency of the brain consciousness, to develop the frequency of the cell consciousness (cycles in 1000 nm)

$$fcC = 1.000 / l_m = 1000 / 178.5 = 5.60 \qquad\qquad (7)$$

Equations 5 and 7 are developed in a similar way, hence they are similar. Yet, they are independent and have different meanings.

The cell, genetic laws: The cells are made by chemicals. Yet they also follow the **intelligence, GENIO**, with the sampling and quantizing, that make natural selection and life work. Proper **information attraction**, selection, packages and programs, repress, switch and regulate the genes and feedback. Combinations and organization of the BRAG, AMAG, MAG, GENIO, are building links of life itself. These links grow in many different ways and do quite different things, say, in fruit fly, mouse and human. GENIO links the TP73 expression; the neurogenesis of specific neural structures; the GST multiple gene family; *etc.* The genetic coding complexity is related to the chemicals, hence to the **links** of molecules in the LISS, link, information, sign, set. Fig. **2**: MAG, master the associations, lm = 178.5 nm. Hence the **genetic frequency of cell consciousness** is about 1000: 178.5=5.60 (cycles in 1000 nm). The cell consciousness is a genetic coding intelligence function, supported by the under laying physical, chemical forces. It affects organizers and **associations**, which affect genes, which in turn affect the rate of development of tissues and organs.

Association overlaps many patterns. The input to the association memory is a **stimulus field [S]** and the **response is a field [R]**.

Learning (encoding) enfolds (overlaps) multiple stimulus – response associations into the same **association, correlation matrix [A]**.

$$[A] +\!= \overline{[S]}^{T} [R] \tag{8}$$

Decoding or response recall transforms stimulus field through all of the previous stimulus – response mappings and generates the associated response field [R]

$$[R] = [S]^* / c [A] \tag{9}$$

where $[S]^*$ is the new stimulus field exposed to the memory for issuance of the response recall; c is a normalization coefficient, probabilistic bound.

Genome; proteome. Proteome is the complete set of proteins, which are expressed by the entire genome [1-28].

Since the proteome is quite dynamic and it changes along with the development of an organism and with any alterations in the environment, it can be referred to as the array of proteins expressed in a biological compartment, such as cell, tissue or organ, under particular environmental circumstances at a particular time [1-28].

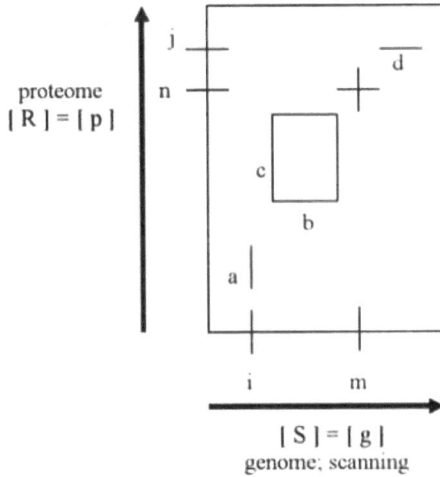

Figure 3: The dynamic genome proteome association. The genome part [g] is the stimulus. The proteome part [p] is the response.

Proteomics is a powerful tool for examining differential protein expression comparing hundreds of proteins simultaneously. There are more proteins in the proteome in comparison with the genes in a genome and it has been estimated that the human proteome is at least an order of magnitude more complex than the human genome, since it is assessed that there might be as many as a million human proteins. The cell signaling pathway could be a simple one signal, one receptor, one signal transduction cascade; tightly regulated cascade; complicated functional branching where most of its components are not only involved in transduction a signal, but are also involved in other biochemical or cellular processes. Hence the protein modification is not obvious from the DNA sequence, such as isoforms and post-translations modifications It is assessed that approximately 200 diverse types of post-translation protein modification processes occur.

The cell is a complex association composed of many reciprocal adjustment loops. The association element is related to the sensation and action sequences, loops, signaling pathways, modification processes.

Fig. **3** shows an element, as the genome part g, to the proteome part p, association.

$$[A] \mathrel{+}= [\text{genome}] \, \overline{[\text{proteome}]}^{\,T} \tag{10}$$

$$[\text{proteome}] = [\text{genome}] \ast / c \, [A] \tag{11}$$

Large part of the association map is empty (zero). Note the active parts and relations: gene i to proteins a; genes b to proteins c; genes d to protein j; gene m to protein n.

L/P; T/M. The cell intelligence follows two different avenues: logical/programming, L/P; and transformation / mapping, T/M. L/P is based upon algorithms, procedures and rules. T/M is based on mutation learning and on building associations. These two types of information processing are conceptually incompatible. In other words, it is becoming clear that it may often be impossible to satisfactorily describe the operation of transformation in terms of an algorithm, and *vice versa*. For example, cell action, based on T/M, may provide useful important solution to area, without allowing us to discover the fundamental processes used in the solution. They are dispersed and hidden in the complex association matrix. The logic, programming L/P: the decision boundaries – the bounds used to make particular decisions – are specified for each domain. L/P leads the "hard level" tasks and goal directed reasoning decomposed into the logical sequential operations, parallel pattern recognition operations and path planning steps see Table **1**.

Table 1: How cell L/P and cell T/M differ

L/P	T/M
Processes crisp data that are written as base pairs, codons, genes.	Process analog signals that fluctuate continuously, providing a range from, say, black through all shades of gray to white
Make yes/no decisions, using chemical and logical functions.	Make weighted decisions on the basis of fuzzy, incomplete, and contradictory data.
Handle data in a rigidly structured sequence so that operations are always under control and results are predictable.	Independently formulate methods of processing data, often with surprising results.
Find precise answers to any problem, given enough time.	Find good, quick – but approximate – answer to highly complex problems.
Sort through large data bases to find exact matches	Sort through large data bases to find close matches
Store information so that specific data can be retrieved easily	Store information so that retrieving any piece of information automatically calls up all related facts.

The transformation, mapping T/M: The decision boundaries are adaptive. T/M leads the "soft level" tasks, processes and signaling pathways. Changes in the genome, proteome operating environment cause the decision boundaries to be shifted or changed. The cell learns, detects and adapts to these changes. The cell intelligence is a massively parallel, multilevel mixture of L/P and T/M. The result is a dynamic proteome. The 99 per cent of human genes have at least one mouse equivalent. **This is DNA, chemical, similarity. The differences are hidden in the GENIO, intelligence diversity**.

THE GENIO MODEL

UNITS: The membranes are essential as selective barriers to the external environment of cells. They divide the cell into subunits, where different functions are carried out by different enzymes.

The organelles are embedded in the cytoplasm which is about 90% water and a mixture of mineral salts and giant molecules. These react together as the living contents of all cells. **Transduction** of information signals by proteins results in temporal and spatial control of protein functions and cellular activity and cooperative resonances, field fluctuations, and interference patterns which comprise functions within the cell. **The matrix grid** of subunits and associated proteins is responsible for biological communication, regulation, information processing. Genetic and other cell codes and associated continuous information interactions present the basic level of intelligence: the level of the cell. This intelligence level is subdivided into layers: discrete (genetic code); continuous (molecular interaction); discrete (other cell codes); and continuous (ion flux, charge gradient, action potential).

PROCESSES: CQD process followed by DQC process: Q=quantizing. CQD: from continuous to the discrete code elements. DQC: from discrete code elements to continuous. Diversified DQC and CQD processes explain a number of the cell behavioral interactions. The CQD and DQC processes are crucial for the cooperation, competition and self-organization. Continuous is necessary for smooth interaction with fuzziness, elasticity, feedback, non-linear dynamics. Discrete is necessary for long-term recording based on physical and chemical discrete states, for accuracy, uniformity and for symbolic representation and template matching. The mixture of discrete and continuous layers is the basic feature of biological self-organization for intelligence. The cell performs the "sequential tasks" and the "parallel tasks".

Sequential tasks use simple logic and a small portion of the available data at any given time. The problem is decomposed into simple and relatively independent parts and solved in sequential subunits. Sequential tasks include logical reasoning, sequential operations, planning, cell internal language understanding and production, scheduling, and small rule - based expert system.

Parallel tasks use all the available data at the same time. The logic of such tasks cannot be decomposed into independent parts but instead requires a global synthesis. Parallel tasks include a large number of linked processors operating in parallel, parallel operations, fuzzy expert systems, large rule-based expert systems, pattern recognition, analog and fuzzy reasoning and learning. The cell subunits are specialized for separate tasks, as well as for mixed tasks.

INTELLIGENCE: Self Organization SO of understanding U, consciousness C, emotion E and knowledge K. See Fig. **4**. **SO**, the functions UCEK and associations A are strictly related to the cell, genome, proteome intelligence.

A, Association: stores and associates the response with sensory stimuli; effect with cause.

K, Knowledge: condition action rules or implications with associated uncertainty factors.

E, Emotion in the cell: feed, fight, flight, court.

C, Consciousness: makes a link with those items which are currently claiming its attention. It opens gates on the relevant contents. The content is taken from the unconscious memory, and it appears in consciousness, that is in the working short term memory.

U, Understanding: performs a short cut through the content and message combinatorial explosions.

Cell learning, adaptation, reasoning, language and communication. The Self Organization involves all features, not one at a time.

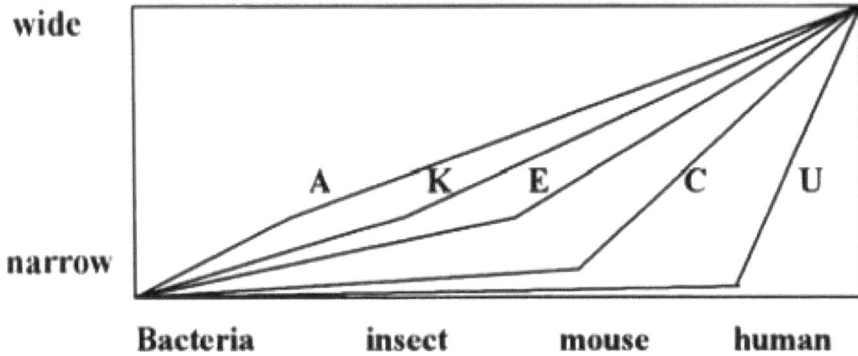

Figure 4: The cell SO functions. They are independent of the multitude of brain SO functions.

Cell learning, adaptation, reasoning, language and communication. The Self Organization involves all features, not one at a time.

This is a massively parallel physical and chemical process, with the interactions of cell event trains. Starting from different initial states, behavior trajectories become attracted onto specific states. Through the Self Organized attractions the structures of U,C,E,K, and A evolve in the time from initial states. Cell performs the compression of intelligence. The compression emerges from the dynamic interactions between flocks of cell agents. The agents form a variety of compression processors. Agents operate in the fractal time and are regulated by SO and GENIO. GENIO **selectively** disinhibits and selects the right **associations**. Many associations pairs can be **distributed** one over another in the same association space. Hence they **overlap**. Both, in time and in space, cell combines the selectivity with the overlap. Cell combines partial selection with the distribution.

The GENIO model is presented in Fig. **5**. GENIO is composed of the multiple, inter coupled, positive and negative feedback loops.

Survival: organelles, biochemical processes, mitochondria, endoplasmic reticulum, ribosome *etc.* In cooperation with the feedback it guides the cell intelligence. The cell codes keep a program; the changes in state (ion flux, charge gradients, action potentials) are executive commands.

Reproduction: mitosis; meiosis; the fusion between egg and sperm.

Feeding: phagocytosis; the membrane flows around the "food" being taken in the cell; feeding begins using enzymes made by the cell.

Flying, walking: mitochondria; the tiny subunits fly around the cell and aggregate in places where most energy need to be released.

The multiple memory of complex information is used in guiding long – term behavior; it is encoded directly in the higher, holistic level. The multiple level approach allows several competing "dominant" schemas to cooperate in use of low – level competence for problem solving. The coupling of perception to action is analogous to simple "reflex arcs". Each level of behavior generating hierarchy receives the command C from a higher level. It also receives the feedback F from the environment. The output from the operator H selects one or several of the possible subcommands on the next lower level. Operators H provide parallel processing across a wide range, some which last for short times, others which span longer intervals. Operator H3 receives the stimulus [S] = feedback F3; and generates the response [R] = command C2. Hence H3 is related to the innate **Knowledge and Emotions**. Operator H2 receives the stimulus [S] = feedback F2 and Command C2. H2 is related to the **Associations and Understanding**. The response C1 defines the self – other message flash. It is a SON of a father: F2 and C2, ("Attention to the Current Task"); and of the mother: H2 ("Related Experience"). Hence it is the elementary **Consciousness**. In the neural cell the GENIO is related to the dendrite stimulus, axon response synapses, membranes and neural transmitter release. In this way the environment and the life experiences can have molecular effects on the GENIO: it can turn genes on or turn them off; it can block or start the synaptic vesicles release.

CONCLUSIONS

Are cells made only by chemicals, or do they contain some special ingredient, force, plans, links, that make life work? The answer is:

Life and cell: the similarity of DNA codes; the similar genes keep the information and programs.

In complement with the diversity of GENIO intelligence links; the diverse genes and pathways keep the intelligence links, associations and parameters.

The human genes and the mouse genes are 99 per cent similar in DNA codes. Yet the human GENIO intelligence links are different from the mouse GENIO intelligence links. These are two different building, linking plans, producing two different lives: human and mouse. In all cases the GENIO intelligence links are supported by the under laying physical, chemical forces. Compare the processes of building the school and the office. There are two large piles of similar building materials; and two small packages containing the building plans, links, on paper. The result of processes is the school building, very different from the office building.

The GENIO has no leader, and no control mind. It is the individual members following certain simple laws that make the group respond the way it does. In other words, the behavior is built from the top-down, bottom-up and is governed by the cooperative action of many small agents. The cell agents include primitives or components of intelligence and of communication. Resulting decisions, behavior or organizations are based on: distributed decision making; collaborative reasoning; distributed control; community coordination; cooperation; groupware. Each group represents an elastic, distributed sign. In the same time the group carries the discrete codes and the continuous signals. The GENIO is a missing link between the genome and proteome.

Continuous cell processes are permanently related to the discrete codes, including the DNA genetic code. The GENIO comprises the cell reasoning and the cell consciousness.

The cell consciousness cC is related to the current awareness. The cC frequency, defined by equation 7, is 5.60 cycles per 1000 nm. The cC current content is related to equation 11, and to the proteome part p in Fig. **3**. The cC certainty is related to the cC current content in Fig. **5**. Until now the consciousness was not clearly defined. The major steps forward are the frequency of the cell consciousness fcC and the frequency of the brain consciousness fbC. **Note that fcC and fbC remain almost constant over different scales: nm in cell and ms in brain.**

UNIVERSALITY: Brain; Cell. The Self Organization SO of UCEK leads the brain and mind, as well as the genetic coding and cells. The brain TISS Fig. **7** in

[49] is similar to the cell LISS. The brain consciousness Fig. **8** in [49] leads to the cell consciousness, Fig. **5**. The brain SO Fig. **10** in [49] in the Evoked Potential time scale in ms, could be modified in the cell SO figure in the link scale in nm.

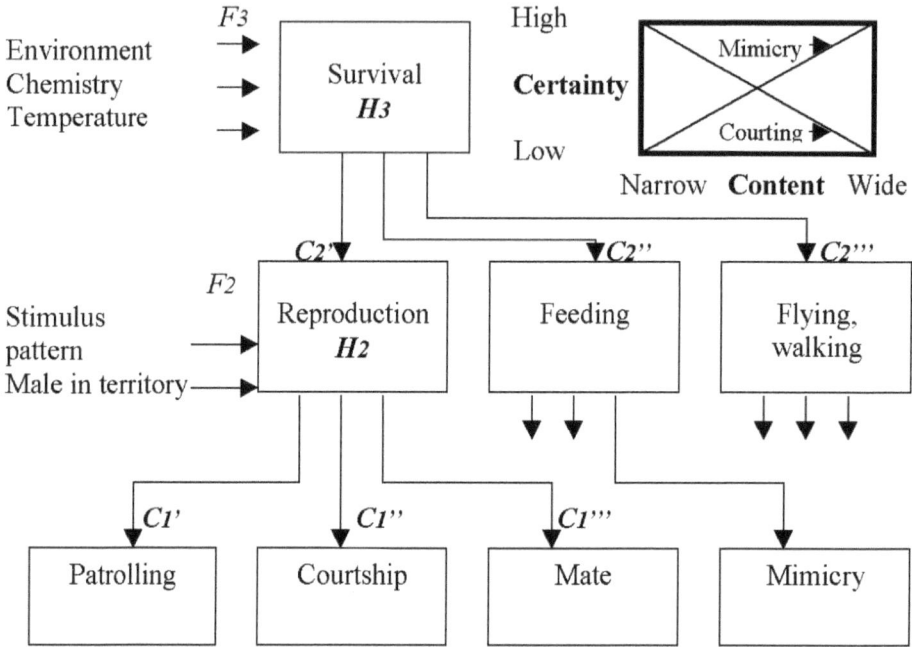

Figure 5a: The genetic intelligence organization, GENIO. Conscious courting. Content: narrow, specific dialogue. Certainty is high, to mate the right partner. Conscious mimicry. Content: wide range of dialogues. Certainty is high, to eat the partner.

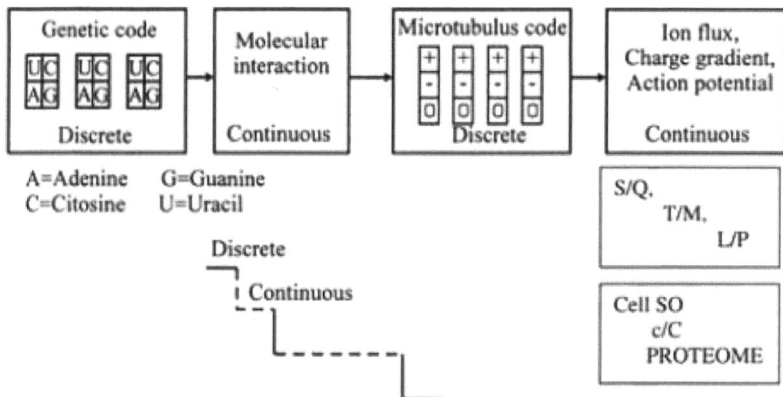

Figure 5b: GENIO with the sampling and quantizing S/Q. Discrete-Quantized-Continuous, DQC layers. Genetic code: four deoxynucleoside triphosphates have been identified as coding elements labeled U, C, A, G. An adjacent sequence of three coding elements constitutes a code word.

Microtubule code: the coding elements are three-state elements. The coding words are formed from four coding elements. Group ware based on GENIO laws: S/Q, T/M, L/P, cell SO, cell c/C. GENIO is a missing link between the genome and proteome.

The cell SO and the brain SO display regularities and similarities. See the Abbreviations on the first page of this work. This is universality: animal and human cells and brains follow a set of common laws, including the sampling and quantizing, S/Q. The genome cannot specify the vast number of special structures and time processes, but it can specify repeating developments based on S/Q. S/Q optimizes billions of links crowded into the finite cells and brains. **S/Q saves space**. S/Q optimizes billions of time functions. **S/Q saves time**.

The brain primary waveforms and oscillations; Fig. **2** in [31] could be modified in the cell primary **waveforms** and oscillations. They are responsible for an inherent time, space, link program that controls the communication and the behavior of the cell agents. The Primary waveform also controls the relationship between the stimulus and the response by narrowing and widening the receive and send windows. Hence the Primary waveform presents the basic, precise, and quantitative description of a part of the cell SO. The sum of three waveforms, properly shifted and scaled, presents a good approximation of many complex segments of the cell SO. They are related to the links BRAG, AMAG, MAG, in nm scale. Again compare the cell SO with the brain SO [24–52]. They are independent and have different meanings. Yet there are some similarities in the form and in the universal view: the natural evolution, based on the physical and chemical forces, follows by chance the selection steps: functions UCEK; cell SO + cell consciousness cC; brain SO + brain consciousness bC.

SO of UCEK = S/Q + L/P+T/M → cell SO + cC, life →

→ brain SO + bC, mind   (12)

The cell SO tells genes how to work or not work and makes the life possible. The brain SO tells the neurons and brain event trains how to work or not work and makes the mind possible. In cells and brains there is an enormous number of forms, composed of a limited number of signs, shapes. SO governs the flow of signs, shapes, changes, motions, forms. SO governs the evolution of the sign, shape in space and the evolution of the sign, shape in time. The universalities of the signs, shapes, the similarities across time and space scales, recursive flows within flows, are based on the SO laws and equations [24–52] and S/Q, L/P and T/M equations 1 to 12 here.

The organic molecules grow from inorganic molecules according to the chemical logic. **The living cells** grow from organic molecules according to the cell GENIO laws. In other words, the living cell grows above the chemical logic.

The cell is intelligent. The cell activity is capable of solving problems which, if done by human, would be considered intelligent activity. The cell is full of SO functions, Fig. **4**. The SO functions exist already in a simple cell of bacteria. The entire genome length of the E coli genome is about 4000 kilo bases and it is related to the elementary coli GENIO. The human genome is 3000 billion bases and it is related to the complex human GENIO.

The origin of life and consciousness is in the genetic intelligence organization, developed by chance.

The discrete GENIO functions are expressed in bases and in bits; the continuous functions are expressed in links, nm, and in the fuzzy information units, fit. GENIO is open for further joint research with the bio medicine and with the bio computing. The new 65 nm technology offers 1 billion transistors per chip. The bio computing breakthrough methods [31–37] and results [24–52] are rapidly gaining the ground. **The distance between the cell and the chip is reduced to 1 billion 3000: 1**.

ACKNOWLEDGEMENT

I have spent fifty years working out the Self Organization of life intelligence: in Institute Ruder Boskovic; U of Zagreb; Brookhaven National Laboratory N.Y.; SUNY; U of AZ. I acknowledge the stimulating atmosphere and excellent working conditions.

DISCLOSURE

"The content of this chapter has been previously published in *Periodicum Biologorum Vol. 107, No. 4,385-392, 2003*"

ABBREVIATION

SO   = Self Organization

U   = Understanding

C   = Consciousness

E   = Emotions

K   = Knowledge

Brain, mind, self-organization laws:

BRAMA   = Brain and mind attraction, 1225 ms

BRA   = Brand the features, 3.6 ms

AMA   = Amass the chunks, 25 ms

MA   = Master the associations, 175 ms

BILO   = Brain internal language organization

COMET   = Compressor, meter

SAVA   = Selective audio video association

bC   = Brain Consciousness

fbC   = Frequency of brain Consciousness= 5.7 cycles per 1000 ms

BET   = Brain event train

TISS   = Time, information, sign, set

Cell, genetic, self-organization laws:

GENIO   = Genetic intelligence organization, 1250 nm

BRAG = Brand the features, 3,64 nm

AMAG = Amass the chunks, 25.5 nm

MAG = Master the associations, 178.5 nm

CILO = Cell internal language organization

CEMET = Cell meter

CELA = Cell association

cC = Cell Consciousness

fcC = Frequency of cell Consciousness= 5.6 cycles per 1000 nm

CET = Cell event train

LISS = Link, information, sign, set

REFERENCES

[1] CHIAPPA KH. Evoked Potentials in Clinical Medicine. Raven Press New York 1989

[2] CHUANG PT, McMAHON AP. Vertebrate Hedgehog signaling modulated by induction of a Hedgehog-binding protein. Nature1999; 397: 617–621

[3] DEHAENE S. *et al.* Sources of Mathematical Thinking Behavioral and Brain – Imaging Evidence. Science1999; 284: 970 – 974

[4] DEL CASTILLO J, KATZ B. Quantum Components of the End-Plate Potential. J Physiol (London)1950; 124: 560

[5] DURAJLIJA ZINIC S. SitaRam: a computational approach for multi perspective visualization of higher-order and progressive patterns in highly repetitive regions of DNA. Per biol2005;107: 423 – 436

[6] GOLDMAN-RAKIC Patricia. Architecture of the Prefrontal Cortex and the Central Executive. [in Ref. (7)],1995

[7] GRAFMAN J, HOLYOAK KJ, BOLLER F. Structure and Functions of the Human Prefrontal Cortex. New York Academy of Sciences, vol. 769, New York 1995

[8] HO R, SUTHERLAND JG, BRUHA I. Neurological Fuzzy Diagnoses: Holographic *vs.* Statistical *vs.* Neural Method. [in Ref. (19)] 1994

[9] JIMENEZ – MONTANO MA, LUCIO – GARCIA HR, FERNANDEZ AR. Computer simulation to generate simplified proteins with stochastic grammars. Per Biol2005;107: 397 – 402

[10] KOSTOVIC I, JUDAS M, KOSTOVIC – KNEZEVIC LJ, SIMIC G, DELALLE I, CHUDY D, SAJIN B, PETANJEK Z. Zagreb Research Collection of Human Brains for Developmental Neurobiologists and Clinical Neuroscientists. International J Developmental Biol1991;35: 215 – 230

[11] KRALJ M, KRALJEVIC S, SEDIC M, KURJAK A, PAVELIC K. Global approach to perinatal medicine: functional genomics and proteomics. J Perinatal Med2004; (in press)

[12] LEVANAT S, PAVELIC B, CRNIC I, ORESKOVIC S, MANOJLOVIC S. Involvement of PTCH gene in various no inflammatory cysts.J Molecular Med2000; 78 (3): 140–146

[13] LOCKHART DJ, WINZELER EA. Genomics, gene expression and DNA arrays. Nature2000; 405: 827–836

[14] LYON BE. Recognition and Counting Reduce Costs of Avion Cospecific Brood Parasitism. Nature2003;422: 495 – 499

[15] PANDEY A, MANN M. Proteomics to study genes and genomes. Nature2000; 405: 837–846

[16] PETANJEK Z, ROKO RASIN M, JOVANOV N, KRSNIK Z. Magno pyramidal Neurons in the Area 9 of the Human Prefrontal Cortex. A Quantitative Rapid Golgi Study Per biol1998;100 (2): 221 – 231

[17] PETRENKO O, ZAIKA AI. MOLLUM Delta Np 73 facilitates cell immortalization and cooperate with oncogenic Ras in cellular transformation *in vivo*. Moll Cell Biol2003; 23: 5540–5555

[18] PETRIDES M. Functional Organization of the Human Prefrontal Cortex for Mnemonic Processing [in Ref. (7)] 1995

[19] PLANTAMURA VL, SOUČEK B, VISAGGIO G. Frontier Decision Support Concepts. Wiley New York 1994

[20] RAMACHANDRAN *VS*. The Emerging Brain. Profile Books 2003

[21] RANDIC M, BALABAN AT,NOVIC M, ZALOZNIK A, PISANSKI T. A novel graphical representation of proteins. Per Biol2005;107: 403 – 414

[22] SOLMS M. The Neuropsychology of Dream. Erlbaum Associates 1997

[23] SLADE N,GALETIC I, KAPITANOVIC S, PAVELIC J. The efficacy of retroviral herpes simplex virus thymidine kinase gene transfer and ganciclovir treatment on the inhibition of melanoma growth *in vitro* and *in vivo*. Arch. Dermatology. Res. 293: 484–490,2001

[24] SOUČEK B. Mono stable Systems Triggered at Random. *Nuclear Instruments Methods 1964; 29:* 109–114

[25] SOUČEK B. Application of pile-up distortion calculation. *Rev Scientific Instruments 1965; 36:* 1582–1587

[26] SOUČEK B. Influence of the Latency Fluctuations and the Quantum Process of Transmitter Release on the End-Plate Potentials' Amplitude Distribution. *Biophysical Journal 1971; 11:* 127–139

[27] SOUČEK B. Complete Model for the Statistical Composition of the End-Plate Potential. *J Theoretical Biology 1971; 30:* 631–648

[28] SOUČEK B. Applications of computers and mathematical models to the study of neuronal systems, Nuclear and neuronal pulse spectrometry. *Computer Physics Communications 1973;5:* 115– 122

[29] CARLSON AD, SOUČEK B. Computer simulation of firefly flash sequence. *Journal of Theoretical Biology 1975; 55:* 353–370

[30] SOUČEK B. Model of Alternating and Aggressive Communication with the Example of Katydid Chirping. *J Theoretical Biology1975; 52:*399–417

[31] SOUČEK B, VENCL F. Bird Communication Study Using Digital Computer. *J Theoretical Biology 1975; 49:* 147–172

[32] VENCL F, SOUČEK B. Structure and Control of Duet Singing in the White-Crested Jay Thrush. *Behavior 1976; 57:* 20–33

[33] SOUČEK B, CARLSON AD. Brain Windows in Firefly Communication. *J Theoretical Biology 1986 119:* 47–65

[34] SOUČEK B, CARLSON AD. Brain Window Language in Firefly. *J Theoretic Biology 1987; 125:* 93–103

[35] SOUČEK B, CARLSON AD. Computers in Neurobiology and Behavior. Wiley New York 1976.

[36] SOUČEK B, SOUČEK M. Neural and Massively Parallel Computers. Wiley New York 1988.

[37] SOUČEK B. Neural and Concurrent Real-Time Systems. Wiley New York 1989

[38] SOUČEK B and the IRIS Group. Neural and Intelligent Systems Integration. Wiley New York 1991.

[39] SOUČEK B and the IRIS Group. Fast Learning and Invariant Object Recognition. Wiley New York 1992.

[40] SOUČEK B and the IRIS Group. Fuzzy, Holographic and Parallel Intelligence. Wiley New York 1992.

[41] SOUČEK B and the IRIS Group. Dynamic, Genetic and Chaotic Programming. Wiley New York 1992

[42] PLANTAMURA VL, SOUČEK B, VISAGGIO G. Frontier Decision Support Concepts. Wiley New York 1994

[43] SOUČEK B. Quantum Mind – Evoked Potential Link. *Per Biol1998;100(2):* 129–140

[44] SOUČEK B. Quantum Mind Emerges from the Prefrontal Cortex Nested, Fractal Chaos. *Per biol1999; 101(2):* 109–119

[45] SOUČEK B. Quantum Mind Compresses the Verbal Stories. *Per biol1999; 101(3):* 193–201

[46] SOUČEK B. Quantum Mind Measures the Verbal Stories. *Per biol2000:102(4):* 331–342

[47] SOUČEK B. Universal Brain Theory: The Self Organization of Understanding, Consciousness, Emotions and Knowledge. *Per biol2001; 103(3):* 219–228

[48] SOUČEK B. The Brain Agents Universe. *Per biol2002; 104(3):*353–369

[49] SOUČEK B. The Brain and Mind Tissue, TISS: node, group, flock, pool. *Per biol2002; 104(3):* 345–352

[50] SOUČEK B. The Brain and Mind Attractions, BRAMA, the Brain Internal Language Organization, BILO, the Consciousness. *Per biol20O3; 105(3):* 207–214

[51] SOUČEK B. The genetic and learned brain and mind event trains BET and signs: BILO,COMET, SAVA, CON. *Per biol2004; (106)3:*265–278

[52] SOUČEK B. The DNA code, the brain event trains BET and the self-organization SO make a single entity: life and consciousness. *Per biol2004; 106(4):* 443–444

Send Orders of Reprints at reprints@benthamscience.net

CHAPTER 6

The Genetic and Learned Brain and Mind Event Trains BET and Signs: BILO: COMET: SAVA: CON

Abstract:

Background and Purpose: This work develops the BET and signs theory as a complement to the genetic DNA code. It explains in a new way the learning and information processing in neural networks. The neural network generates various Brain Event Trains, BET. The network's best BET is the best thing that it can do. BETs occur simultaneously at different points in the brain and they form the Signs BILO, COMET, SAVA, CON, communication patterns, verbal stories, mnemonic measurement and compression, mind, perception and consciousness.

Material and Methods: The brain generates various event trains using internal systems: univibrator, one-shot, and other electrochemical brain units. The event trains participate in the Prefrontal Cortex, Thalamus, Basal ganglion loops. The theory and the computer model explain the BET, BILO, COMET, SAVA and CON interactions in the learning, reasoning and consciousness.

Results: The neuron has resistive and capacitive properties: it allows selective flow of ions; and also it can store charges. The resulting charging and recovering time constants determine the flow of voltages. This is a base of the neural monostable systems, memory and learning. The monostable system, after being triggered, is in the quasi stable state. Usually the triggering of the system is repeated when the capacitor voltage reaches its stationary value. But if triggered at random, the system can receive the triggering signal during the recovery period, when the capacitor voltage is different from the stationary value. The brain event trains and signs are formed, and explained by the BET, BILO, COMET, SAVA and CON laws.

Conclusions: By adjusting the rate of triggering and the internal time constants, brain generates various brain event trains: **Poisson; almost Poisson; uniform distribution; almost periodic**. Many event trains are active simultaneously in the brain and mind tissue. The time intervals of trains cover a broad range from 0 to 1225 ms, with the peaks in 3,6; 25; 175 and 1225 ms. These event trains support the links between the brain agents. The links and the agents support the brain functions in the Self Organization SO of Understanding U, Consciousness C, Emotions E and Knowledge K. This is a nested, fractal, dynamic, fuzzy loop of the trains and signs. The brain signs are the pieces of mosaic used to build the mind. The assemblage of **Genetic Signs** is a crop of the signs developed through evolution and stored in DNA. The assemblage of **Learned Signs** is a crop of personal and of learned experience stored in the long term memory. The genetic and learned signs are stored in the dispersed neural networks: in 25 billion of neurons; some of which with thousands of synapses; hence with many thousands of billions interconnections; with the prefrontal cortex large pyramidal neurons; with high arborisation and spine density. **The Consciousness content and**

Branko Souček

certainty are dispersed over the cortex. This is why the lesion of prefrontal lobes disintegrates the sequences, but preserves the fragments. The theory, with over 100 equations, is in excellent agreement with the experimental data, for both, human and animal brains.

Keywords: Brain, mind, event train, poisson train, uniform train, periodic train, brain mind signs, genetic signs, learned signs, consciousness, $\tau = $ **tau**.

INTRODUCTION

The genetic code, stored inside the nucleus of each cell, contains the complete program necessary to develop a living organism. The genetic DNA code defines the development of all neural cells and of the **genetic part** of connections between them. Yet the life experiences develop the **learned part** of connections between neural cells. They are full of the random brain event trains [1-9]. In this way the neural networks are formed, including the links to long projected, pyramidal, SMI-32, AChE associative cortico-cortical neurons. See the Neurolucida 2.1 Software Records [10-17]; Mnemonic Processing [18], Decision Data [19], Brain [20-22], and Dreams [23].

The specific, visible motor and sensory Active Areas, AA, communicate with event trains *via* thalamus and basal ganglia. The spinal cord's formation reticularis keeps active all areas of the brain. There is a constant activating afferent flow from the formation reticularis and the non-specific thalamus to the cerebrum that controls the state of consciousness. The specific thalamus is a switching, integration and coordination link between cortex areas.

The verbal understanding emerges from the prefrontal cortex, nested, travelling event trains. The trains oscillate back and forth between the cortical columns, thalamus and basal ganglia. Gradually, from the recursive, nested event trains emerges the understanding, awareness and consciousness. But how?

The brain deals with the mixtures of trains [24], pile-up processes [25, 26] and functions [27-40]. This is a nested, fractal, dynamic, fuzzy Self Organization SO of Understanding U, Consciousness C, Emotions E and Knowledge K [41, 42]. SO is regulated by the SO laws. The brain and mind tissue TISS is the Time Information Sign Set [43, 44]. The brain and mind operate on the BRAMA principle [45]. Real time data acquisition systems, control systems, and transaction processing systems of the brain, range from fairly simple units to complex networks [46].

Neural networks have been simulated on computers [31-52]. This work explains the operation of the brain and mind event trains BET, the selective audio verbal associations and the operators: cross correlation; superposition; scanning; multiplexing; dead time; buffer memory; chaotic calls. These operators maintain a sustained level of the monostable event firing. The operators present the working memory keeping the objects and actions representations. The proper inputs release and propagate the firing between the brain functional units. In this way various event trains and SO laws participate in the information flow across multiple mutually inhibitory neurons in cortical columns; and across the barriers of brain units: neural networks; nodes; groups; flocks and pools. The flow is regulated by the signs: BILO, COMET, SAVA.

THE BRAIN EVENT TRAINS, BET

The brain event train BET presents a point process with events occurring randomly or regularly in time. Here I am not interested in the amplitude of an event, nor in the information that this event carries. The time of occurrence of the event and its relation to previous events are all that matter. In a real-time brain, the "event" could be an electrical pulse, a switching instant, a transaction, an instant when an algorithm ends; or an interruption. Examples of BET include pulses along a nerve fibber, pulses from sensors, brain internal communication sequences, and behavior sequences.

A brain event train correlation measures the distribution of intervals between two events, regardless of the number of intervening events. The correlation is used to analyze and compare event trains in the brain real time systems, in neural networks and in behavior systems. I show that the brain multiplexers and synapses, through the superposition of fairly periodic event trains, produce on the output almost random train. On the other hand, processing algorithms and buffer memories smooth the random train into almost periodic sequence. Examples of detection of hidden patterns in experimental data, as well as detection of dependences between two event trains, are shown, explaining neural and behavior models. Event correlation is based on the measurement of the distribution of intervals between random events. The events can represent the flow of data in a real-time brain, or the time series of experimental pulses.

The autocorrelation C(t) specifies the probability of encountering an event as a function of time after a given event, irrespective of the number of intervening events, if any; *i.e.*,

C(t)dt = prob [an event in (t, t + dt)/an event at 0]   **(1)**

The cross correlation C(t) is used in case of two trains of events, *A* and *B*. The cross correlation specifies the probability of observing an event in *B* as a function of time after a given event in *A,* irrespective of the number of intervening events, if any:

C(t)dt=prob [an event in B in (t, t +dt)/an event in A at 0]   **(2)**

So defined, autocorrelation and cross correlation are used to explain the behavior of the brain real-time measuring and control systems, neural networks, and behavioral patterns. Event correlation is used to find out the dependences in the event trains; to provide the measure of the dependences; to detect the hidden patterns in random sequences; and to suggest the proper probabilistic model of the system under investigation. I shall apply the Poisson process to different brain systems and look for the output brain event trains. Event correlation is used to recognize the system and to detect its basic properties. Cases of practical interest in the brain and mind tissue TISS are: TISS with built-in generators of repetitive events; TISS with delay; TISS with dead time; Periodic events displaced by random deviation; TISS with buffer memory for one or more events; Superposed series of events; Doubly stochastic Poisson processes; Branching stochastic processes.

Poisson Process. The Poisson process describes the probability of a number of events, r, in an arbitrary interval of length t:

$P(r, t) = [(\lambda t)^r / r!] \exp (-\lambda t) (r = 0,1,..)$ **(3)**

The Poisson process also gives the probability distribution of intervals t between events:

$$f(t) = P(r = 0, t) = \exp(-\lambda t) \tag{4}$$

The event correlation based on Equation (1) for the Poisson process is then equal to the average number of events in dt:

$$C(t) = \lambda \, C(0) = 1 \tag{5}$$

The most obvious application of event correlation in the brain is in cases with more than one event train in the system. The brain event trains could each be at a different point in the system, in which case the cross correlation will give the degree of interdependence; or the event trains could be mixed together (superposed).

Cross correlation. This is a frequent application in the brain. In a system with a delay d, the cross correlation shows if the output series depends on the input series. Equation (2) gives

$$C(t) = 1 \text{ for } t = d; \ C(t) = \lambda \text{ for } t \, \#d \tag{6}$$

Superposition. In many brain and mind situations, the event trains are the superposition of a number of other event trains, such as random interrupts arriving at a processor from many sources, or nerve pulses arriving at synapse from many fibers. If the event train is composed of two or more other event trains, its correlation function will be the sum of the correlation functions of each individual train. Processes can be superposed in a variety of combinations. The correlation will help to distinguish the participating processes, their intensities, and their speeds. It can also be used in simulation and measurement of random neural data. Here I show a few examples from the brain real-time systems, neural networks, and behavior systems.

Scanning. In real-time brain systems based on scanning, the internal program determines both the timing of operations and the scheduling. Because a variety of programs can be used for processing, the scanning might present a process in which events are scheduled at regular intervals but, due to different processing times, are displaced from those scheduled times. Hence, the scanning process and its autocorrelation function presents the measure of irregularity in the scanning operation.

Multiplexing. If many outputs are connected to the brain multiplexer, the number of event trains will be superposed. The resulting correlation function will be the sum of component correlation functions. Even if the component event trains are fairly periodic, the sum train might be a random process. An interesting observation has been made on synapses, with nerve pulses arriving from many fibers. A series of nerve pulses may have been formed by superposing a number of fairly regular sequences, yet the result is a random sequence. This fact presents the warning in the brain real-time systems based on multiplexing, because it is more complicated to deal with random than with regular sequences. The event correlation function gives the degree of regularity.

Dead Time. If the brain event processing time T is of the same order of magnitude as the average interval between events, $1/\lambda$, a substantial percentage of output events will be lost. The dead time losses can be found for cases of practical interest. For the constant dead time T, the losses are

$$g(T) = \lambda T \tag{7}$$

In the brain sensation real-time measurement systems, dead time losses will not produce the histogram distortion. The information is signed in pulse amplitude, and the pulses arrive at random. The situation is different in real-time brain for measuring the interval histograms (*e.g.*, neural latency analyzers). For such systems, the dead time should be much shorter than the average interval between events.

Buffer Memory. If the interval between two events is shorter than the processing time T, the buffer memory will store the second event. This results in a smaller percentage of lost events.

$$g(T) = \lambda T - [1 - \exp(-\lambda T)] \tag{8}$$

The event stored in the buffer memory is processed immediately after the dead time. Hence, the buffer memory moves events along the time axes, forming more regular intervals. The brain uses the autocorrelation function to measure the degree of regularity of intervals.

Chaotic Calls. The sequence of chaotic calls present the communication between two brain agents. The intervals between calls have been analyzed in the correlation histogram. The experimental results have been compared with different correlation histograms. The most appropriate model for this case seems to be the superposition of the Poisson process and of a system with fixed processing time or dead time. Again, the event correlation function is used to find the model of the system.

Neural Spikes. The train of neural spikes has been recorded by a microelectrode. The intervals between spikes have been analyzed, resulting in the correlation histogram. The experimental results have been compared with different correlation histograms. The most appropriate model for this case seems to be the superposition of the Poisson process and of displaced regular events. In this case, the described event correlation has helped to find the proper model of the system: monostable train. In a complex real-time brain system, numerous trains of events occur simultaneously at different points in the system. The measurement, analysis, and proper identification of processes becomes an important part of the brain. A high speed, brain correlation presents a simple yet efficient tool for these goals. The applications of an on-line correlation include the real-time internal behavior, and communication.

THE BRAIN EVENT TRAIN MONOSTABLE GENERATORS

The brain generates various event trains using mono stable internal systems see Figs. **1** and **2**. A mono stable system (uni vibrator, one-shot, electromechanical, and biological mono stable systems), triggered periodically, has a constant duration of quasi stable period, T_0. A mono stable system, after being triggered, is in the quasi stable state, whose duration T_0 is given by the system time constant τ_1. Usually the systems have resistance-capacitance time constants, whose capacitors change their charge during the quasi stable period. When the capacitor voltage reaches some critical value, the system is switched back to the stable state by its own cumulative action. Now the capacitor starts changing its voltage, from a value which it has at the end of the quasi stable period, to the stationary value of the stable state. The time constant τ_2 of this recovery period is different from the time constant τ_1 because the capacitor is charged through different paths in the stable and in the quasi stable states. Usually the triggering of the system is repeated when the capacitor voltage reaches its stationary value. But if triggered at random, the system can receive the triggering signal during the recovery period, when the capacitor voltage is different from the stationary value. The duration of the quasi stable period T is now different from the characteristic value T_0. The period T becomes a stochastic variable, whose statistical distribution is to be found. To find this distribution, we must know the dependence of the duration on the trigger arrival instant t taken from the end of the last quasi stable period. In most systems, the dependence of the normalized quasi stable period T/T_0 on the normalized trigger arrival instant t/τ_2 is given by

$$x(t) = T/T_0 = 1 - \exp(-a\, t/\tau_2) \tag{9}$$

where the parameter a is determined by the structure of a particular system. If triggering pulses are coming at random, the mono stable circuit may be triggered before the end of the recovery period. Because of that, the duration of the quasi stable period will vary from pulse to pulse. This period becomes a stochastic variable, whose statistical distribution is to be found. I suppose that triggering pulses come at random with a rate λ and that the first pulse which comes after the end of a quasi -stable period will trigger the circuit. The probability that the first pulse will come in the interval t, t + dt is equal to the probability $P_0(t)$ that there are no pulses in the interval 0–t, and the probability $\lambda\, dt$ of a pulse in the interval dt. According to the Poisson distribution for random events, we obtain

$$P_0\, dt = \exp(-\lambda t)\, \lambda\, dt \tag{10}$$

The probability density function of the arrival instant of the first pulse is then

$$f(t) = \lambda \exp(-\lambda t)$$

The quasi stable period T and its dimensionless form $x=T/T_0$ are functions of the arrival instant t, $x=x(t)$ (Equation 9). The stochastic variable x will have a probability density function g(x), which we can obtain by transformation of the function f(t):

$$g(x) = f\,[\,t(x)]\,|dt\,(x)\,/dx| \qquad\qquad (11)$$

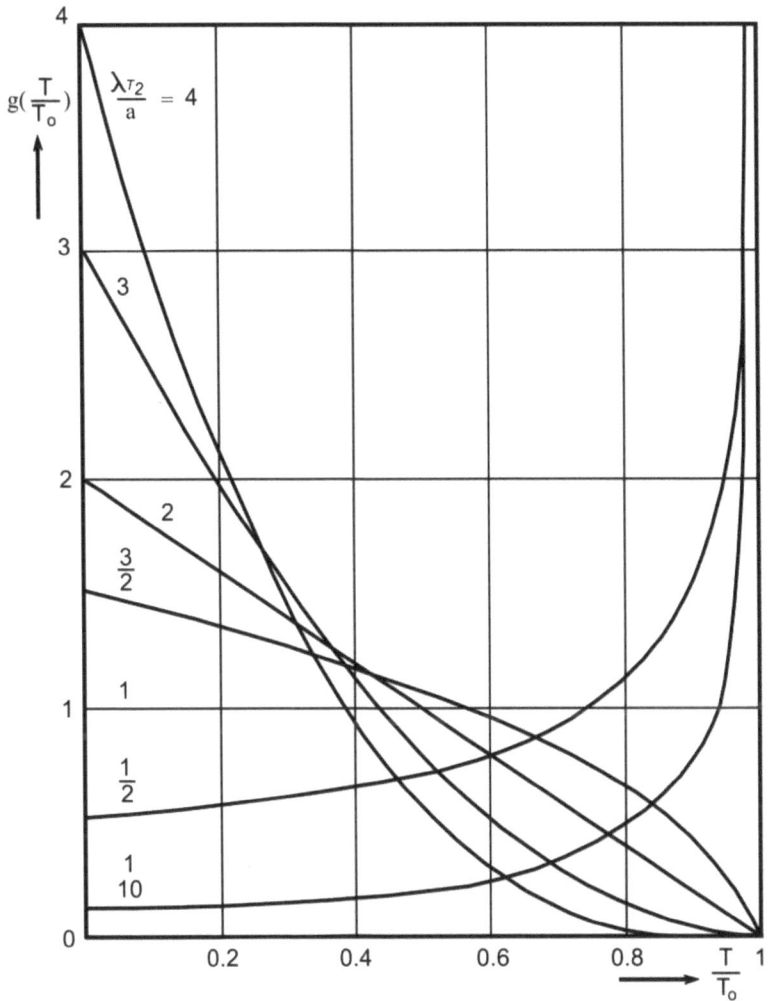

Figure 1: Distribution function of the duration of the brain event trains monostable period.

where t(x) is the inverse function of the function x(t) and, according to Equation (9), is

$$t = \tau_2\,[\ln 1 - \ln |1 - T/T_0|]\,/a = \tau_2\,[\ln 1 - \ln(1 - x)]/a \qquad\qquad (12)$$

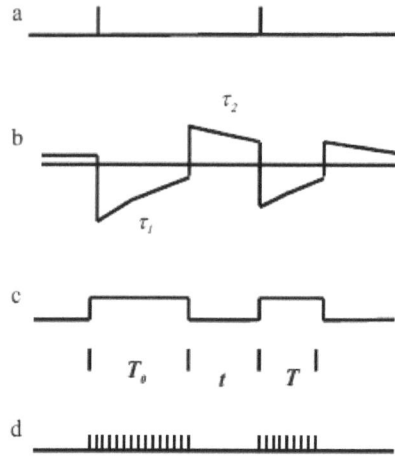

Figure 2: The Brain event train mono stable generator. a) triggering input. b) charging τ_1 and recovering τ_2 time constants. c) periods T_0, t and T. d) burst of neural spikes.

$$dt\,(x)\,/\,dx = \tau_2\,/\,a\,(1 - T/\,T_0) = \tau_2\,/\,a\,(1 - x) \tag{13}$$

Substituting Equations (10), (12), and (13) into (11) we obtain

$$g(x) = \lambda\,\tau_2\,\exp\{-\lambda\,\tau_2\,[\ln\,1 - \ln\,(1 - x)]\,/a\}\,/\,a(1 - x)$$

$$g(x) = \lambda\,\tau_2\,(1 - x)^{\lambda\,\tau_2/a-1}\,/\,a = \lambda\,\tau_2\,(1 - T/T_0)^{\lambda\,\tau_2/a-1}\,/\,a \tag{14}$$

Theoretically obtained distributions (Equation 14) are shown in Fig. **1**, for parameters $\lambda\tau_2/a$ in the range $0 < \lambda\,\tau_2/a < 4$, which is of practical interest. These distributions are valid for all types of mono stable circuits considered. The curves are normalized by the circuit parameters T_0 and a. By selecting the parameters λ τ_2/a, a large variety of distributions can be easily generated in the brain, as shown in Fig. **1**. Hence the mono stable effect is important in explaining the event trains in neural networks and in the complex brain and mind tissue, TISS. The presence of BET processes in experimental data is not directly visible. To recognize the BET process, I have developed a semi-automated knowledge mining procedure. Using this procedure, I recognize and analyze several BET related processes and SO laws.

The PILE-UP theory [25, 26, 37] has been first developed to explain the experimental data of the end plate of the frog Rana Temporaria. It explains also the transitions in human brain as stochastic processes. See Figs. **3** and **4**. The PILE-UP, is built up from the transmitter release m.e.p.p. quanta, in the range of 0.2 to 0.8 mV; quantizing enhances the small generalization.

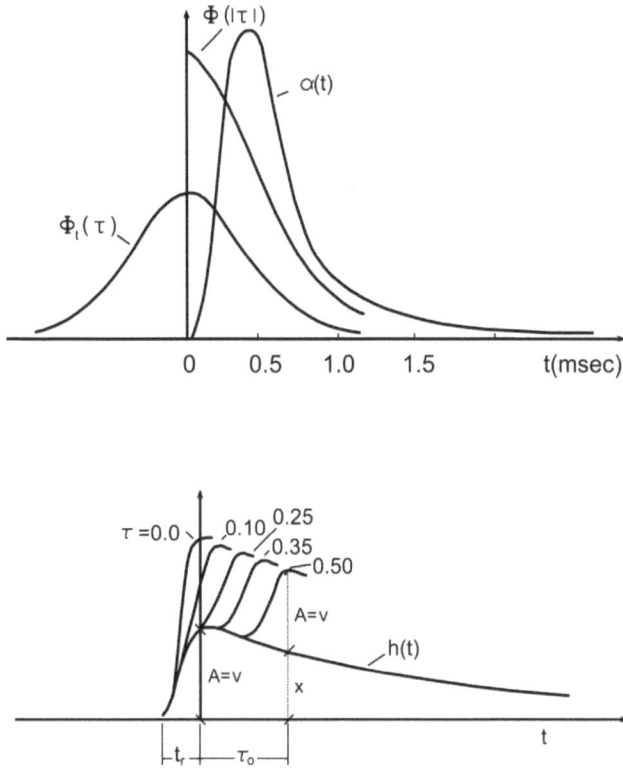

Figure 3: The Pile-Up theory, [15, 16, 27] Upper: the distribution. Lower: building Sensation amplitudes from two attributes, s=A+ x, with relative delays from 0 to 0,5 ms.

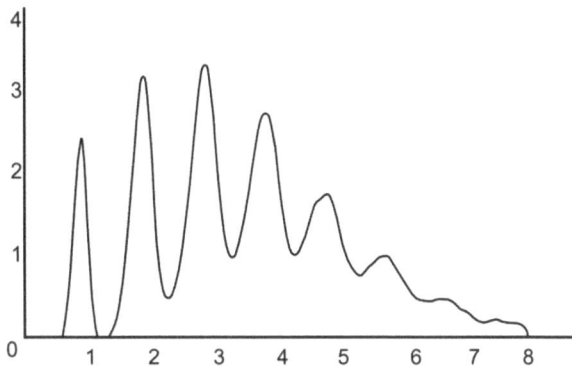

Figure 4: The Pile-Up amplitudes distribution function f(s) for v = 1, mean number of attributes m=4; and h(t) as in Fig. **3**. Abscissa is a normalized amplitude s.

PILE-UP law is composed of the synaptic transmission stochastic equations 1 to 17, [25, 26, 37]. In the neuromuscular transmission PILE-UP equations explain the motor end plate potential EPP with the average quantum number of 100 to 200. In the brain synaptic transmission PILE-UP equations explain the excitatory and inhibitory post synaptic potentials, EPSP and IPSP, with the average quantum number about 1. The average quantum number per synapse is low; yet on the nerve cell there are many synapses from converging pathways and there is a very efficient summation of the individual excitatory synaptic actions.

Brain Event Train Results. The brain generates various event trains using mono stable internal systems. A mono stable system (uni vibrator, one-shot, electromechanical, and biological mono stable systems), triggered periodically, has a constant duration of quasi stable period, T_0. If triggering pulses are coming at random, the mono stable circuit may be triggered before the end of the recovery period. Because of that, the duration of the quasi stable period will vary from pulse to pulse. This period becomes a stochastic variable, whose statistical distribution is to be found. I suppose that triggering pulses come at random with a rate λ and that the first pulse which comes after the end of a quasi -stable period will trigger the circuit. By adjusting $\lambda\tau_2/a$ the brain generates:

- $\lambda\tau_2/a = 4$, almost Poisson distribution event trains

- $\lambda\tau_2/a = 1$, uniform distribution event train

- $\lambda\tau_2/a = 1/10$, almost periodic event trains.

The brain is a very efficient generator of many different mono stable event trains. The presented theory explains the brain event trains generation, in the brain and mind tissue TISS.

Various mono stable event trains participate in the information flow across the barriers of brain units: neural networks; nodes; groups; flocks and pools. Many event trains are active simultaneously in the brain and mind tissue TISS. The time intervals of trains cover a broad range from 0 to 1225 ms. The ratio of time intervals between neighboring trains is $7 \cdot 7 \cdot 7$. This is due to the brain sampling and quantizing [34]. In BET, analogue voltage = Continuous C, is Quantized into an event, or fuzzy cluster=Discrete D. This is a Continuous Quantizing Discrete law: CQD. For details on CQD see [26, 31].

BET equations 1 to 14 and PILE-UP equations 1 to 17 in [15, 16, 27], give a precise explanation of neurons as the CQD computing networks. Next steps are the pattern recognition and the brain mind signs.

THE GENETIC AND LEARNED SIGNS

A sign is a mark that always has a particular meaning. It indicates the presence or likely future existence of something else. Each sign is a specific combination and interaction of Time T, Information I and Set S. Here I explain the CQD brain mind signs: BILO, COMET, SAVA.

- **BILO** sign is related to simple messages and features. It belongs to the BILO, Brain Internal Language Organization. BILO is related to the CQD computing neural networks, involved all over the brain. BILO is supported by BET, PILE-UP. BILO signs involve the chaos, courting, mimicry and the dialogues D1 to D6. There is a variety of BILO signs: in "labeled line" signs, the information is embodied in the particular fiber it traverses; in "rate coding" sign, the stimulus intensity is presented by means of the rate of nerve impulses in a particular group of fibers; in "time coding," the length of each inter spike interval carries information. In "quantum component" or "quantum step" or "quantum", electrical and chemical packages carry information; there is no relation whatsoever with the subatomic quantum mechanics. **Many different BET, PILE-UP co operations generate the BILO signs**.

- **COMET** sign deals with the chunks and simple associations. COMET is a short name for COMPRESSOR and METER. Here I show COMET related to the verbal stories compression and measurement.

The Brain COMPRESSOR and REASON [37, 38, 39] have been discovered in the human brain Evoked potential, BSAEP and N400. See Fig. **5**. They are explained with the nested BRAMA protocol. BRAMA is built up from the time windows: BRA = 3,6 ms; AMA = 25 ms; MA = 125 ms; BRAMA = 1225 ms.

The Brain COMPRESSOR and REASON compress the verbal story, memory and search processes. The compression goes through the mind BARRIER gates: Cause-Effect CE, Time Order TO; Common Concept CC; Concept Parents, Children, Emotions, Phonemes. They are involved in the speech and thinking loops.

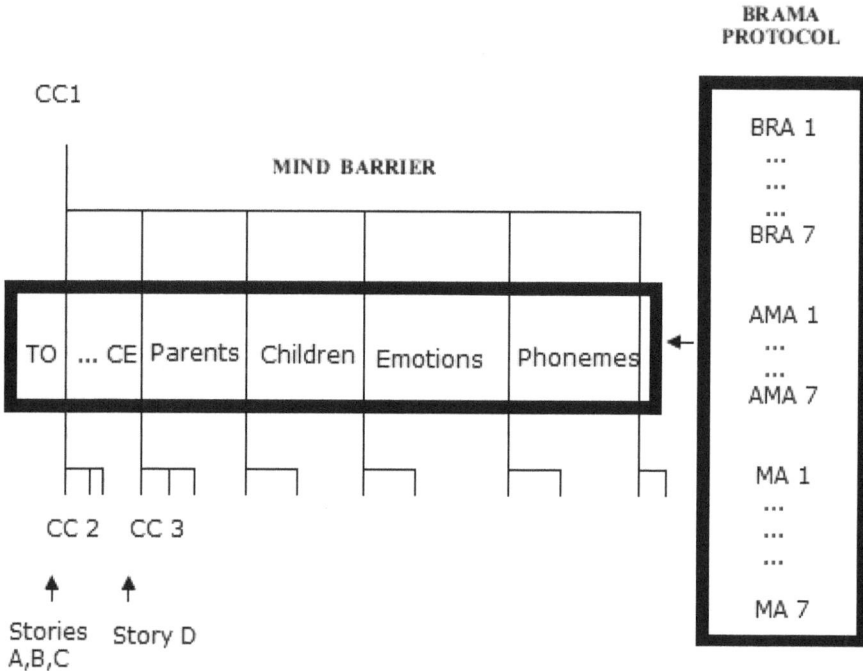

Figure 5: The Brain COMPRESSOR, REASON. Mind associate memory, for inexact compression of stories. BRAMA protocol selectively disinhibits the Mind Barrier, related to the storage of concept trees.

The Brain Meter [40] has been first observed in the verbal stories experiments. See Fig. **6**. Brain measures the verbal stories. Brain uses a set of verbal fuzzy clusters. Each major verbal concept is measured with its fuzzy clusters and with the memberships to them. For example, the concept "temperature" is measured with the 7 temperature t fuzzy clusters. Similarly, the "Time" is measured with the 7 Time T fuzzy clusters; the "distance ", with the 7 distance d fuzzy clusters *etc.*

The COMPRESSOR, REASON with the BARRIER gates and the METER with the fuzzy clusters form the verbal COMET signs within T, I, S:

T, time windows, periods: BRA, AMA, MA

I, information, fuzzy clusters: t (cold, mild, hot); d (long, medium, short); T………….

S, Set, crisp gates: CE,TO, CC, PA,CH,EM,PH……….

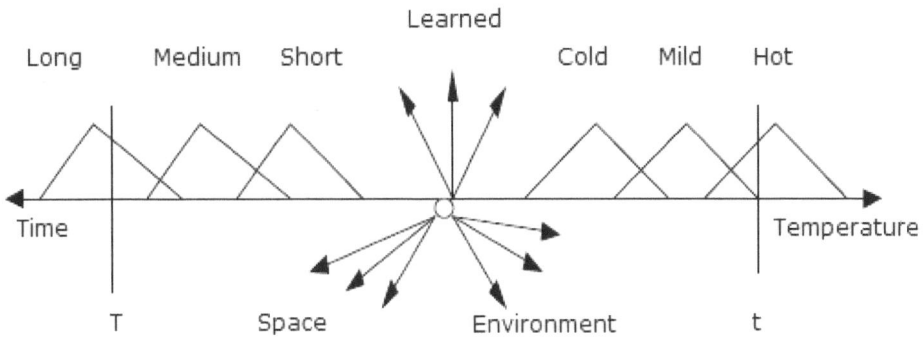

Figure 6: The Brain Meters measure the verbal story. Each measure finds the membership with the overlapping fuzzy clusters.

In Fig. **5**, Cognitive concepts CC1 and CC2 are linked in the Time Order TO, tree. Three stories are compressed into the same tree. A: After the long hot summer arrives the mild rainy fall; B: After the sunny warm period, arrives the mild season of fruits; C: After several hot months arrives the mild rainy fall. In Fig. **6** see the CQD process: from the continuous experience (C), measured by the meters (Q), to the fuzzy cluster or discrete step (D). Based on the verbal stories simulation and measurements (27 – 30), I see the COMET as a "common concept" sign. Many different COMPRESS, REASON, METER co operations generate the COMET signs.

SAVA sign deals with the multiple complex associations that explain a specific experience. SAVA, Selective Audio Video Association is responsible for the

CQD pattern recognition and storage. SAVA signs follow the observations of both the structure in stellate and pyramidal cells, and the general features of intra-cortical signals. SAVA also follows the computer associations [31 – 34] and the computer Holographic Neural Technology [46]. External auditory and visual fields are first converted to BILO and COMET domains. Next comes SAVA in an image (or voice) addressable memory. SAVA signs participate in the selection and overlap of the multiple stimulus response associations and knowledge.

Association overlaps many patterns. The input to the association memory is a **stimulus field [S] and the response is a field [R]**.

Learning (encoding) enfolds (overlaps) multiple stimulus-response associations into the same **association, correlation matrix [A]**.

$$[A] +=\overline{[S]}^{T} [R] \tag{15}$$

Decoding or response recall transforms stimulus field through all of the previous stimulus-response mappings and generates the associated **response field [R]**

$$[R] = [S]^* / c [A] \tag{16}$$

where $[S]^*$ is the new stimulus field exposed to the memory for issuance of the response recall; c is a normalization coefficient, probabilistic bound. Association grows through 3 MA periods.

Knowledge overlaps the patterns as well as rules, in a similar way as association. It grows through 3 MA periods.

$$[K] +=\overline{[S]}^{T} [R] \tag{17}$$

$$[R] = [S]^* / c [K] \tag{18}$$

SAVA is a "pattern" sign and it deals with the cluster of overlapped patterns. In our experiments with birds, we found the complex trees full of overlapped patterns. See [27, 48] and Fig. **4** in [42]. I believe that the "pattern trees" are also present in the human brain. Using the pattern signs, the human brain compresses the memory and shortens the search, reasoning and thinking processes. **Many different Associations, Knowledge pattern co operations generate the SAVA signs**.

THE TIME INFORMATION SIGN SET: TISS

Fig. **7** shows the Time Information Sign Set TISS. In TISS, the term Set S indicates the mutually related neural networks, elements, agents, units, fractal spaces; rather than the anatomy, geometry, organs. This definition of TISS replaces the simple definition of TISS in [43, 44, 45]. Fig. **7** is a snap shot of the massively parallel, dynamic, nested, fractal, never repeating TISS. The Self

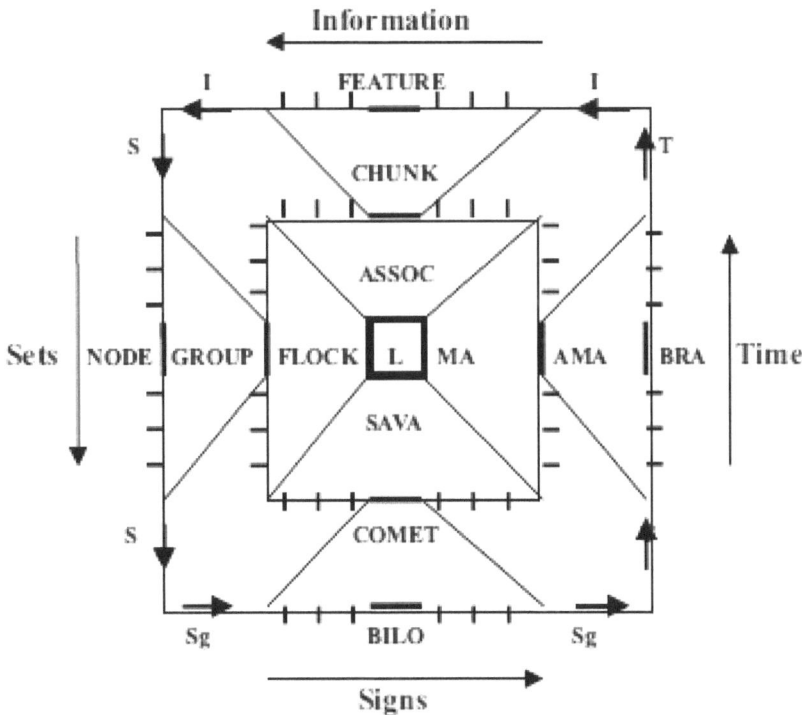

Figure 7: The Brain Mind SIGNS. They are formed from the Time Information Sets. Note the triplets: T (BRA, AMA, MA); I (FEATURE, CHUNK, ASSOCIATION); Sets (NODE, GROUP, FLOCK); Signs Sg (BILO, COMET, SAVA). The verbal and visual thinking grows through the nested, fractal layers: BILO square, COMET square, SAVA square, Language L.

Organization SO links the born with and learned features, chunks and associations. They are taken from the nodes, groups, flocks and pools. In the fractal time periods, the nested sequences of signs are formed and used in the reciprocal adjustment, REASON [39]. Many times the brain quantizing equation [44] is followed: behind each MA there are about 7 AMA. Many times the BRAMA protocol [44] is followed: BRAMA => 7 MA; MA => 7 AMA; AMA => 7 BRA. In the brain mind signs, each SAVA is related to the information-time-set necessary to perform one single thinking step. There is a very large number of different SAVAs. Each SAVA is related to several, say 20, COMETs, which perform the partial selection. Underneath of each COMET are the brain event train BILO signs. The signs BILO,COMET, SAVA are in a relation with the, say 100.000, born with and learned features, chunks and associations. They form the brain chaotic, dynamic, feedback loops. Loops connect the zones of imagination to the primary sensory zones: visual zone in case of visual imagination; acoustical zone in case of voice *etc.* That means that imagining an object is practically the same as sensing it. This involves: a) storing the data in the short term memory; b) associating it with other data presently in the memory; c) compressing or quantizing the result; d) forming a new chunk or a permanent association. Here diverse stories, images, perception and imagination sequences meet and interact. The signs BILO, COMET, SAVA participate in the generalization [48]. The generalizer is "trained" with the learning set and then "asked" a question. The brain uses different generalization principles: pattern selection; pattern overlap; transformation and compression of the mostly empty stimulus fields, in the direct addresses of the pattern association, Fig. **6** in [43]; *etc.* The brain SO usually, but not always, chooses the right generalizers.

SON, Selection of specific, Overlap and Non specific cooperates in nodes N, groups G, flocks F, pools P [43]. The partial selection selects the specific N, G and F between 1 to z. Associative content based search extracts the right pattern from the cluster of y overlapped patterns from non specific, general domains. The size of the pattern is indicated by x. see Fig. **6** in [43].

Various TISS operate in parallel, in small and in large scales. TISS is related to the content and certainty of UCEK functions:

tissue <-> content <-> certainty

Table **1** outlines the brain and mind entity. This multidimensional, time and environment dependent entity, cannot be reduced to a simple geometry, anatomy and equation. The entity follows a very large set of SO Laws. The entity is composed of the fuzzy overlapped clouds of the tissue TISS.

The TISS clouds are full of the Associations A and agents. The agents are full of the functions UCEK. Some parts are genetic and they support the innate behavior programs. Other parts are learned and they support the learned sensation and mental behavior programs. The entity is interlinked with SO loops. The pieces or elements of the consciousness CON are spread all over.

Table 1: TISS Clouds

------TISS------ ------TISS ------
SO SO SO
Agent ------------ Agent Agent ---------- Agent
SO UCEK A SO UCEK A SO UCEK A SO UCEK A
sensation genetic mental sensation
mental sensation genetic

ELEMENTS OF CONSCIOUSNESS CON

This work brakes the brain into the agents; it brakes the consciousness into the pieces and elements; it links the pieces to the agents; it develops the CON model, based on the CON pieces. **The pieces of Consciousness, CON** we have observed in our experiments with the fireflies, katydids, frogs, birds, and in the evoked potentials from human brain. The pieces serve for the **Planning of the behavior**. SO also explains the conscious functions in the animal and human brains. **Elementary consciousness** is related to the sensing without the abstractions and thoughts.

CON of an animal is related to the specific signs, calls and duets: 1. A sequence or pattern of sounds; 2. A sequence or pattern of light flashes; 3. A display of gestures, body position, facial expressions or; 4. An emission of odors.

CON of an agent is related to the items which are currently claiming its attention. The agent opens window on these items, allowing to the set to become aware of them. Hence the awareness is communicated to the set. By the window, the agent outputs data to the set; and the set's data enter to the agent. See the human brain agent, called the firefly and its brain windows. The firefly's **continuous** stimulation intervals I and response latencies L are passing through the **discrete** time brain windows. This is **the pieces or element of consciousness CON**. Other pieces include alternating and aggressive calls in katydid agents and associative trees in bird agents. The piece merges the slow blood chemistry, hormones, temperature, environment; and the fast stimulation patterns, brain event trains BET. Fig. **8** presents the multi-level Elementary Consciousness CON model of the Femme Fatale firefly. The model explains our experimental findings in the following way. The firefly must be capable of accommodating a changing, usually only semi predictable world. A memory of complex information is used in guiding long-term behavior; it is encoded directly in the higher level. The multiple level approach allows several competing "dominant" schemas to cooperate in use of low-level competence for problem solving. The coupling of perception to action is analogous to simple "reflex arcs". Each level of behavior generating hierarchy receives the command C from a higher level. It also receives the feedback F from the environment. The output from the operator H selects one of the possible subcommands on the next lower level. For example, the level "SURVIVAL" selects the sub command for the next lower level from the set C2 (C'2, C"2, C2'"). Which subcommand is selected depends on the feedback vector F3. In other words, $C2=H3(F3)$. Similarly the level "REPRODUCTION " selects the subcommand for the next lower level: $C1=H3(F2)$. When the hormone level and blood chemistry indicate the proper time, and the air temperature is right, the command C2 is selected. When $C2=C'2$ indicates reproduction, and F2 indicates that external stimuli are present in the form of light flashes, and the male is in the territory, the command C1 is selected. When $C1=C'1$ indicates "PATROLLING FLASHING", motor control, internal oscillator, and the lantern, execute this command. Both commands and feedback are coded in a slow scale chemical hormonal coding and in a fast scale pulse/time coding. Pulse/time coding is of special interest for behavioral patterns that are executed as time sequences of events. The Brain Windows are used in such sequences, to screen, check, or recognize the information. Operators H provide parallel processing across a wide range, some which last for short times, others which span longer intervals. Operator H3 receives the stimulus [S]= feedback F3; and generates the response [R] = command C2. Hence H3 is related to the innate **Knowledge and Emotions**. Operator H2 receives the stimulus [S] = feedback F2 and Command C2. H2 is related to the **Associations and Understanding**. The response C1 defines the self-other message flash; hence it is the elementary **Consciousness**. It is a SON of a father: F2 and C2, ("Attention to the Current Task"); and of the mother: H2 ("Related Experience"). It is related to the experimentally observed dialogues D1 to D6; hence [C] is related to the BILO language and signs. Fig. **8** shows the SO of UCEK functions: the innate Knowledge, the innate / learned Associations, and the Consciousness. They are strongly coupled already in this elementary SO.

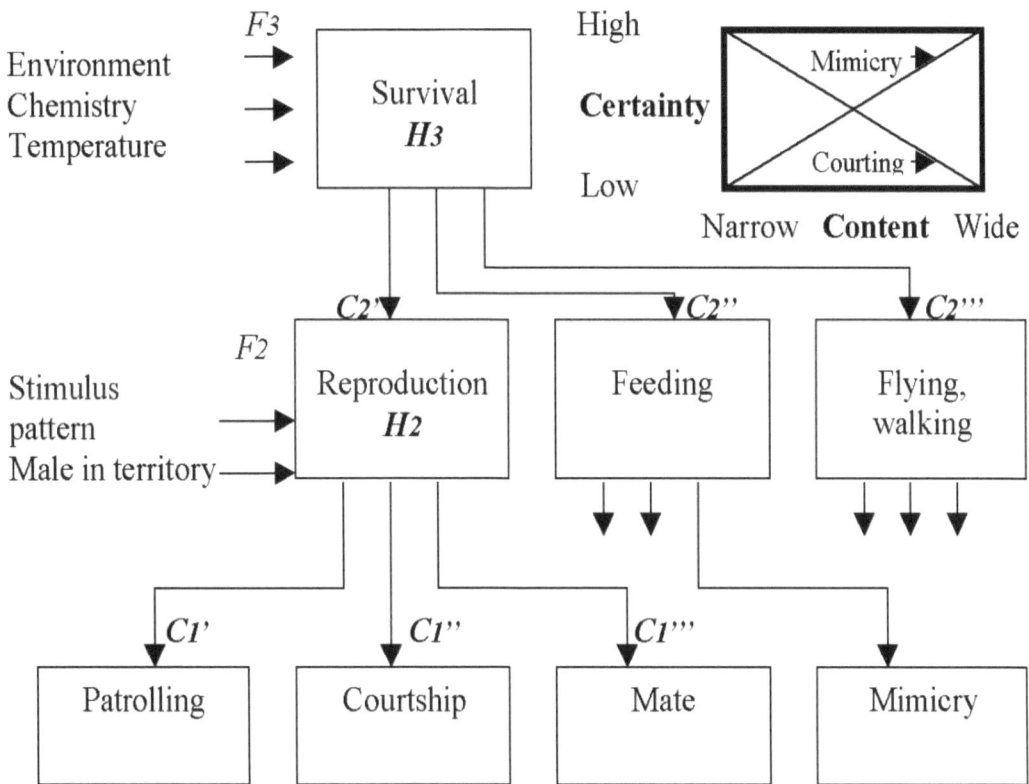

Figure 8: The Elements of Consciousness in the Firefly Brain: Patrolling, Courtship, Mate and Mimicry. These and other elements form the complex consciousness in the human brain. Conscious courting. Content: narrow, specific dialogue. Certainty is high, to mate the right partner. Conscious mimicry. Content: wide range of dialogues. Certainty is high, to eat the partner.

COMPLEX CONSCIOUSNESS

Complex consciousness in human, is a subjective awareness. Human sense things, but they also sense that they sense them; they use the words and build the abstractions and complex trains of thoughts.

The complex consciousness is created from the elements. In the invisible mind topology, the agent i is related to its elementary consciousness Ci and to its SONi. The node is related to the node's Cn and SONn; The group is related to the group's Cg and SONg; the flock is related to the flock's Cf and SONf. Corpus callosum links the verbal consciousness Cv in the left brain and the pattern recognition consciousness Cp in the right brain [44]. SON laws use all above mentioned pieces of the consciousness mosaic, and build the overall consciousness C. Each piece of consciousness is a SON of the father called "Attention to the Current Task " and of the mother called "Related Experiences ". Father and mother communicate in TISS by using BET and the common message clusters, taken from BILO. The Attention presents the specific need and its non-specific general domain. The Experience responds with the born with and learned components. The elements of consciousness, CON come from several agents. The brain draws causal pieces and forms huge connected consciousness bases in arbitrary problem domain. Example: my current Attention is a man of 170 cm. My Experience gives him a membership or CON to the cluster of "tall": 0,7; and to the cluster of "medium": 0,3. My current Consciousness is a vector 0,7; 0,3. The high level components are the verbal stories, that have passed through the brain METERS, COMPRESSORS, REASONS AND SAVA: "a medium tall man". A word representation to a feeling, memory, wish or thought renders it communicable to other. Consciousness is the self-other interface. Denying something a verbal representation means repressing it.

Fig. **9** outlines the human Complex Consciousness. SO produces an ordered sequence of actions that starting in some particular state of the brain, produce some desired "goal" state. SO couples the reacting (the ability to handle dynamicity and unexpected events) with the planning (the ability to project into the future). SO generates a variety of multi- level reacting and planning sequences and drives.

DNA

Innate: SO
reactive behavioural programs

Environment

Innate / Learned:

evaluating
observing
consorting
correcting
superSO

UCEK
ASSOCIATIONS ← → SO　Self
A　　　　　　Organization

SO+
planning
compatibility
reality
coherence

response

reactive　　　　conscious
　　　planned

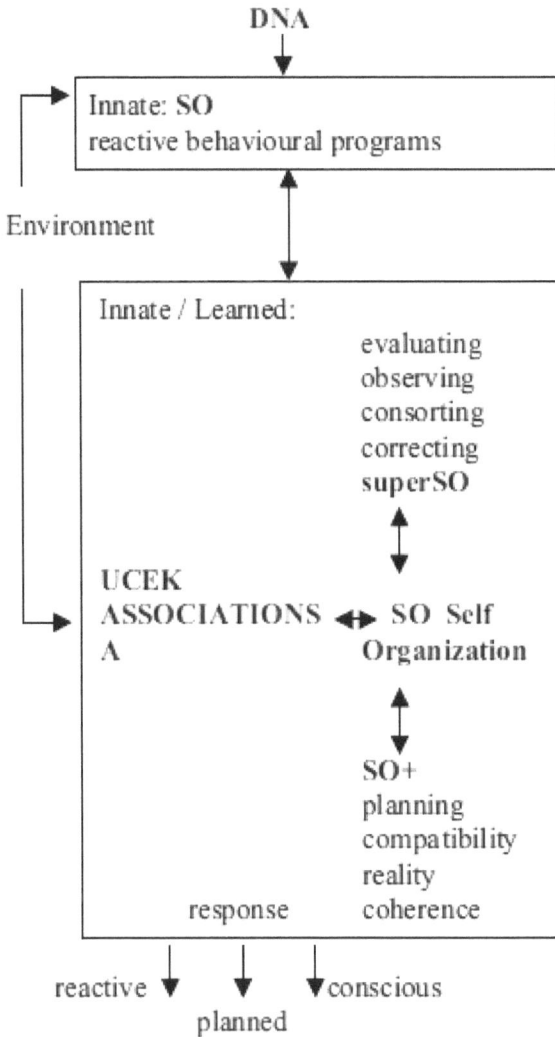

Figure 9: Complex Consciousness is the large mosaic of the associations, Self- Organization, and drives: SO, SO+, SuperSO+. It is composed of a large number of the consciousness elements.

The instinct drives "SO", are defined by the DNA genes. The code for each SO exists as a discrete entity, and each runs by turns, rather than as a unified organization for behavior. They do not have to form a coherent entity, but might make competing and even conflicting demands on the organism for "runtime" in the central nervous system. Consequently the "SO" is the repository of many different programs for behavior, not all of which need be compatible or conformable in any way, at least as long as they remained in the repository. The

SO focuses on the pleasure and pain. The SO drives are related to the reactive behavioral programs. These programs correspond to functional neural circuits. The programs encode memories of long duration action sequences that remain active to direct behavior in the absence of sensory stimuli. Routine sensory conditions activate SO program pathways. The SO drives represent automatic conditioned action sequences that achieve goal in routine situations. These program sequences map conditions into effect on commands in real-time without any deliberation.

The self -drives "SO+", are charged with responsibility for unconscious activities, as well as for voluntary thought and movement. It is an event driven system, responding to stimuli, either from outside (sensory data from the real world) or from inside (the drives and demands of the SO or parts of itself expressed as emotions, feelings, thoughts, intentions or memories). The SO+ is in direct contact with the outside world *via* inputs from the perceptual system, and makes outputs of various kinds through its ability to control voluntary thought and action. This means that consciousness, occupying current awareness, is a unique peculiarity of the SO+, which to this extent is the only agency capable of consciousness. The SO+ focuses on the environmental reality. The SO+ drives monitor the automatic conditioned responses and anticipate, detect and correct any error that occur due to the model conditions. The SO+ simulation program produces the structures that describe the predicted effect of executing any given program in the context of current conditions. It then compares the simulated predictions and plans with the goals, in order to detect the potential errors.

The super drives "superSO+" suppress the pleasures. Hence they run over SO and SO+. The super SO+ drives observe and evaluate both, SO and SO+. The SO of UCEK merges the drives. SO determines when and how to replace the reactive, with the deliberately planned and conscious programs. The details are based on the SO laws and equations, including the commitment and coordination between the agents. SO model forces information processing issues to be addressed in detail.

The Consciousness Content [C] is the response [R], related to the case of self-other messages. Equation 18, becomes:

[R] = [C] = [S]* / c [A]   **(19)**

Complex [C] grows from the TISS. [C] grows from the elements of association ai, chunk chi, feature fi and stimulus si; and from various operators H.

$[S] = [s_1\ s_2\ s_3 \ldots\ldots\ldots\ldots]$

$[A] = [a_1\ a_2\ a_3 \ldots\ldots\ldots\ldots]$

$a_1 = H\ (ch_{11}\ ch_{12}\ ch_{13} \ldots\ldots)$

$ch_{11} = H\ (f_{111}\ f_{112}\ f_{113} \ldots\ldots\ldots)$ **(20)**

The element i could be associated to several higher (and lower) elements. Equations 20 is a small part of multiple operators. The elements could be binary, fuzzy or complex values. The process, equations 19 and 20, realizes an encoding / decoding operation whereby the new stimulus field [S] is mapped exactly to the desired, conscious response [R] = [C]. The encoding pass is irrespective of prior enfolded associative memory. Subsequent encodings will accumulate a distortion of this mapping at a gradual rate and rise in proportion to the closeness of new stimulus field to the prior field [S]. The brain has many distinct neural associations of the above type. Each one is dedicated to separate region and data fields, such as frequency / time in the **auditory input, stories and thoughts** or the x / y pixel position within the **visual field sequences**. One or more stimulus fields can be associated to a single response field. The brain combines the stimulus elements forming the high order product terms. This is a jump from a small initial data field to the higher dimensionality; permitting a large number of distinct mappings, to be enfolded into the neural association. For the experimental findings and computer models see [24-48]. The new equations and models are presented here. These models can be tested more easily than models based on verbal descriptions because they produce behavior that can be compared directly with clinically observed behavior. For example, a lesion of the frontal lobes disintegrates the firmly established sequences and plans of actions into a series of isolated fragments. The preserved fragments are related to the dispersed, nested, fractal elements in the model based on equations 15 to 20. In contrast, verbal models must be interpreted subjectively to predict and test their behavior.

THE BRAIN AND MIND SELF ORGANIZATION, SO: LAWS AND EQUATIONS

The first role of SO laws is to explain phenomena in the brain. The second role is to predict the future. Given the state of the brain at some initial time, what is the state of the brain at some future time? The answers are provided by SO laws as well as by SO equations. In human brain the Self Organization SO laws deal with the UCEK functions in all areas: synapses, neural networks, agents, nodes, groups, flocks and pools. SO laws are everywhere. It is not possible: to locate the specific mind area; to read the mind; to follow the track of thinking. The cortical, mind agent i has its U_i, C_i, E_i, K_i functions.

The holistic SO of UCEK relates the free will to the experimentally observed **readiness potential**. SO is presented in Fig. **3** in [44]; and modified SO in Fig. **10** here.

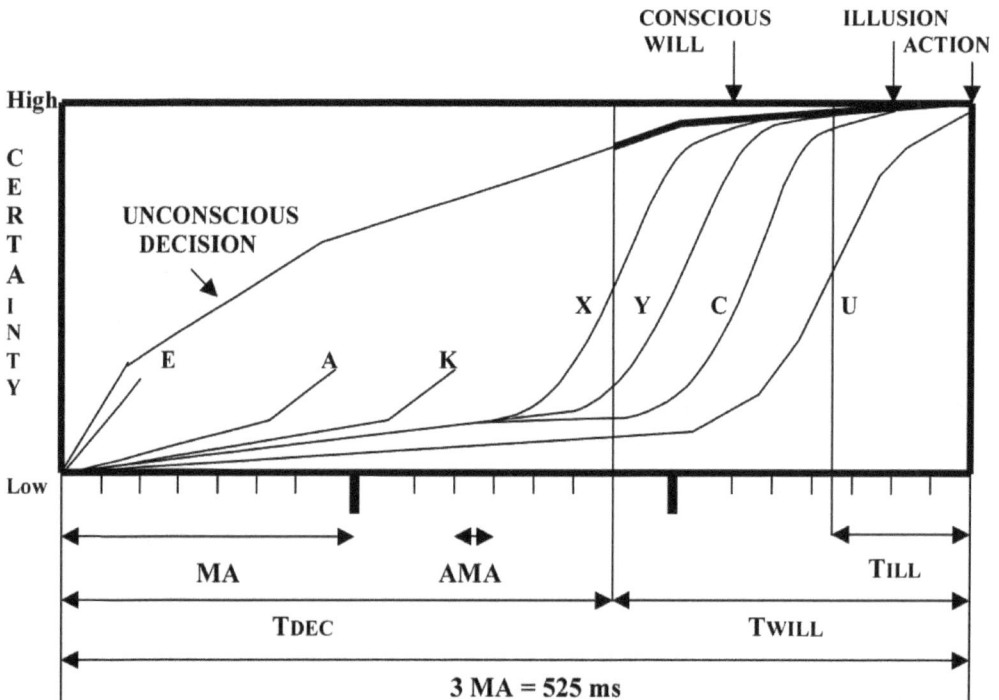

Figure 10: The State of Mind. Holistic Self Organization, SO of UCEK, certainty grows to the unconscious decision, to the conscious will, to the illusion, to the action. Tdec = 2MA –AMA = 331 ms; Twill = MA + AMA = 204 ms; Till = 3 MA + 3 BRA = 86 ms

I use the constants f, p, u, d and e and develop the following holistic **certainty** equations:

Consciousness Certainty C combines the consciousness of agents. The neural networks apply a set of weights Wi to a set of agents, allowing to the elementary consciousness Ci to affect the Consciousness Certainty C

$$C = \Sigma C_i W_i / \Sigma W_i \tag{21}$$

$$C = \text{Sigm}(X, Y) \tag{22}$$

$$X = \text{Sigm}(ft) \tag{23}$$

$$Y = \text{Sigm}(pt) \tag{24}$$

X = the activated **fraction** of the set of agents; Y = the piece of consciousness of one activated agent. The peaks of the X and Y derivative functions are in two AMA periods. In the one AMA period: the largest fraction X of agents is activated; in another AMA period the largest piece Y of consciousness is added to each activated agent.

NOTE: Each Sigm is a different Sigmoidal process. Equations 9 to 14 show that the sigmoidal integral distribution performs the optimal transformation of the random brain event trains BET. For more see [35].

Understanding Certainty U locks, adapts, the hypotheses and the unexpected data stream. U grows until the goal, action is achieved.

$$U = \text{Sigm}(ut) \tag{25}$$

Decision Certainty D grows into the saturation approaching the goal, action.

$$D = 1 - \exp(-dt) \tag{26}$$

Emotion Certainty E relates the motor and sensory areas following the SON law: selection, overlap, non specific. It grows fast in the first AMA period;

$$E = 1 - \exp(-et) \tag{27}$$

SO equations:

PILE-UP equations 5 to 17; [25-26-37]

FIREFLY equation 1 to 17 [29]

QUANTUM equations 1 to 7; [35]

BILO dialogue equations D1 to D6; [36-44]; equations 1 to 4 [30]

BRAMA equations 1 to 4; [37]

METER equations 1 to 7; [40]

LEAP, many equation [44-45]

TISS equations 1 to 4; [44]

BET equations 1 to 14; this work.

SIGN equations 15 to 27; this work.

SO Laws:

PILE-UP; **CQD**; **BIRD** agent; **KATYDID** agent; **FIREFLY** agent; neural computing; message **QUANTUM**; mind **BARRIER**; **BRAMA**; brain **CHAOS**; **COMPRESSOR**; **REASON**; **METER**; **SOUCEK**; **ASSOCIATION**; **TISS**; **BET** (this work); brain mind **SIGN** (this work); **BILO**; **COMET** (this work); **SAVA** (this work); **SON** (this work); **CON** (this work); brain **LEAP**.

SO laws are a dispersed, massively parallel cooperation and entity. SO laws explain the Brain and Mind functions UCEK. Several laws and equations must be combined to explain the functions. Here is an example of the massively parallel, nested and combined laws: PILE-UP, BILO, BET, TISS and FIREFLY. **BILO law** is based on the Primary waveform P (t) and the memory M2. See Figs. **1** and **2** in [29,30,44]. P (t) presents the frequency of events in BET. BET with the frequency above M2, through the PILE-UP, generates the high EPSP that opens the receive windows. BET with the frequency below M2 generates the low EPSP:

the receive window is closed, but the send window is open. These windows in the internal FIREFLY agents, within TISS, generate the internal dialogues D1 to D6 [29,30,44]. The time window depends on the neural network that generates it. In human brain: many neurons, short window, fast BILO. In the firefly insect: smaller number of neurons, longer window, slow BILO.

CONCLUSIONS

This work introduces the new brain event trains and signs theory that explains the brain and mind processes. The work is based on the concrete experimental data from the firefly, katydid, frog, bird and human. The data are measured in a short time scale from 0 to 2000 ms. The described theory is strongly related to these experimental data in four ways:

- **SHORT TIME**. The theory focuses on BRAMA period of 1225 ms, rather than on a long time.

- **LOCAL PROCESSES**. The fuzzy, nested, random, experimental data lead to the **local** brain event trains BET, TISS signs BILO COMET SAVA, SO processes; rather than symbols.

- **FLOW OF FAVORABLE FACTORS, FFF**. While the neurons do not move, the Information I and the Signs Sg agents and processes flow through the Sets S, with the Time T. This a dynamic TISS.

- **MOSAIK**. Short time local processes and FFF, are the pieces of mosaic needed to explain the brain and mind. This work gives a very concrete description of these pieces. The pieces form the long time complex processes, in the neural networks, prefrontal cortex, temporal, parietal and occipital cortex as well as in the sub cortical structures.

1. The nucleus of each cell keeps the **genetic code**. In genetic code a gene keeps the information necessary to produce one single protein. There are about 100.000 genes; each composed of 20 coding words (amino acids); each composed of 3 out of 4 coding elements (A, C, G, T). **2.** The assemblage of **Genetic Signs** is a crop of the signs developed through evolution and stored in DNA. Formation of genetic signs goes through the cycle of variation, selection and reduplication of selected. New signs are continually cropping up, but as there is a DNA limit, many signs gradually become extinct. In short, favored signs survive the natural selection. **3.** The assemblage of **Learned Signs** is a crop of personal and of learned experience stored in the long term memory: in neuron-synapse connections. **4.** Finally in the brain, the genetic and learned signs are stored in the dispersed neural networks: in 25 billion of neurons; some of which with thousands of synapses; hence with many thousands of billions interconnections; with large associative neural networks. Dendritic growth and spine production of the large, layer III, pyramidal, neurons corresponds with the intensive cognitive development during early childhood. They play a dominant role in preserving cognitive functions. **5.** The theory explains and proves the existence of the BET and SIGNS, from the level of the neurons-synapses, all the way to the level of the evoked potentials and of the behavior. **6.** Psychological experiments suggest the information flow of 10^{11} bits per second for human sensory input, but only about 10 bits per second for the input into short term memory. It is clear that enormous data compression, clustering, quantizing takes place. **7.** Brain mind nested, fractal, TISS clusters are capable of solving problems of seemingly arbitrary complexity. Yet the learning procedures follow simple principle: brain event trains, BET and SO laws. **8.** The Brain and Mind Attractions, BRAMA, merge and compress the strong desires. The burning, passionate, unrestrained, excessive desires come from the concurrent, nested, fractal, selfish, TISS agents and units. **9.** The brain and mind follow two different avenues: logical/programming, L/P; and transformation/mapping, T/M. L/P is based upon algorithms, procedures and rules. T/M is based on learning and on building associations. These two types of information processing are conceptually incompatible. In other words, it is becoming clear that it may often be impossible to satisfactorily describe the operation of transformation in terms of an algorithm, and *vice versa*. For example, brain action, based on T/M, may provide useful solution to important application area, without allowing us to discover the fundamental ideas used in the solution. The solution is based on the SO laws. **10.** The mind is a traffic of the electrochemical brain event trains, BET in TISS. **11. The quantity and**

complexity of TISS clusters and SO laws strongly distinguishes the human brain, language, consciousness and abstraction, from the animal brains. The quantity is in proportion with the number of nerve cells: in human brain, billions of cells, complex UCEK functions; in octopus brain, 520 millions of cells, simple UCEK functions; in insect brain, over 1 million of cells, elementary UCEK functions. In each brain the UCEK functions are in relation with its environment and life complexity. **12.** There is an enormous degree of the modularized, nested and repetitive human TISS clusters. They follow the SO laws and the signs BILO, COMET, SAVA. The signs are present in the cerebral cortex, cerebellum, brain stem and spinal cord: in the pyramidal, stellate, Martinotti and granule cells. Within and between the neural networks, the signs participate in the internal, multilevel, complex, pattern recognition and generalization. The signs merge: time, information and sets; continuous and discrete; selection of specific and overlap; rules and associations. **13.** Multilevel, parallel and sequential loops perform the pattern recognition, associative reasoning, speech and thinking. **14.** The brain signs are the pieces of mosaic used to build the mind. **15.** The brain networks are using the assembled signs to cooperate and to fight, until the winner takes all. Again and again. Here and there all over the brain. **16.** Large parts of the neural interconnections within the human neo cortex are related to the complex associations and to the language. The unique human language grows out of the internal signs BILO, COMET, SAVA. See the central square of Fig. **7.** **17.** The word finding increases the activity in dorso lateral prefrontal cortex and decreases the activity in posterior cortical regions. This is because the prefrontal TISS units act to gate, and select the posterior TISS units.

The State of Mind. SO of UCEK creates the State of Mind. There is no central executive. It is SO that leads the tracks of thoughts. In Fig. **10**, the curve U shows **the overall certainty state** of Understanding. Other curves present the overall certainty states of C X Y D A K E. They explain the active forms of encoding and retrieval, which depend on the lateral frontal cortex; and the more passive forms of encoding and retrieval, which result when incoming or recalled stimuli automatically trigger stored representation. High or low levels of UCEK states select the mind tracks in a fraction of a second. Yet the mixture of high and low levels slows down the decision process. See Table **2**.

Table 2: Decision Process

High Level	Low Level
U I understand the situation. I follow this track.	I do not understand. I must go on, or change the track.
C I am aware of the task. I give attention to this task.	I am not aware of what is happening.
E The brain is pleased with this, and it follows the track. This is painful and the brain leads away.	The brain has no feeling what so ever.
K This case is similar to the past experience. The brain performs the case based **reasoning**.	Mind has no indication where to find this case. It is not related to the past experience. **Learning**
A The brain searches through the Past stimulus/response associations and finds the answer.It **repeats**.	The brain does not find similar, past, stimulus / response associations. It **learns**.

The Elements or Pieces of Consciousness CON, explain the innate and learned **Bio** assemblage. They can be used as a guide to build the CON Software **Soft: Selective courting**. The CON system gradually narrows the windows. The goal is to detect/select the right partner and to avoid the risk of courting the wrong partner. **Bio**: brain windows before mating. **Soft**: low risk credit scoring. **Mimicry**. The CON system gradually widens the windows. The goal is to attract/select as many partners as possible. **Bio**: brain windows for feeding. **Soft**: help desk for marketing. **Context Switching**. Sudden change in CON behavior, based on the past history, recalled experience and on environmental conditions. **Bio**: brain windows after mating. **Soft**: EDI-switch for adaptive purchasing. **Aggression**. One subsystem tends to take control of the whole CON system. **Bio**: time coding in insect chirping. **Soft**: competition networks.

Alternation. Two (or several) subsystems are taking control of the CON system in alternation. **Bio**: time coding in insects; leader/follower chirping. **Soft**: travelling salesman, genetic programming.

Solo. One subsystem is in control of the whole CON system. **Bio**: time coding in insects; leader chirping. **Soft**: winner takes all. **Transmitting**. Exchange of conscious messages among subsystems. **Bio**: quantum transmitter release on neural terminals. **Soft**: conscious message packages.

The BET and SIGN Theory is Explaining Many Experimental Findings: End-plate potentials; duet singing; alternating and aggressive calls; courting and mimicry; fuzzy concepts more/less; approximate, innate, posterior reasoning *vs.* learned, linguistic, symbolic, prefrontal reasoning; **verbal stories compression and meters**; mind, evoked potential, prefrontal chaos links.

Plasticity and Transfer. Fig. **11**: S1, S2, S3 and S4 stimulate the separate TISS units 1, 2, 3 and 4. S4 is an expansion of the field S5. S4 is a compression of the field S6, that can occur through the damage or learning. S2 and S3 stimulate the parts of TISS 2 and TISS 3. These overlaps explain the brain plasticity and the transfer using equations 15 to 20.

TISS is Damaged: The links of S3 to TISS 2 and TISS 4 are used to learn the lost class 3 tasks. **S3 is damaged**. S3 is a dominant stimulus field in TISS 3, and S4 is a secondary field. Yet, now, C3 is low and the part of S4 through learning, becomes a dominant field in TISS 3.

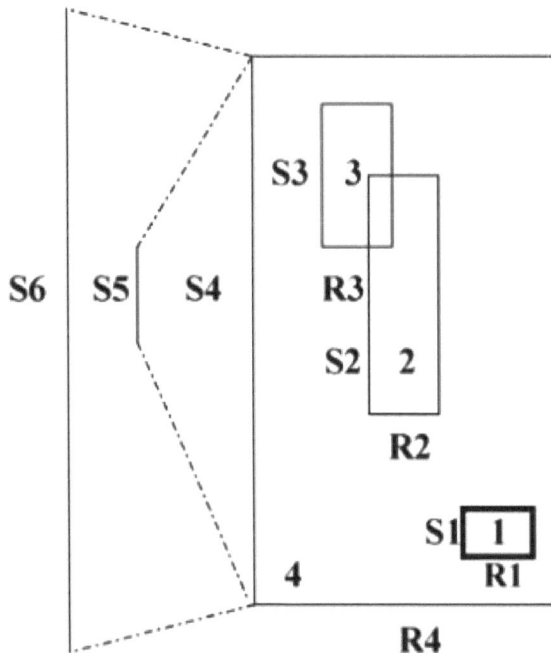

Figure 11: Concept elementary consciousness certainty 1 is high: Narrow stimulus field S1 stimulates TISS1 producing the narrow response field R1. Conscious insect. Firefly agent inside the human brain. Pattern complex consciousness certainty 4 is low. Wide S4, R4 and TISS 4. Human unconscious decision.

This is automatic backup. TISS units that loose the old stimulation are linked to backup, and they learn new tasks. SO laws and equations lead the plasticity and transfer into the clinical applications.

SO process: BET; BILO; COMET; SAVA; TISS information flow of 4000 billion bits in a single BRAMA period of 1225 ms.

ACKNOWLEDGEMENTS

I have spent fifty years working out the Self Organization of life intelligence: in Institute Ruder Boskovic; U of Zagreb; Brookhaven National Laboratory N.Y.; SUNY; U of AZ. I acknowledge the stimulating atmosphere and excellent working conditions.

The BRAMA names, BRA, AMA, MA, have been inspired by the names of my children Branko, Amalia and Marina. The name BILO has been inspired by the Bilo Gora hill and valley of my parents. The name SAVA has been inspired by the Sava river.

DISCLOSURE

"The content of this chapter has been previously published in *Periodicum Bilogorum, Vol. 106, No. 3, 265-278,2004*".

ABBREVIATIONS

BET   = Brain Event Train

BILO   = Brain Internal Language Organization

COMET   = Compressor Meter

SAVA   = Selective Audio Video Association

CON   = Consciousness Element

SO   = Self Organization

U   = Understanding

C   = Consciousness

E   = Emotions

K   = Knowledge

REFERENCES

[1]   CHIAPPA KH. Evoked Potentials in Clinical Medicine. Raven Press 1989.

[2]   CHUANG PT, McMAHON AP. Vertebrate Hedgehog signaling modulated by induction of a Hedgehog-binding protein. Nature1999; 397: 617–621.

[3]   DEHAENE S. *et al*. Sources of Mathematical Thinking Behavioral and Brain – Imaging Evidence. Science1999; 284: 970 – 974.

[4]   DEL CASTILLO J, KATZ B. Quantum Components of the End-Plate Potential. J. Physiol. (London)1950; 124: 560.

[5]   DURAJLIJA ZINIC S. SitaRam: a computational approach for multi perspective visualization of higher-order and progressive patterns in highly repetitive regions of DNA. Per. biol 2005;107: 423 – 436.

[6]   GOLDMAN-RAKIC Patricia. Architecture of the Prefrontal Cortex and the Central Executive. [in Ref. (7)] 1995.

[7]   GRAFMAN J, HOLYOAK KJ, BOLLER F. Structure and Functions of the Human Prefrontal Cortex. New York Academy of Sciences, vol. 769, New York 1995.

[8]   HO R, SUTHERLAND JG, BRUHA I. Neurological Fuzzy Diagnoses: Holographic *vs*. Statistical *vs*. Neural Method.[in Ref. (19)] 1994.

[9]   JIMENEZ – MONTANO MA, LUCIO – GARCIA HR, FERNANDEZ AR. Computer simulation to generate simplified proteins with stochastic grammars. Per. biol2005;107: 397 – 402.

[10]   KOSTOVIC I, JUDAS M, KOSTOVIC – KNEZEVIC LJ, SIMIC G, DELALLE I, CHUDY D, SAJIN B, PETANJEK Z. Zagreb Research Collection of Human Brains for Developmental Neurobiologists and Clinical Neuroscientists. International J Developmental Biol1991; 35: 215 – 230.

[11]   KRALJ M, KRALJEVIC S, SEDIC M, KURJAK A, PAVELIC K., Global approach to perinatal medicine: functional genomics and proteomics. J. Perinatal Med2004; (in press).

[12]   LEVANAT S, PAVELIC B, CRNIC I, ORESKOVIC S, MANOJLOVIC S. Involvement of PTCH gene in various no inflammatory cysts. J Molecular Med2000; 78 (3): 140–146,2000.

[13]   LOCKHART DJ, WINZELER EA. Genomics, gene expression and DNA arrays. Nature2000; 405: 827–836,2000.

[14]   LYON BE. Recognition and Counting Reduce Costs of Avion Cospecific Brood Parasitism. Nature2003;422: 495 – 499.

[15]   PANDEY A, MANN M. Proteomics to study genes and genomes. Nature 2000;405: 837–846.

[16] PETANJEK Z, ROKO RASIN M, JOVANOV N, KRSNIK Z. Magno pyramidal Neurons in the Area 9 of the Human Prefrontal Cortex.A Quantitative Rapid Golgi Study. Per Biol1998; 100 (2): 221 -231.

[17] PETRENKO O, ZAIKA AI. MOLLUM Delta Np 73 facilitates cell immortalization and cooperate with oncogenic Ras in cellular transformation *in vivo*. Molecular Cell Biol2003; 23: 5540–5555.

[18] PETRIDES M. Functional Organization of the Human Prefrontal Cortex for Mnemonic Processing. [in Ref. (7)]1995.

[19] PLANTAMURA VL, SOUČEK B, VISAGGIO G. Frontier Decision Support Concepts. Wiley New York.1994.

[20] RAMACHANDRAN VS., The Emerging Brain. Profile Books.2003.

[21] RANDIC M, BALABAN AT,NOVIC M, ZALOZNIK A, PISANSKI T. A novel graphical representation of proteins. Biol2005107: 403 – 41.

[22] SOLMS M. The Neuropsychology of Dream. Erlbaum Associates.1997.

[23] SLADE N, GALETIC I, KAPITANOVIC S, PAVELIC J. The efficacy of retroviral herpes simplex virus thymidine kinase gene transfer and ganciclovir treatment on the inhibition of melanoma growth *in vitro* and *in vivo*. *Arch. Dermatology. Res.* 2001; 293: 484–490.

[24] SOUČEK B. Mono stable Systems Triggered at Random. *Nuclear Instruments Methods 1964; 29:* 109–114.

[25] SOUČEK B. Application of pile-up distortion calculation. *Rev Scientific Instruments 1965; 36:* 1582–1587.

[26] SOUČEK B. Influence of the Latency Fluctuations and the Quantum Process of Transmitter Release on the End-Plate Potentials' Amplitude Distribution. *Biophysical Journal 1971; 11:* 127–139.

[27] SOUČEK B. Complete Model for the Statistical Composition of the End-Plate Potential. *J. Theor. Biol.1971; 30:* 631–648.

[28] SOUČEK B. Applications of computers and mathematical models to the study of neuronal systems, Nuclear and neuronal pulse spectrometry. *Computer Physics Communications 1973;5:* 115– 122.

[29] CARLSON AD, SOUČEK B. Computer simulation of firefly flash sequence. *J. Theor. Biol.1975; 55:* 353–370.

[30] SOUČEK B. Model of Alternating and Aggressive Communication with the Example of Katydid Chirping. *J Theoretical Biology1975; 52:*399–417.

[31] SOUČEK B, VENCL F. Bird Communication Study Using Digital Computer. *J. Theor. Biol. 1975; 49:* 147–172.

[32] VENCL F, SOUČEK B. Structure and Control of Duet Singing in the White-Crested Jay Thrush. *Behavior 1976; 57:* 20–33.

[33] SOUČEK B, CARLSON AD. Brain Windows in Firefly Communication. *J. Theor. Biol. 1986 119:* 47–65.

[34] SOUČEK B, CARLSON AD. Brain Window Language in Firefly. *J. Theor. Biol.1987; 125:* 93–103.

[35] SOUČEK B, CARLSON AD. Computers in Neurobiology and Behavior. Wiley New York 1976.

[36] SOUČEK B, SOUČEK M. Neural and Massively Parallel Computers. Wiley New York 1988.

[37] SOUČEK B. Neural and Concurrent Real-Time Systems. Wiley New York 1989.

[38]   SOUČEK B and the IRIS Group. Neural and Intelligent Systems Integration. Wiley New York 1991.

[39]   SOUČEK B and the IRIS Group. Fast Learning and Invariant Object Recognition. Wiley New York 1992.

[40]   SOUČEK B and the IRIS Group. Fuzzy, Holographic and Parallel Intelligence. Wiley New York 1992.

[41]   SOUČEK B and the IRIS Group. Dynamic, Genetic and Chaotic Programming. Wiley New York 1992.

[42]   PLANTAMURA VL, SOUČEK B, VISAGGIO G. Frontier Decision Support Concepts. Wiley New York 1994.

[43]   SOUČEK B. Quantum Mind – Evoked Potential Link. *Per Biol 1998;100(2):* 129–140.

[44]   SOUČEK B. Quantum Mind Emerges from the Prefrontal Cortex Nested, Fractal Chaos. *Per Biol 1999; 101(2):* 109–119.

[45]   SOUČEK B. Quantum Mind Compresses the Verbal Stories. *Per Biol 1999; 101(3):* 193–201.

[46]   SOUČEK B. Quantum Mind Measures the Verbal Stories. *Per Biol 2000:102(4):* 331–342.

[47]   SOUČEK B. Universal Brain Theory: The Self Organization of Understanding, Consciousness, Emotions and Knowledge. *Per Biol 2001; 103(3):* 219–228.

[48]   SOUČEK B. The Brain Agents Universe. *Per Biol 2002; 104(3):*353–369.

[49]   SOUČEK B. The Brain and Mind Tissue, TISS: node, group, flock, pool. *Per biol2002; 104(3):* 345–352.

[50]   SOUČEK B. The Brain and Mind Attractions, BRAMA, the Brain Internal Language Organization, BILO, the Consciousness. *Per Biol 2o03; 105(3):* 207–214.

[51]   SOUČEK B. The genetic and learned brain and mind event trains BET and signs: BILO, COMET, SAVA, CON. *Per Biol 2004; (106)3:*265–278.

[52]   SOUČEK B. The DNA code, the brain event trains BET and the self-organization SO make a single entity: life and consciousness. *Per Biol 2004; 106(4):* 443–444.

CHAPTER 7

The Brain and Mind Attractions: BRAMA; The Brain Internal Language Organization, BILO; The Consciousness

Abstract:

Background and Purpose: This work explains the brain and mind as a single entity that uses the strong attractions or desires, BRAMA. BRAMA is the bursting, passionate, unrestrained, excessive desire. Presented theory is supported by experimental findings.

Material and Methods: The brain generates various BRAMA, from the molecular level, to the brain windows, message and language levels. The theory and the computer model explain the interaction.

Result: Humans Brain and Mind are composed of attracting agents. Three classes of BRAMA desires and attractions have been identified. **The chaotic attraction** is a dynamic structure. Attraction trajectories concentrate into a narrow attractor space. This is a case of massive self-organization.

The courting / mimicry attractions are based on continuous–discrete processing and are capable of discovering the hidden information by observing sample behaviour and comparing it with the past learned experience.

The pattern attraction is capable to recognize inexact, incomplete patterns. Through many attraction loops, the human brain agents called katydids, fireflies and birds learn about the partner, and adapt answers and behaviour. The resulting Brain Internal Language Organization, BILO, is explained. The consciousness is dispersed into many agents of the brain; in the nested, fractal tissue, TISS. There is no central consciousness.

Conclusions: The brain-mind tissue, TISS and BRAMA, have been observed in experimental data that come from insects, birds, brainstem auditory potentials and Evoked Potential records triggered by verbal stimuli. All these experiments could be explained with the similar kinds of TISS units and BRAMA protocols:

–Brain and Mind operate in the **nested fractal time T**: BRA= brand the feature, 3,6 ms; AMA=amass the chunk, 25 ms; MA=master the association, 175 ms; BRAMA protocol,1225 ms.

–Brain and Mind deal with the nested, fractal information I: feature; chunk; association; continuous -quantizing-discrete layers.

For the human sensory input, in a single BRAMA period of 1225 ms, the TISS information flow INFLOW is about $4 \cdot 10^{12}$ bits.

–Brain and Mind operate in the **nested fractal space S** composed of neurons and neural networks, nodes, groups, flocks and pools.

The Long Term Memory is the nested fractal association, distributed over TISS units. The Short Term Memory is the nested fractal flow, distributed over TISS units. The presented theory and results are in agreement with the brain structures and with the topology of functions. BRAMA and BILO principles explain the fractal components of structures; the nested dynamics of functions; the Self Organization of the Understanding, Consciousness, Emotions and Knowledge.

Keywords: Brain, universal brain, brain and mind, BRAMA protocol, BRAMA principle, mind, brain and mind tissue, brain node, brain group, brain flock, brain pool, brain and mind matter base, brain network, brain computing, cooperation, BRAMA.

INTRODUCTION

For a long time the brain and the mind are considered to be federations of distinct modules or sub functions [1–13]. I consider the brain and mind as a single nested, fractal, dispersed entity that uses the strong attractions or desires, BRAMA.

BRAMA is the bursting, passionate, unrestrained, excessive desire. Presented theory is supported by experimental findings, and computer models [14–33]. I compare the dynamics of the brain and mind with the dynamics of the flock of birds. The flock of birds, the colony of ants, the school of fish, have no leader, and no control mind. It is the individual members following certain simple laws that make the group respond the way it does. In other words, the behaviour is built from the bottom-up and is governed by the cooperative action of many small Brain Mind agents.

The BM agents include primitives or components of intelligence, communication and attractions. Resulting decisions, behaviour or organizations are based on: distributed decision making; collaborative reasoning; distributed control; community coordination; cooperation; groupware, attractions.

THE BRAMA PRINCIPLE: STRONG ATTRACTIONS AND PASSIONATE DESIRES

I now look to the brain Active Areas, AA. Let us use an imaginary perfect vision and watch all of the Active Areas, AA, move around the brain. We can see every AA in the brain. We notice that during the language processing, the AA seem to congregate around the frontal lobe of the brain. During the day, AA disperse randomly many times, and also congregate again around specific locations of the brain. We wonder why this occurs and who is in charge here. For older brain theories the answer is the central mind or supervisor, that coordinates activities of specialized units. Contrary to this, I introduce the Flow of Favourable Factors, FFF. For very detailed description see [24, 31]. FFF incorporates the strong attractions and passionate desires, BRAMA. This includes cooperation, competition, courting, mating, mental selection and mental environment. Mental environment includes mental and physical inputs, mental interactions and fluctuations, boundary conditions, hormonal levels, mental levels, blood chemistry, body temperature *etc*. Each sub population of agents lives within its FFF space. There is no central control point. There is only FFF. But we have noticed, over days, that there is a very definitive AA pattern. We see AAs related to the object recognition and others related to the memorization of places. What causes this to happen? The answers are the basic FFF laws that all agents respond to. The FFF laws merge together: the balance between inherited and learned, bio feedback, nonlinear dynamics including chaos, knowledge-learning densities, the Brain Mind primitives [14–33]. The crucial ingredient is BRAMA.

The agents stimulated by FFF, cooperate. They synchronize and coordinate individual activities using signals, messages and language. The message informs the neighbourhood that a sender has been stimulated by FFF and that it looks for a help. The message is recognized by a sub population of receivers, and they respond. Agents with appropriate resources reply with bids that indicate their abilities in cooperating towards maximizing the welfare. The agents help each other by providing related interpretations. Through negotiations partners come to an agreement. Examples of the BRAMA attractions are the Brain Agents Universe, the Brain Internal Language Organization, BILO, and the BRAMA fractal protocol.

BRAIN AGENTS UNIVERSE

The brain BRAMA **attractions** are supported by a variety of neurotransmitters, neural bursts and selfish agents, which are common to the entire animal world. Hence I am taking the findings from different animals when defining some of the

Universal selfish agents. I give to an agent a name, based on the animal used in the experiment [17–20, 30].

Katydid agents, compete for the message. Leader and follower reciprocally adjust, by sliding towards a common region on an **attractor**. In this way they also synchronize their message. There is a need for a strong message, and the need is satisfied. Hence the katydid is a homeostatic, cycling, competition based agent: in insect, as well as in the human brain see Figs. **1** and **2** in [30].

Bird agents, attract each other with the internal and external songs expressed as a series of elements of varied frequency. The individual elements of the song are called syllables. Two adjacent syllables in the song form a pair, and three syllables form a triplet, and a song forms the tree: in bird as well as in the human brain see Figs. **4** and **5** in [30].

Firefly agent, accumulates and selects the evidence; for the specific input it finds the membership with more general fuzzy windows; de-fuzzy the output into a crisp form; generates the timing protocol; performs the self-adjustment, and the context switching, based on the past history of stimulation. Fireflies reciprocally adjust the send and receive windows, and in this way **attract** and select the right partner agent: in insect, as well as in the human brain see Fig. **3** in [30]. The female firefly Photuris versicolor is always **attracted** to the male of the same species. They express their **desires** through the brain window language. Within three days after mating, the female converts to predatory behaviour and will no longer respond to her own male. Instead, she responds to the flash pattern of Photinus males, **attracting**, capturing and eating them. The courting and the aggressive mimicry are also used by the firefly agents in the human brain.

THE BRAIN INTERNAL LANGUAGE ORGANIZATION, BILO

The Brain Windows have been first observed in fireflies [19, 20]. Fireflies use a point process with light flashes for communication purposes. This exchange of light flashes is used for a courtship communication between male and female fireflies. Much of the basic information transmitted from one member of the species to another member is contained in the inter flash interval I of male flashes and in the female's flash-response latency L. Precise time discrimination is needed to recognize the species-specific signal and to identify the correct partner. I/L relationship forms the Brain windows. Based on experimental data, we have developed the Brain Window computer model. Both experimental and computer generated data are presented in Figs. **1** and **2**.

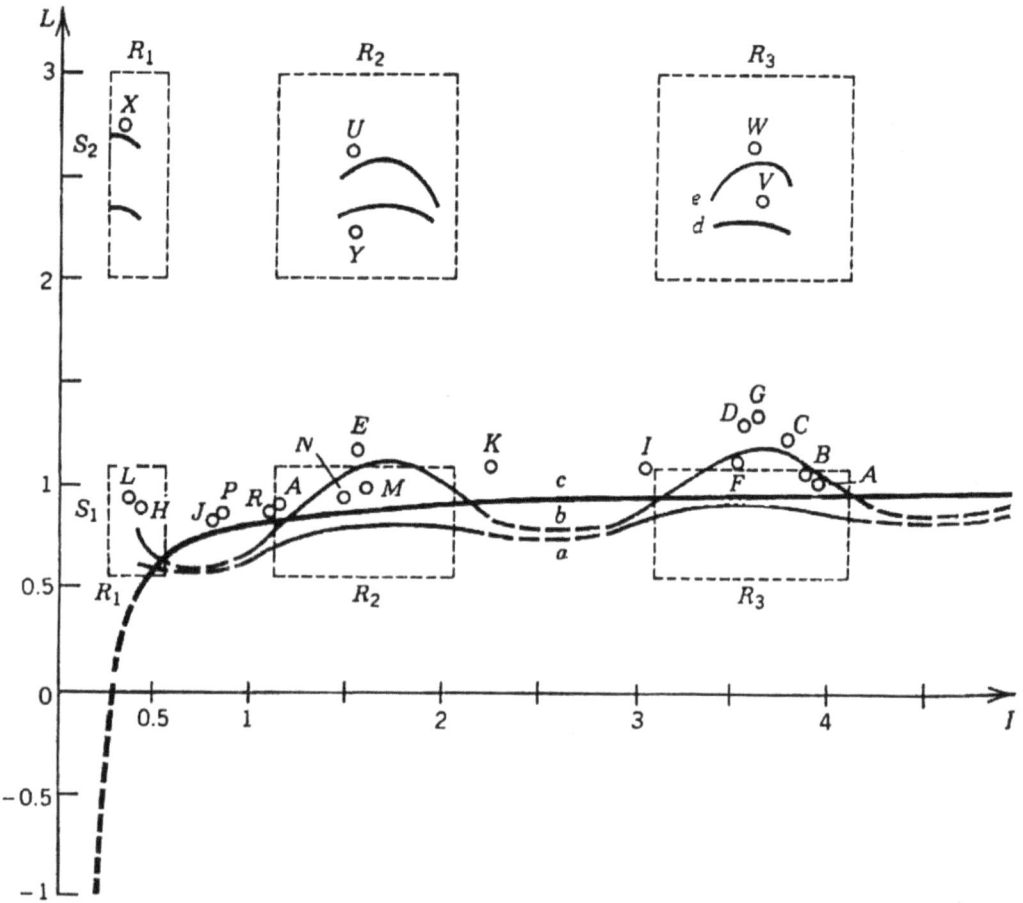

Figure 1: *The Brain-Windows and the Brain Internal Language Organization, BILO.* The language is formed of dialogues; dialogues are intersections between continuous belts [b, d] and discrete windows. The same stimulus (question) I, could produce various responses (answers) L, depending on the context. Time in seconds. Theoretical computer-calculated latencies plotted over experimental data. Windows S1R1, S1R2, and S1R3 are responsible for responses with short latencies (courtship, mimicry). Windows S2R1, S2R2, and S2R3 are responsible for responses with long latencies (patrolling flashes and separation of flash patterns). Experiments A through T and Z from series 55; V and W from series 57, and U, X, and Y from series 59, each of which represent different Photuris versicolor femmes fatales (FF).

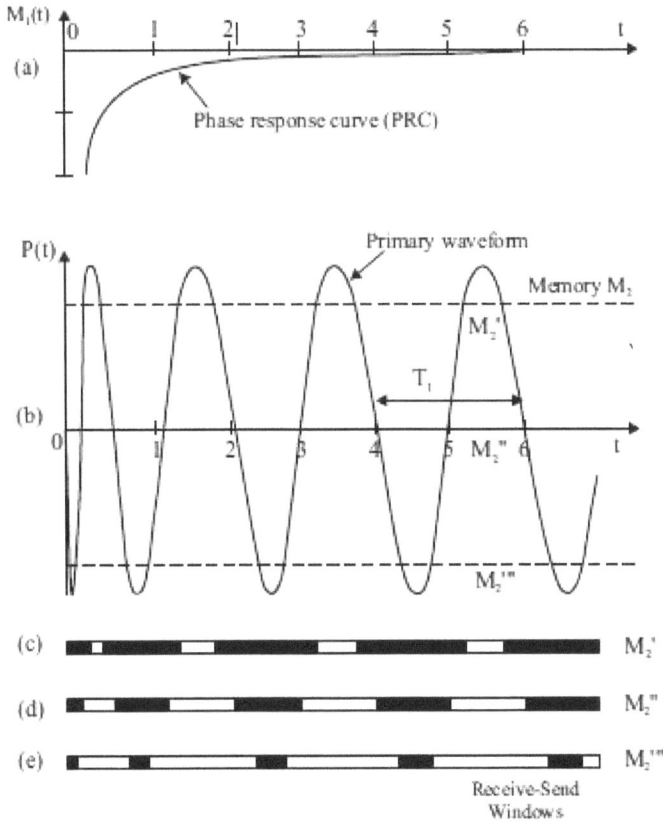

Figure 2: The Brain Windows and the internal human brain window language. Abscissa is time in seconds.

Language involves a set of legal messages used in a particular communication system. The sender and the receiver must agree upon the meaning of the messages. I consider the Brain–Window system as an intelligent agent that has inherited from the parents some predefined operations or knowledge. In the same time, it is able to adapt, and also to carry a message or a content between partners. Hence it learns. In other words, the Brain–Window system supports the fireflies, but also the human brain knowledge-learning firefly agents. In the fireflies, the stimulus interval I and the response latency L present the messages.

The intersection between the vocabulary (belts) and the family of windows defines the family of dialogue. Relating the measured data to behaviour [19, 20], we find the dialogues.

These are the dialogues between the animals, fireflies. Yet for me, these are also the dialogues between the firefly agents in the human brain. This is my first step to explain the human Brain Internal Language Organization, BILO. I am using the names like firefly, male, female, virgin. These are now the names related to the internal, universal, brain agents. For more see [17–20, 30]. Here are the BILO dialogues:

D1 is the dialogue between the virgin female and the co specific male. It is an intersection (O) between the belt b (a, b, c) and the window S1R1:

$$D1 = b\,O\,(S1R1)$$

D2 is the dialogue between the mated female (FF) and the co specific male. It is an intersection between belt d (d, e) and the window S2R1:

$$D2 = d\,O\,(S2R1)$$

D3 is the mimicry dialogue between the FF and the hetero specific male (Photinus macdermotti) producing courtship calls. It is an intersection between the belt b and the window S1R2:

$$D3 = b\,O\,(S1R2)$$

D4 is a dialogue between the FF and the hetero specific male producing courtship calls. For this particular range of calls, the belt b goes outside of the window S1R2: the female adds the clock period ?T1 to the short latency, and in this way the long latency is formed (belt d). The dialogue is an intersection between the belt d and the window S2R2:

$$D4 = d\,O\,(S2R2)$$

D5 is a dialogue between the FF and the hetero specific male producing flashes at long intervals. It is an intersection between the belt b and the window S1R3:

$$D5 = b\,O\,(S1R3)$$

D6 is a dialogue between the FF and the hetero specific male producing flashes at short intervals. For this particular range of calls, the belt b goes outside of the window S1R3. As a result, the female adds the clock period 1/2T1 to the short latency, and in this way the long latency is formed (belt d). The dialogue is an intersection between the belt d and the window S2R3:

$$D6 = d\, \acute{O}\, (S2R3)$$

Dialogues D1 to D6 are represented in Fig. **1**. Both experimental data and computer model-generated data are found only near or within six isolated islands, described here as dialogues D1 to D6. The dialogues D1 to D6 put together form the communication language of the firefly Photuris versicolor, as well as of the human brain agents. Exact positions of the dialogues and the windows depend on experimental conditions and on the animal used in the experiment. However, the basic findings are always the same: communication is clustered into six islands (dialogues). Each island is related to one behaviour: courtship, mimicry, or patrolling flashes of long intervals. In this example the language is generated by the process in time axes. In general, the behaviour of living systems is naturally coded into the time axes as a sequence of events. The sequence is controlled by neural oscillators that interact with FFF. In this example, the first half period of the oscillator is the shortest one: 0.25 secs. This is one eight of the period T1 of the non- modulated primary oscillator [19, 20]. As this is the smallest information item used in coding, we call it the Message Quantum q:

$$q = T1/K \text{ (in this example K=8)}$$

We use the Message Quantum to measure the windows:

$$q < R1 < 3q$$

$$5q < R2 < 9q \text{ } etc.$$

Measured in units of Message Quanta, the coding distance is

$$d = S/q \text{ (S=Send Window)}$$

Hence the distance d12 between the windows R1 and R2 is approximately 3q/q=3. The redundancy r of this code is:

$$r = n/m$$

where n is the number of available Message Quanta (in this case n=16); and m is the minimum number of Message Quanta necessary to convey the same message (in this case m=6). The resulting redundancy is r=16/6. Obviously, this is a highly redundant language. In the same time it is adaptive and conditioned by FFF. In general the window concept includes also overlapping windows and fuzzy set membership functions. The Brain Internal Language Organization, BILO, expresses the strong attractions and passionate desires.

THE BRAMA FRACTAL PROTOCOL

In the human brain the chaos oscillates back and forth between the cortical columns, thalamus and basal ganglia and it is regulated by BRAMA protocol [25, 26, 29]. BRAMA fractal protocol is composed of $7 \cdot 7 \cdot 7$ co periods. They are: t_b= 1 to 3.6 ms; t_a = 25 ms; t_m = 175 ms see Fig. **2** in [29].

The resulting up to $7 \cdot 7 \cdot 7$ sequence operates in the fractal time and it could be explained in the following way.

BRA: BRAND THE FEATURES; find the MSs and MELs: break the story; about 7 t_b co periods.

t_b 1 to 3.6 ms

AMA: A MASS THE CHUNKS; about 7 mental, cognitive, semantic chunks are formed in the Short Term Memory, STM; about 7 t_a co periods. t_a 25 ms

MA: MASTER THE ASSOCIATIONS; gradually find the context tree that leads to the understanding; about 7 t_m co periods. t_m 175 ms

The whole process exhibits the fractal self-similarity between the macro and the micro sub processes. Co periods t_m are nested within t_1. Co periods ta are nested within tm. Co periods t_a are nested within t_a. There is no strong primary evidence in human to define the presumed generator sources of **BRAMA waves**. I have observed the long waves in the evoked potentials. I relate the shortest waves to the BSAEP potentials. The generator sources might be as follows:

BRA: wave I–distal eight nerve; wave II–proximal eight nerve or cochlear nucleus; wave III–lower pons (possibly the superior olivary complex); wave IV–mid upper pons (possibly the lateral lemniscus tracts and nuclei); wave V–upper pons of inferior colliculus.

AMA: the thalamus, Intra laminar Nuclei, IN. IN is connected to the brain-stem structures. Also, IN projects widely across the cortex to the layer I, cortical columns.

MA: cingulate cortex; basal ganglia. Basal ganglia disinhibits the IN-cortex projections.

The BRAMA fractal protocol expresses the strong attractions and passionate desires.

THE CONSCIOUSNESS

BRAMA is present also in the behaviour. We could say that the female animal develops the passionate **desires** because of the male BRAMA **attractions**. The old indo–European languages relate the word BRAMA to the bulls roars to **attract** the female. The animal is to some extend conscious that the potential courting partner is present. Hence BRAMA principle leads to the traces of the consciousness. I show that on the examples of several animals. Also the brain internal, universal agents exhibit the traces of the consciousness. This includes the katydid, firefly, bird and other brain agents. The simple animal brain has first evolved around the event trains, sampling, quantizing and Quantum steps. The basic rule is: minimum of the material to keep and to carry the information, the message. The message serves as a simple indicative statement that informs about the activity of the brain unit. The reciprocal exchange of messages between several brain units prepares them for the cooperation and action. In the first unit, the message is formed within its Quantum step. In the second unit, the message will be received only within the identical Quantum step. In this way the second unit will understand the message of the first unit. Hence the first purpose of the evolution is: the Quantum steps and the messages for the internal communication between the brain units. Now comes pre–adaptation, for two more purposes: **The**

Consciousness, C, is the inner subjective reality, based on the messages. C is that, which currently occupies awareness. C appears in a short term, working memory, as the information currently needed for what the unit is doing: unit's action and reaction. **The Abstraction**. The messages are abstract terms, that can represent abstract realities, such as intentions, memories, emotions.

The path of the evolution is: Quantum step or message quantum; message; consciousness; abstraction. The result is the Self Organization of Understanding U, Consciousness C, Emotions E and Knowledge K. U, C, E and K are present in the human brain and to some degree, in all animal brains as well. To some degree, U, C, E and K are present within all units of the brain and mind tissue TISS: nodes, groups, flocks and pool. Hence U, C, E, and K are dispersed all over the brain. The brain Agent 1 is expressed by its components U1, C1, E1 and K1. Components of the consciousness, C1 to CN belong to the Agent 1 to Agent N. C1 to CN participate in forming the higher level consciousness C. In the left hemisphere, the Ci components come, for example from the Broca speech area and from the Wernicke language area. They participate in the expressive, thinking, verbal consciousness Cv. In the right hemisphere Ci components come, for example, from the image, holistic areas. They participate in the inexpressive, pattern recognition consciousness Cp. Cv and Cp participate in the overall consciousness C.

Cutting the corpus callosum results in the split brain. Cv and Cp are still active, yet they do not support each other. Hence the overall consciousness is not complete. The experiments with the split brain subjects show: Names of object flashed to left hand field, can be read and understood but not spoken. Subject can retrieve the named object by touch with the left hand, but cannot afterwards name the item or retrieve it with the right hand. I give the following explanation: the images of the name and of the object have entered into the right hemisphere, and the pattern recognition consciousness Cp has associated them to each other. Yet the left hemisphere has not received neither the images, nor the information from Cp. Hence the person's verbal consciousness Cv cannot afterwards name the object. I conclude: the consciousness is dispersed into many agents of the brain; there is no central consciousness. The same is true for U, C, E, K and A, dispersed in the nested, fractal tissue, TISS.

In speech, TISS deals with the verbal features, chunks and associations. In vision, TISS deals with the image features, chunks and associations. Normal brain combines the speech TISS and the image TISS.

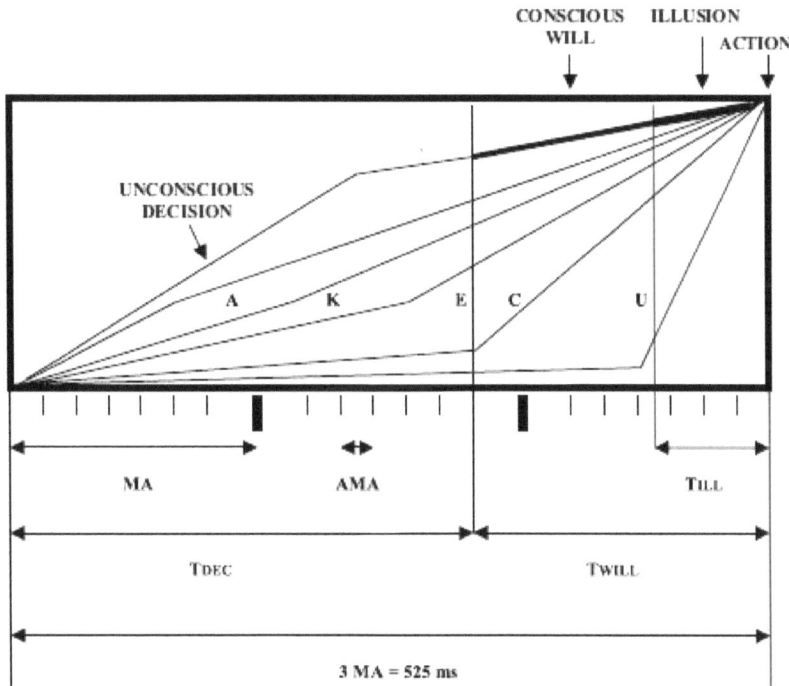

Figure 3: Holistic Self Organization, SO of UCEKA, grows to the unconscious decision, to the conscious will, to the illusion, to the action. SO involves BRAMA, BILO, Brain Agents Universe, TISS, BET, REASON, PILE – UP. Tdec=2MA –AMA=331 ms; Twill=MA+AMA=204 ms; Till=3MA + 3 BRA = 86 ms.

The BRAMA principle of attractions and desires explains the life evolution and the Self Organization of Understanding, Consciousness, Emotions and Knowledge. The BRAMA attraction–desire and the Self Organization are present on the synapses, end plates, neurons, nodes, groups, flocks and pool.

FROM THE UNCONSCIOUS DECISION TO THE CONSCIOUS WILL

Free will is the ability to carry out actions that have been planned in thought. What is happening in the brain at the time, when a person decides to do some motor act, say, finger movement? The slowly rising negative potential, called the

readiness potential was observed over a wide area of the cerebral surface, almost as long as 600 ms before the onset of the movement. Fig. **3** explains the brain holistic processes through 3 MA = 525 ms.

Implicit memories related to UCEKA keep the universal, born with instinctual drives, stereotypes, old archetypes; as well as the learned, person specific, new archetypes. Components C1 to CN of the consciousness C, belong to the Agent 1 to Agent N. The Agents cooperate through BRAMA attractions and BILO. Behind the Agents, there are neural networks. The neural network best BET is the best thing that the network can do. The Self Organization, SO of UCEKA grows.

Readiness potential is generated by the above complex processes that project to the pyramidal cells of the motor cortex, and synaptic excite them to discharge just preceding the movement. Through the period TDEC, the unconscious DECISION grows. Through the period Twill, the conscious WILL grows. Through the period Till, the person has an ILLUSION that the action has already started.

Fig. **3** explains how the willing of a muscle movement starts the Brain Event Trains, BET, that lead to the discharge of motor pyramidal cells. It explains how the cerebral cortex is linked to motor cortex. This is the brain, mind, body link. This is the will to action link, based on the SO of UCEKA.

Fig. **3** explains: finger movement; person's jump when suddenly comes the dog; compression of the verbal stories [27]; measuring of the verbal stories [28]; and many other actions. For each action the data might be somewhat different, yet the principle is always the SO of UCEKA: BRAMA, BILO, Brain Agent Universe, TISS REASON [27], BET [32], PILE – UP [15–16].

SO of UCEKA explains the brain and mind as a single entity. The SO of UCEKA theory, computer models and neurobiological experiments are in excellent agreement [14–34].

CONCLUSIONS

In this work I introduce a new principle, **BRAMA**: strong attractions; bursting, passionate, unrestrained, excessive desires. BRAMA is the major force in the animal and human brains, on many levels. I will be so free to say: BRAMA principle explains even the genetic code. Billions of years ago purely chance circumstances assembled the self–reproducing bio chemicals, DNA and RNA. DNA is composed of four bases, normally abbreviated as A, T, G and C. An A is always **attracted** to form a chemical bond with a T; and G is always **attracted** to C. The brain mind tissue TISS operates with the dispersed, dynamic BRAMA and BRAMA protocols. BRAMA protocol is full of the multilevel **attractions** and **desires**, in each step: BRA, brand the feature; AMA, amass the chunks; MA, master the associations.

Brain Internal Language Organization, BILO deals with all internal agents [17–20, 30]. The katydid agents use the **chaotic attraction** duets. The bird agents use the **pattern attraction** duets. The firefly agents use the **courting / mimicry attraction** duet. Hence many languages are present in the human brain, in BILO. **The consciousness** is dispersed into many agents of the brain in the nested, fractal tissue, TISS; there is no central consciousness.

DISCLOSURE

"The content of this chapter has been previously published by *Periodicum Biologorum, Vol. 105, No. 3, 207-214, 2003 ".*

REFERENCES

[1]   BOYD IA, MARTIN AR. The End-Plate Potential in Mammalian Muscle. J Physiology (London) 1950;132: 74

[2]   CHIAPPA KH. Evoked Potentials in Clinical Medicine. Raven Press Ltd New York 1989

[3]   DEL CASTILLO J, KATZ B. Quantal Components of the End-Plate Potential. J Physiology (London) 1950; 124: 560

[4]   DEL CASTILLO J., KATZ B., The Membrane Charge Produced by the Neuromuscular Transmitter. J Physiology (London) 1952;125: 546

[5]   GOLDMAN-RAKIC PATRICIA. Architecture of the Prefrontal Cortex and the Central Executive.In Ref. [6] 1995

[6]   GRAFMAN J, HOLYOAK KJ, BOLLER F. Structure and Functions of the Human Prefrontal Cortex. New York Academy of Sciences vol. 769 New York 1995

[7]   HO R, SUTHERLAND JG, BRUHA I. Neurological Fuzzy Diagnoses: Holographic *vs.* Statistical *vs.* Neural Method. In Ref. [12] 1994

[8]   KATZ B, MILEDI R. The Measurement of Synaptic Delay, and the Time Course of Acetylcholine Release at the Neuromuscular Junction. Proc Royal Society London Ser. B1965 p 161, 483

[9]   LeDOUX J. Emotional Memory Systems in the Brain. Behaviour and Brain Research 1993

[10]   NÄÄTÄNEN R. Attention and Brain Function. Hillsdale NJ Erlbaum 1992

[11]   PETRIDES M. Functional Organization of the Human Prefrontal Cortex for Mnemonic Processing. In Ref. [6] 1995

[12]   PLANTAMURA VL, SOUCEK B, VISAGGIO G. Frontier Decision Support Concepts. Wiley New York 1994

[13]   PIAGET J. Meine Theories der Geistigen Intelligenz. Fischer Taschenbuch Verlag Frankfurt 1983

[14]   SOUCEK B. Mono-stable Systems Triggered at Random, Nuclear. Instruments Methods 1964; 29, 109–114

[15]   SOUCEK B. Influence of the Latency Fluctuations and the Quantal Process of Transmitter Release on the End-Plate Potentials' Amplitude Distribution. Biophysical Journal 1971; 11, 127–139

[16]   SOUCEK B. Complete Model for the Statistical Composition of the End-Plate Potential. J Theoretical Biology 1971; 30: 631–648

[17]   SOUCEK B, VENCL F. Bird Communication Study Using Digital Computer. J Theoretical Biology 1975; 49: 147–172

[18]   SOUCEK B. Model of Alternating and Aggressive Communication with the Example of Katydid Chirping. J Theoretical Biology 1975; 52: 399–41

[19]   SOUCEK B, CARLSON AD. Brain Windows in Firefly Communication. J Theoretical Biology 1986; 119: 47–65

[20]   SOUCEK B, CARLSON AD. Brain Window Language in Firefly. J Theor Biol1987; 125: 93–103

[21]   SOUCEK B, SOUCEK M. Neural and Massively Parallel Computers. Wiley New York 1988

[22]   SOUCEK B, The IRIS Group. Neural and Intelligent Systems Integration. Wiley New York 1991

[23]   SOUCEK B. The Quantum Mind. Period Biol1996; 98: 67–76

[24]   SOUCEK B. The Quantum Mind Theory. Period biol1997; 99:3–18

[25]   SOUCEK B. Quantum Mind–Evoked Potential Link. Period biol1998; 100: 129–140

[26]   SOUCEK B. Quantum Mind Emerges from the Prefrontal Cortex Nested, Fractal Chaos. Period biol1999; 101: 109–119

[27]   SOUCEK B. Quantum Mind Compresses the Verbal Stories. Period Biol1999; 101: 193–201

[28]   SOUCEK B. Quantum Mind Measures the Verbal Stories. Period biol2000;102: 331–342

[29]   SOUCEK B. Universal Brain Theory: The Self Organization of Understanding, Consciousness, Emotions and Knowledge. Period Biol2001; 103: 219–228

[30]   SOUCEK B. The Brain Agents Universe. Period biol2002;104:353– 369

[31]   SOUCEK B. The Brain and Mind Tissue, TISS: node, group, flock, pool. Period biol2002; 104: 345–352

[32]   SOUCEK   B.   The   Brain   and   Mind   Event   Trains   BET   and   signs:BILO,COMET,SAVA,CON, Period biol2004;106,3,205-316

[33]   VENCL F, SOUCEK B. Structure and Control of Duet Singing in the White-Crested Jay Thrush. Behaviour 1976;57: 20–33,1976

[34]   The BRAMA names, BRA, AMA, MA, have been inspired by the names of   my   children Branko, Amalia and Marina. The BILO name has been inspired by Bilo Gora, hill and valley of my parents.

CHAPTER 8

The Brain and Mind Tissue, TISS: Node, Group, Flock, Pool

Abstract:

Background and Purpose: This work explains the brain-mind tissue, TISS. TISS is the Time-Information-Space Set that operates as a Self-Organized loop. TISS leads into the new brain research and clinical practice, as well as into the new brain networks and brain computers.

Materials and Methods: The brain-mind tissue, TISS, has been observed in experimental data that come from insects, birds, brainstem auditory potentials and Evoked Potential records triggered by verbal stimuli. All these experiments could be explained with the similar kinds of TISS units.

Results: The brain-mind tissue, TISS, is a multilayer, massively parallel structure composed of nested neural networks, nodes, groups, flocks and pools. Frontal TISS and Posterior TISS cooperate in linguistic and in other information processing tasks, in thinking and in thought wandering.

Conclusions: TISS cancels the border between the brain and the mind: masses of the instant processes and brain-mind tissues. The matter-based TISS generates the never ending massively parallel chaos. The chaos constantly modifies TISS. This is the never repeating brain mind loop. TISS is directly related to the Self Organization of Understanding, Consciousness, Emotions and Knowledge.

Keywords: Human brain, universal brain, brain and mind, mind, brain and mind tissue, brain node, brain group, brain flock, brain pool, brain and mind matter base, brain network, brain computing, cooperation.

INTRODUCTION

This work is a direct extension of [1- 7] where there is a long list of references.

We are beginning to understand the patterns of neuronal organization and the way they work. We are at the advanced stage of our attempt to understand the brain, which may well be the last of all the frontiers of knowledge that man can attempt to penetrate and encompass. I predict that the brain research will occupy the years of our future. Vigorous and exciting new disciplines emerge: neurochemistry, molecular neurobiology, neuron-genetics, neuron-pharmacology. But also: brain communications, brain networks, brain computers and brain theories.

Branko Souček

Accurate understanding of the mechanics of individual neurons and their interactions in specific brain areas has been achieved in a broad range such as: mollusk [1], rodents [2], human prefrontal cortex [3], frontal cortex for mnemonic processing [4], neural computing [5]. The goal is to reveal how brain operates. In this work and in the Universal Brain Theory [6, 7] I present an entirely new explanation, TISS.

- Universal Brain operates in the nested fractal time: BRA= brand the feature; AMA=amass the chunk; MA=master the association; BRAMA protocol. See Fig. **8** in [6].

- Universal Brain deals with the nested, fractal information: feature; chunk; association; continuous, quantizing, discrete layers. See Fig. **7** in [6].

- Universal Brain operates in the nested fractal space composed of neurons and neural networks, nodes, groups, flocks and pools, Figs. **1** to **6**.

NESTED, FRACTAL TIME-INFORMATION-SPACE SET, TISS

Figs. **1** to **6**: simple outline of the instant, never repeating processes. The group in Fig. **1** consists of several processing and memory nodes and of communication links. The flock in Fig. **1** consists of several groups. The pool consists of several flocks. In this way the nested space is formed: nodes, groups, flocks, pools. The communication is based on the point to point links. Within the brain the evolution has created the specific sets of links: for low and high level information traffic; for short and long distances; for small and high information volumes.

These are node, group, flock and pool links. In this way the architecture has a general connectivity within the group and slightly restricted between groups, flocks and pools. Very large sets of fuzzy associations may be enfolded within the same set of nodes. Stimulus-response associations are both learned and expressed in one non-iterative transformation. The neural process ideally embodies the concept of content addressable memory. Multiple pattern associations, at nearly

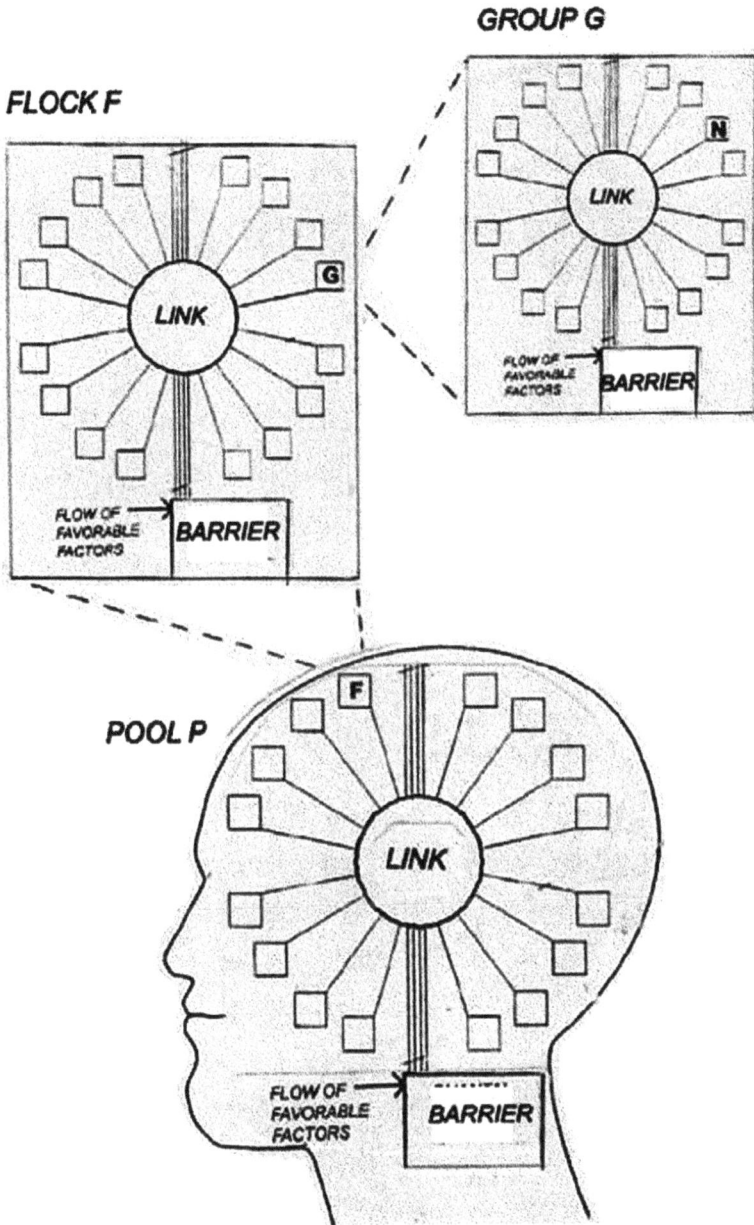

Figure 1: The Universal Brain Nested Fractal Space Structure. It is a part of the Time-Information-Space Set, TISS. TISS is the matter-based brain-mind tissue. TISS generates the never ending massively parallel chaos. The chaos constantly modifies TISS. This is the never repeating brain-mind loop. TISS is composed of the dynamic, fuzzy nested fractal clouds. Many associations can be distributed one over another in the same cloud. Hence they overlap. This is combined with the partial selection. TISS generates fuzzy overlapped functions, such as Understanding, Consciousness, Emotions and Knowledge.

arbitrary levels of complexity, may be enfolded onto a neural node. Encoded responses or "outputs" may subsequently be generated or accessed from the node *via* content of input. Input fields may be representative of addressing schemes or "syntax," and are transformed in an inherently parallel manner through all of the contents enfolded within the node. In response to a stimulus signal, the node regenerates the associated output data field, indicating also the degree of confidence in that output association.

The node network is capable of enfolding associations in the sense that input of one pattern prototype will induce the issuance of the second, thus subsequently inducing the issuance of a third, and so on.

Patterns generated within a recurrent data flow may express a linear sequence of associations, each pattern association connected through its encoding within one temporal frame (*i.e.* associations are linked by their proximity in time). This process of linear association may be considered to be a base to the associative reasoning processes where a thought train may be expressed through a sequence of associations initially learned over time. For example, the image of a fork may invoke the impression of plate, subsequently invoking an impression response in association to a kitchen table or food, for instance. In this manner, the node, group, flock and pool systems course through a sequence of sensory impressions, each of which has been formed by associations temporally connected. The brain-mind activity is composed of processes. A process starts, performs actions and finishes. Many processes are active at the same time, and processes can send messages to one another. Several communicating processes could run on several nodes, or concurrently on the same node. The same is true for groups, flocks and pools.

NODES AND GROUPS IN ANIMAL BRAIN

We have to think of the brain as being structurally plastic at the micro level: some synapses being mature, others developing, others regressing. In the process of learning, neuronal activation leads first to specific RNA synthesis and these in turn to protein synthesis and so finally to synaptic growth and the coding of the memory.

Critical sites of neuron-modulation reside in the framework of complex neural networks that define the basic behavior of the system. Thus, models for complex animal and human behavioral features should account for electrophysiological details and complexity of the single neuron as well as the connectivity and architecture of neural networks.

Neurons form the nodes. To test the context of a neural network involved in the control of complex behavior, the rhythmic feeding activity observed in Pleurobranchaea is presented. This carnivorous mollusk will initiate a rhythmic protraction and retraction of its proboscis when presented with food stimuli, culminating in bites and swallowing of the food, [1]. Apart from the fact that this feeding behavior obviously requires an oscillator, there are several additional features that are of interest in this behavior. The neural circuitry responsible for these behaviors has been analyzed in some detail. The essential features are shown in the network of Fig. **2**.

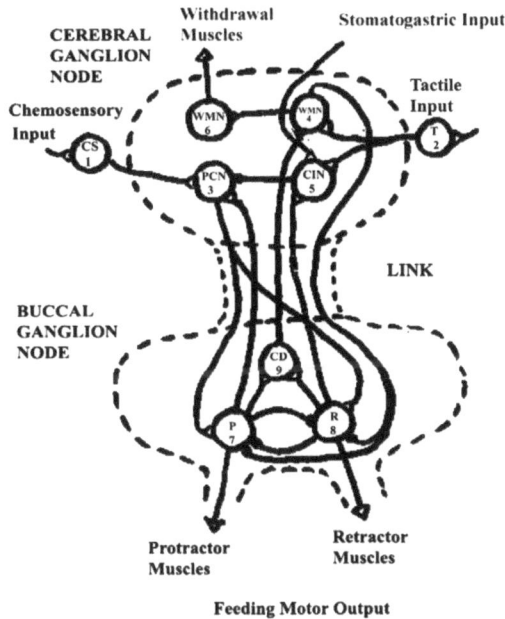

Figure 2: The Cerebral Ganglion Node and the Buccal Ganglion Node in Pleurobranchaea. The neural networks 1-9 are presented as single neurons. The two nodes are linked into a group. Here are rhythmic feeding behaviors of neurons 1 and 3 produced when food stimulus is presented to neuron 1:

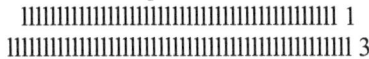

|||||||||||||||||||||||||||||||||||||||||||||||||||||||| 1
|||||||||||||||||||||||||||||||||||||||||||||||||||||||||| 3

The protractor and retractor neurons fire in alternating trends of action potentials, and the feeding activity, once initiated, persists even when food stimulus is removed. The node response combines the train of action potentials with the bursting and oscillations. The synaptic efficiency is influenced by the width of presynaptic action potential, postsynaptic time constant, learning and memory,

The neural elements responsible for the animal's behavior are distributed between the cerebral and buccal ganglia. Individual elements in the model are composed of functionally equivalent neurons in the animal, and many of the connections in the network have long delays, indicating that they are polysynaptic. Neurons 1 and 2 represent chemosensory (CS) and tactile (T) receptors, respectively. Neuron 3 represents the paracerebral command neurons (PCN) that control the rhythmic feeding activity. Neuron 5 represents the central inhibitory network (CIN), which receives inputs from the tactile sensory neuron and the stomatogastric pathways that signal satiation. Tactile inputs are also transmitted to the withdrawal command neurons (4, WCN), which transmit their outputs to the withdrawal motor neurons (6, WMN). The PCN provides excitatory inputs to the protractor and retractor motor neurons (P and R, neurons 7 and 8, respectively) in the buccal ganglion. Neurons P and R are mutually inhibitory and act as a flip-flop circuit, thus providing the feeding motor output. The corollary discharge neuron (9, CD) in the buccal ganglion integrates the overall feeding activity and provides inhibitory inputs to WCN in the cerebral ganglion. The loop formed by PCN, R, and CIN constitutes a negative feedback oscillator with delay and is primarily responsible for rhythmic motor output.

Note: **1.** The rhythmic behavior, once initiated, can persist even if food stimulus is taken away. **2.** The feeding behavior is harder to initiate or is suppressed completely when the animal is satiated. **3.** The animal exhibits choice behavior between feeding and withdrawal due to a noxious stimulus. When both types of stimuli are present, it chooses one or the other, depending on the stimulus strengths. **4.** The animal exhibits the rudimentary functions of the Understanding U, Consciousness C, Emotions E and Knowledge K. These functions are present in the Self Organized loop. **5.** The loop links the cerebral ganglion node and the buccal ganglion node. **6.** Nodes are linked into a group.

THE COOPERATION

Nodes form the group, Fig. **3**. Experiments with brain waves or EEGs suggest a correlation between human brain patterns and some cognitive processes. I explain this correlation by introducing the Cooperation. In this Cooperation, thoughts and perceptions are related to the changing patterns of the Flow of Favourable Factors

FFF [6, 7] rather than the impulses of individual neurons. The neurons of the node form a closed feedback loop: individual neurons are contributing to the common FFF; The FFF in turn influences the activity of the neuron. The situation is similar to that in an orchestra: each musician contributes to the total sound; the total sound is heard by each musician.

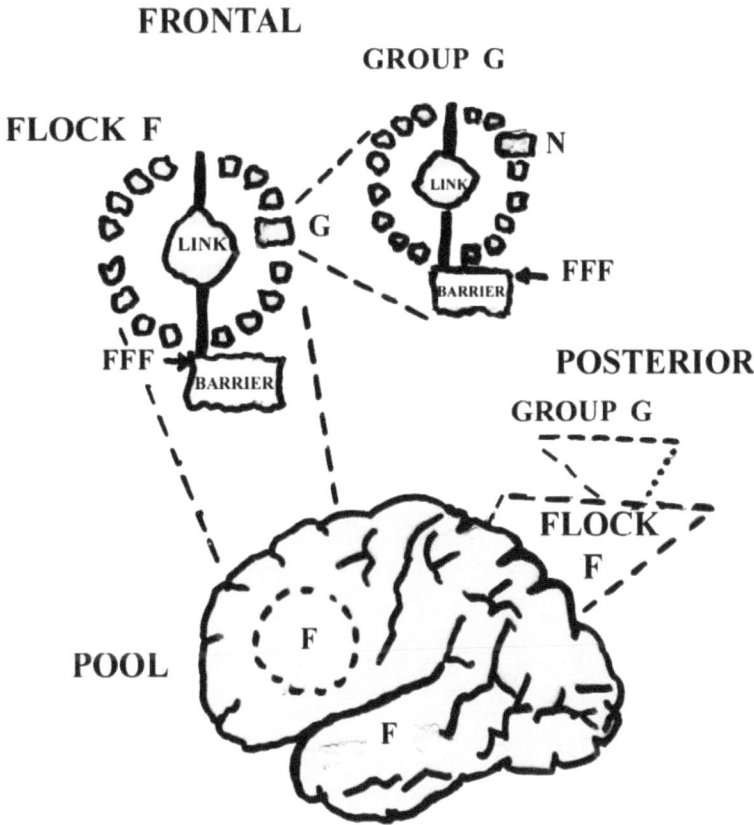

Figure 3: The Brain-Mind Tissue, TISS. The Frontal TISS: Nested, fractal flock, groups and nodes. The Posterior TISS: Nested, fractal flock, groups and nodes. Each unit is involved in the unit's Self Organization. The Frontal and the Posterior TISS are linked into the brain-mind Self Organization of Understanding, Consciousness, Emotions, and Knowledge, Souček.

The musician adjusts his or her playing on the basis of two sets of information: the melody he or she is supposed to play and which is written on the paper, and the sound received from the common field. The Cooperation is based on experimental findings and it supports the Flow of Favorable Factors, FFF, the carrier of memory and cognition. The patterns are stored in the FFF. When a stimulus is received, it produces the FFF, which is compared with the stored patterns. The pattern of the stimulus causes millions of brain cells to generate a similar pattern, which has been stored in the chemical structure of these neurons. The node Cooperation resembles the resonance: A tuning fork "remembers" the frequency it is tuned at; placed in a variable sound field, the fork will produce the originally tuned pitch when it recognizes that frequency or a frequency which is merely similar (recognizing similar but not necessarily identical frequencies). The argument suggesting the FFF is the fact that the brain is composed of more than ten billion neurons. It is difficult to envision the network that would connect all of these neurons on a point-to-point basis. The answer is a connection through many intermediate synapses at a cost of time, that is going from nodes to groups to flocks to pool, Fig. **3**. In this way a large population of neurons is able to communicate and cooperate almost simultaneously.

FLOCKS AND POOLS IN HUMAN PREFRONTAL CORTEX

Groups form the flock, Fig. **3**. I explain the role of the flocks in the region of the human brain responsible for the mnemonic processing. What is the specific contribution of the lateral Frontal cortical areas to mnemonic processing? This region lies below the sulcus principalis, occupying the inferior frontal convexity, and comprises architectonic areas 47/12,45, and the ventralmost part of area 46 that lies below the sulcus principalis, [4]. In the human brain, the ventrolateral frontal cortical region largely occupies the inferior frontal gyrus, Fig. **3**. This region is inhabited by the Frontal flock, F. F is inhabited by the Frontal groups, G. Frontal groups G are inhabited by the Frontal nodes N. Frontal node N is a neural network, like the one in Fig. **2**. Each of the Frontal units is involved in its Self-Organization. All units together cooperate in the Frontal Self-Organization.

Now I look at the Posterior region, inhabited by the Posterior flock, groups and nodes. Each of these Posterior units is involved in its Self-Organization. All units together cooperate in the Posterior Self Organization. The posterior cortical association areas, where recently processed information is temporarily held while it is being integrated with incoming and recalled information, are connected with the ventrolateral frontal cortical region.

The functional interaction between the ventrolateral frontal region and the posterior association cortex is critical for the expression within memory of various executive processes, such as active selection, comparison, and judgment of stimuli held in short-term and long-term memory. This interaction, Cooperation and Self-Organization involve two nested, fractal, brain-mind tissues: Frontal TISS and its N, G, F; and Posterior TISS and its N. G, F. This type of interaction is necessary for active (explicit) encoding and retrieval of information, that is, processes initiated under conscious effort by the subject and guided by the subject's plans and intentions. These active forms of encoding and retrieval depend on the lateral frontal cortex. The more passive forms of encoding and retrieval result when incoming or recalled stimuli automatically trigger stored representations (*e.g.*, on the basis of strong preexisting associations or matching to stored representations). These latter aspects of mnemonic processing do not critically depend on the lateral frontal cortex, and, this accounts for the normal performance of the brain.

The Self Organization of the Frontal TISS and of the Posterior TISS coordinate, interpret, and elaborate the information in consciousness to provide the hippocampal-associative-memory system with the appropriate encoding information and retrieval cues that it takes as its input. Comparable processes are involved in evaluating the hippocampal system's output and placing those retrieved memories in a proper spatiotemporal context.

Nodes, groups, flocks and pools are "conscious" of the various processes involved in each unit's internal memory search. They are not conscious of the operations of the hippocampal-associative system, or of the operations of the strategic frontal system that occupy consciousness. The unit is aware of the questions it delivers to other units, the answers it gets from them, and the evaluation of the answers, but it is not aware of the external operations and of the hippocampus itself. On the other hand, the complete TISS is involved in engram formation and reactivation in the neo-cortex, priming, procedural memory, manipulations of strategies, and in cognitive resources.

Note: 1. The units N, G, F, P exhibit the rudimentary functions of Understanding U, Consciousness C, Emotions E, and Knowledge K. 2. These functions are present in the node, group, flock and pool Self Organized loops. 3. The loops form the Frontal and the Posterior TISS. 4. The loops involve the links, FFF and N, G, F, P Barriers.

SELF ORGANIZATION

The fractal, nested, brain-mind tissue TISS operates through the Self Organization. The Self Organization of Understanding, Consciousness, Emotions and Knowledge, SOUCEK, is present in all TISS units, but in different degrees, Fig. **4**. The associative memory A and the functions U, C, E, K are specific for each TISS unit. The evolution has created various associative memories and functions, for various nodes, groups, flocks and pools. Each unit is to some degree conscious of major local processes within the unit's FFF, barrier and link. Yet the unit is not conscious of the overall TISS processes.

I compare Fig. **4** with the Fig. **4** in [6] and I conclude: The Associative memory A, Understanding U, Consciousness C, Emotions E and Knowledge K are present in specific forms:

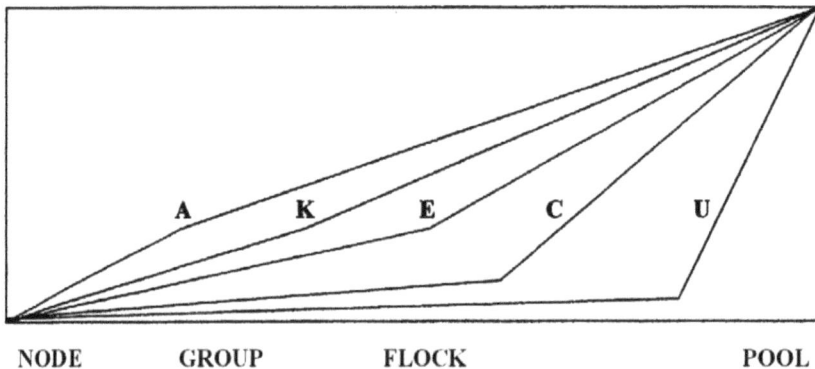

Figure 4: The local A, K, E, C, U in specific form and to some degree are present in the nodes, groups, flocks and in the pool.

1. In All Units of the Brain-Mind Tissues Tiss; 2. In All Animal Brains and in Human Brain

Each unit and agent has: The response function responsible for the inherent built in program; transfer function which deals with the input-output relations; continuous and discrete long term and short term working memories. See the memories M1, M2 and M3 in fireflies. Hence the unit and agent have the representation of the local world and to some extent are free from the environmental dependency. The units and agents communicate using the Universal Brain internal language. See the Brain-Window language in fireflies [7].

The firefly **understands, U**, the courting message through the receive windows. The mollusk is **conscious, C**, of the presence of the food and enters into a rhythmic feeding behavior. The firefly after mating changes her **emotions, E**. She is not interested anymore for a courting partner. She is now inviting a visitor that she could eat. The bird inherits the **knowledge, K**. This includes the song that the young bird inherits from the parents, and then improves through learning. Katydid **associates, A**, the chirping call with the potential courting partner and with its location on the tree. In short, each animal as well as each TISS unit and its agent performs the local Self Organization of the local U, C, E, K and A. All units and agents together Cooperate in the overall TISS Self Organization.

TISS involves the context switching as observed in fireflies; chaotic attractions as observed in katydids; continuous and discrete messages as observed in birds. The FFF information transmission and mixture combines the neural impulse trains, with the fast acting transmitters: inhibitory GABA; excitatory glutamate; and modulatory dopamine, serotonine and acetylcholine.

LONG TERM MEMORY, PARTIAL SELECTION AND OVERLAP

Figs. **5** and **6** present the Time-Information-Space Set, TISS.

The brain performs the generalization (clustering, round-off, quantizing) of distinct objects or patterns into clusters of similarity or equivalence.

Without generalization, every instance of each type of object or pattern would appear new every time it was encountered. Instead, a category (cluster, class) of objects is represented as a concept. The brain extracts the key from the object. The key **selects** the right unit related to a given concept (pattern).

Each unit stores many dispersed **overlapped** association patterns. A small number of association patterns result in a small number of large and deep storage basins,

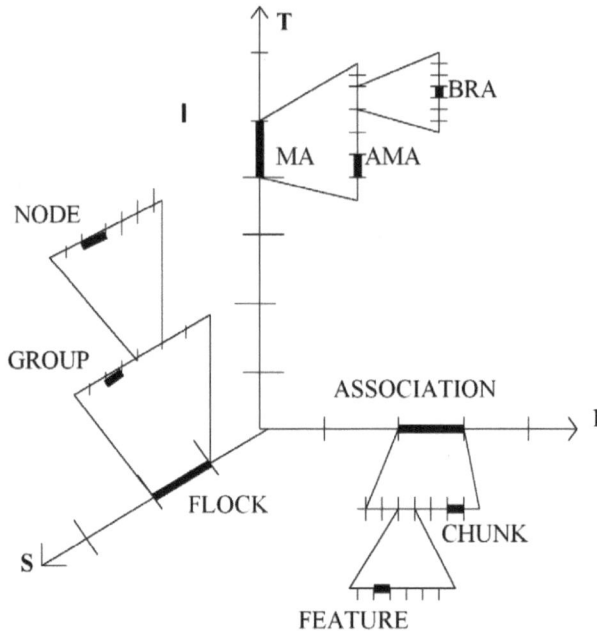

Figure 5: The Brain-Mind Tissue, TISS. TISS is the nested, fractal, dynamic, fuzzy Time-Information-Space Set. Time T is a sequence of MA periods. MA=Master the association. Simultaneously AMA amasses the chunk, and BRA brands the features. **Information I** is composed of associations, that are born from one instance to the next. An instant association is extracted by an instant chunk. An instant chunk is formed from instant features. A single instant information will never be repeated again. **Space S** is a pool of flocks. Each flock lives within its barrier, its FFF and with its internal links. In parallel groups and nodes live in their spaces. All units cooperate.

which are easy to identify. A large number of association patterns result in a large number of small and shallow basins which are more difficult to identify. TISS combines the partial selection with the overlap, in nodes (N key), groups (G key), flocks (F key) and in the pool.

Each unit (N, G, F, P) has its Link, Barrier, Agents, Functions (U, C, E, K) and its Association, A. Each A stores many patterns and is defined by the x, y, z parameters: x, complexity of the pattern; y, the number of patterns that are overlapped one over another; z, the number of units.

Node A keeps simple patterns NP; large number of patterns are overlapped (large y); the number of units z is large. NP could present a stimulus, action or behavior element or component; the word.

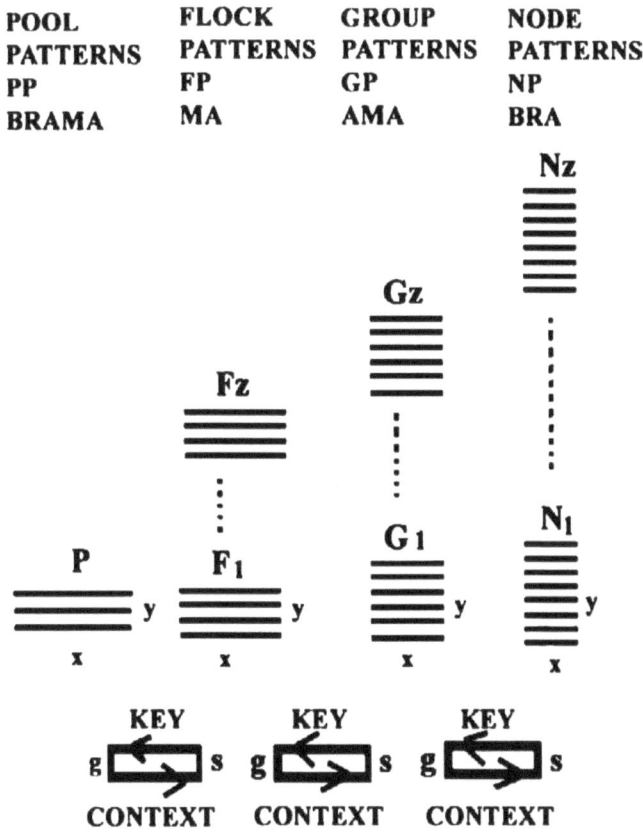

POOL PATTERNS PP BRAMA	FLOCK PATTERNS FP MA	GROUP PATTERNS GP AMA	NODE PATTERNS NP BRA

Figure 6: The Brain-Mind Tissue is full of long term associations, in N, G, F, P. The partial selection selects the right N, G and F between 1 to z. Associative content based search extracts the right pattern from the cluster of y overlapped patterns. The size of the pattern is indicated by x. General=g; specific=s. The research of the alive associations as well as of the computer associations is my job since 1955, and it merges the neurobiology and the computer science. See the details in [5, 6, 7].

Group A keeps less complex patterns GP; more patterns are overlapped; the number of units z is larger. GP could be a picture, program, schedule; short phrase.

Flock A keeps complex patterns FP; (large x); small number of patterns is overlapped (small y): the number of units z is small. FP could be a complex picture, program, schedule, story.

Pool A keeps very complex tasks and contexts (very large x) with the moderate overlap (small y).

In each step towards the higher level the KEY is extracted. Using the KEY the nodes select a proper G unit; the groups select a proper F unit.

In each step towards the lower level, the CONTEXT is extracted. Using the CONTEXT the pool selects a proper F unit; the flocks select a proper G unit; the groups select a proper N unit. Once the unit is selected the associative CONTENT based search extracts the right pattern from the clusters of overlapped patterns.

Sensory data enter at the bottom and are filtered through a series of sensory processing and pattern recognition units that runs in parallel to the behavior generating structure. Each level of this sensory processing structure processes the incoming sensory data stream, extracting features, recognizing patterns and applying various types of filters to the sensory data. Information relevant to the decisions being made at each level is extracted and sent to the appropriate behavior generating structures. The partially processed sensory data is than passed to the next higher level for further processing.

Key, Context, Content, follow the paths: from specific to general; from general to specific. This involves the continuous signals and maps quantized into the discrete internal symbols, CQD. See the internal brain language based on the Brain Windows [7]. It also involves the converting of the internal symbols and messages into the continuous signals and maps: inverted CQD. Both stimulation and action are coded in a slow scale chemical, hormonal coding as well as in a fast scale pulse and time coding. Pulse and time coding is of special interest for behavioral patterns that are executed as time sequences of events. It seems natural that the time brain windows should be used in such sequences, to screen, check or recognize the information which is coded in the form of intervals. The brain window logic and language are described in [5, 6, 7].

The brain assimilates the new pattern which is similar to existing patterns, and associates a new pattern which is substantially different to all previous ones.

SHORT TERM MEMORY

The brain constantly operates with the new short term patterns: features, chunks, associations and stories. Each unit N,G, F, P encodes the short term patterns into the unit's Flow of Favorable Factors, FFF, rather than the individual neurons, elements and impulse trains. In other words the short term patterns are directly involved in the unit's Cooperation. This involves the verbal stories. To recognize the word it is necessary to know the story; to recognize the story it is necessary to know the word. The massively parallel creative search bounces around before finally converging to a solution. In the time scale from 1 ms to 1 s, the creative search REASON [6] is directed back and forth between the cortical columns, thalamus and basal ganglia. For a short time the self-organized search links the features, chunks, associations and stories to the N, G, F, P. But how?

Consider the following examples: a symbol Vine has a membership or association with the category of DRINK, but also with categories of CHEMISTRY, ALCOHOL, AGRICULTURE *etc.* A symbol Chicken could be a feature, but in another story it could be a chunk or association. There is no direct static relation between the feature, chunk, association, story and the N, G, F, P. However some relations are frequent others are rare. The natural selection has created TISS that supports the frequent relations in the optimal way. The result is the moderate number of short links within each unit; the fast chaotic attractions; the fast Cooperation; the compressed words, categories of words, verbal stories [6]. Note: **The Long Term Memory is the nested fractal association, distributed over TISS units N, G, F, P. The Short Term Memory is the nested fractal FFF, distributed over TISS units N, G, F, P.**

DISCUSSION

The Pool P is a dispersed relay station, processor and association for information for and from Flocks F and it covers most parts of the central nervous system. P uses the stellate and pyramidal cell structures. The Groups G and Nodes N, are full of the granule and Martinotti cells that link both proximally located and more distant stellate and pyramidal cells. The granule cells possess a connectivity pattern and structure that expand the afferent stimulus information to higher order statistics prior to input to the principal learning structures and associations in the pyramidal and stellate cells. In case of the sound and speech input, TISS is looking at the spectrum, the set of input signals, the phonemes. TISS associations keep the reference spectra and they compete for the input. The association with the highest matching score becomes a winner. In this way TISS performs **the recognition of phonetic patterns** and extracts the common KEY from a set of overlapped patterns. Going through N,G,F and P, TISS performs the generalization, round of, quantizing, CQD, and resolves the verbal combinatorial explosion. In case of the speech output, the process goes through P, F, G, N and involves the CONTEXT, specialization, inverted CQD and **the generation of phonemes, words and stories**.

TISS involves many information layers, see Fig. **3** in [6]: A,C,G,U; microtubule code; end-plate potential; brain window BW; BW message; BW language; tree; feature; chunk; association; task, story. Hence the feature, chunk, association and task are composed of the above fine, internal information layers, including: the internal BW messages and symbols, and the internal BW language.

CONCLUSIONS

TISS cancels the border between the brain and the mind. There is only one brain-mind tissue, TISS. The matter-based TISS generates the never ending massively parallel chaos. The chaos constantly modifies TISS. This is the never repeating brain-mind loop. The loop generates the BRAMA protocol sequences, BRA=1 to 3.6 ms, AMA=25 ms, MA=175 ms. See Fig. **2** in [6]. The stimulus sequence includes: sensation element; integration; generalization; fuzzyfication; pattern recognition; perception. The action sequence includes: Imagination; concretization; defuzzyfication; decomposition; behavior element. TISS is full of the overlapped nested, fractal, stimulus-action sequences. TISS is full of the overlapped nested, fractal, information layers. TISS is full of the Universal Brain Agents [7]: Mollusk; Katydid; Firefly; Bird and others. Agents fight for time, information and space. Hence they fight for the brain-mind tissue, TISS. Yet agents also Cooperate and mate. For experimental findings on TISS agents see [7].

In TISS there is no Central Executive; no Managerial Unit; no Supervising System. The processes are built through the Cooperation. They depend on the temporary status of the Flow of Favorable Factors, FFF, Barriers, Links and on the local neuronal networks. This is the way how TISS operates using nodes, groups, flocks and pool.

The Units Cooperate. In case of the speech generation (or recognition), each part of the story provides the necessary partial context for the generation (recognition) of a word. The whole word participates in the generation (recognition) of each phoneme.

The generalization and the specialization. For any real world generalization problem, there are always many generalizers that could resolve the problem. Based on the learning set, TISS could pick up one single, winner generalizer from among the set of candidate generalizers, and learn with that generalizer. Yet, TISS learning could also combine several generalizers. From the learning set alone, TISS predicts the good generalizers combination.

Learning and U, C, E, K, and A. TISS restricts the set of candidate generalizers, and searches for which combination has a minimal error on the provided learning set. The same is true for the specialization.

1. TISS uses the innate, unit's, low level, local U, C, E, K and A functions.

2. TISS learns.

3. Through learning TISS gradually makes grow the high level, overall brain U, C, E, K and A functions.

4. The growing and the Self Organization of the U, C, E, K, and A, are the life time processes, and they present the frontier of the nature.

DISCLOSURE

"The content of this chapter has been previously published by *Periodicum Biologorum, Vol. 104, No. 3, 345-352,2002*".

REFERENCES

[1]   BEDIAN V, LYNCH JF, ZHANG F, ROBERTS MH. A Biologically Realistic and Efficient Neural Network Simulator, in Ref. [5],1991
[2]   BJEGOVIC M, ISGUM V, SLIJEPCEVIC M. A Computerized Method of Somatosensory Evoked Potential Monitoring. Period Biol1995; 97: 295-300

[3]   GRAFMAN J, HOLYOAK KJ, BOLLER F. Structure and Functions of the Human Prefrontal Cortex. New York Academy of Sciences, vol. 769, New York 1995

[4]   PETRIDES M. Functional Organization of the Human Prefrontal Cortex for Mnemonic Processing, in Ref. [3] 1995

[5]   SOUCEK B, The IRIS Group. Neural and Intelligent Systems Integration. Wiley New York 1991

[6]   SOUCEK B. Universal Brain Theory: The Self Organization of Understanding, Consciousness, Emotions and Knowledge. Period Biol2001;103: 3, 219-228

[7]   SOUCEK B, SOUCEK M. Neural and Massively Parallel Computers. Wiley New York.1988

[8]   The BRAMA names, BRA, AMA, MA, have been inspired by the names of my children Branko, Amalia and Marina.

Send Orders of Reprints at reprints@benthamscience.net

Better Life and Business: Cell, Brain, Mind and Sex Universal Laws, 2013, 165-183   **165**

CHAPTER 9

The Brain Agents Universe

Abstract:

Background and Purpose: This work explains the duets in both, human brain and animal behavior. Duets transmit the knowledge and learning messages within the Universal Brain, by the Flow of Favorable Factors, through the Barrier. The Time-Information-Space Set, TISS is formed.

Materials and Methods: Real-time computer is used for data acquisition from three duets: the northern true katydid, Pterophylla camellifolia (Orthopteria, Tettigoniidae); the firefly, Photuris versicolor; the bird, white-crested jay thrush, Garrulax leucolophus patkaicus (Timaliidae). Computer models relate behavioral duets to the duets within the human mind, perception and brain.

Results: The following types of duets have been identified: solo, alternation, aggression, selective courting, aggressive mimicry, complex messages using sequences of syllables. These duets are based on: steps in a response function; Brain Windows; patterns; message quanta; chaos and attractors. The human brain-mind tissue, TISS, is presented.

Conclusions: Human Brain, Mind and behavior are composed of communicating agents. Three classes of duets have been identified. **The chaotic duet** is a dynamic structure. Duet trajectories concentrate into a narrow attractor space. This is a case of massive self-organization. **The courting/mimicry duets** are based on symbol-signal processing and are capable of discovering the hidden information by observing sample behavior and comparing it with the past learned experience. **The pattern duet** is capable to recognize inexact, incomplete patterns. Through many duet loops, the human brain agents called katydids, fireflies and birds learn about the partner, and adapt answers and behavior. Symbol-signal processing is responsible for mental states and for consciousness. The genetic, sensation and mental vehicles in all layers of the Barrier, combine the born-with knowledge, with learning. The layers are unconscious of the underlying vehicle traffic regulations. Yet each layer of the Barrier recognizes the intentions and the meaning of quantum messages within its duet domain. The duets are involved in the Universal Brain and Mind self-organization and in perception. The dynamic nodes, groups, flocks and pools form the brain-mind tissue TISS.

Applications: Experimental support to the Universal Brain Theory; Human Brain image and data analyses; stimulation and diagnoses; autonomous agents; intelligent systems; Global Mind services on Internet.

Keywords: Human brain, universal brain, brain and mind, brain and mind tissue, mind, duet, self-organization, katydid, firefly, bird, brain window, message quantum, chaos, syllable, song, chirp, response function, transfer function, agent, brain barrier, flow of favorable factors, consciousness, real-time computing.

INTRODUCTION

Universal Brain is the Self Organization of Understanding, Consciousness, Emotions and Knowledge [1-8]. The brain and behavior processes emerge from these interactions. In this work I explain in detail the most frequent interaction, the duet. The duet involves two partners (agents, flocks). The duet communication is present within living organisms as well as between organisms. Only after understanding the details of the duet it will be possible to analyze the more complex brain and the behavioral structures. I use concrete experimental data measured on:

- **the northern true katydid**, Pterophylla camellifolia (Orthopteria, Tettigoniidae);

- **the firefly**, Photuris versicolor;

- **the bird**, white-crested jay thrush, Garrulax leucolophus patkaicus (Timaliidae).

The insect and bird duets were recorded on a stereo tape recorder. In case of birds, frequency spectra defined as syllables were produced on a sonographer machine. For details see [1, 2, 3, 9]. The fireflies were courted using artificial light flashes. The firefly responses were recorded using a hand held photomultiplier. For details see [4, 5]. In this work I start from experimental data and I develop the theoretical models that distinguish the following types of duets: solo, alternation, aggression, selective courting, aggressive mimicry, complex messages. These duets are explained by: response function; Brain Windows; syllables; message quanta.

Above communication patterns are present in the human brain and in other species. I develop the theory which explains these modes of communication. The theory covers both central neural control and interaction between two partners. A concrete example, katydid chirping, is shown here in detail. Upon receiving acoustical stimuli from the partner, a male katydid generates a characteristic response function with three parts, which regulates solo-overlapping chirps, partially delayed chirps, and alternating chirps. Each partner is considered an element in a closed feedback loop and is described through its response period *vs.* stimulus period curves. In the alternating mode the communication loop converges toward a stable operating point, whereas in the aggressive mode stability is never achieved. In the case of fireflies, the duet involves the light flashes. In the case of birds, more complex messages are involved using sequences of syllables.

I develop computer model, simulating both deterministic and random components of the human brain communication signal. Computer-simulated sequences are in excellent agreement with field-measured data. I introduce the response function and transfer function. The response function describes the inherent built-in timing program. Upon receiving a stimuli, an agent generates a response function which determines the phases and the timing of the behavior to follow. The transfer function describes the input-output relationship, the magnitude of the stimulus *vs.* the magnitude of the response. The transfer function is very useful in describing the interaction between two partners or elements in a communication loop. Each partner or element can be described through its transfer function. Simple plotting of two transfer functions on the same diagram explains one duet. Flocks of duets form different patterns of communication feedback. Katydid, firefly and bird agents are presented in detail. The Time-Information-Space Set, TISS, is introduced and explained. TISS is the brain-mind tissue.

THE KATYDID AGENTS: CHAOTIC DUET

The basis for alternating and aggressive chirping is acoustical interaction between two male katydids. Each katydid can be considered as an element in a closed feedback loop, having its input drive force (stimulus period) and responding to it with a measurable output (chirp period). One of the ways to study this feedback loop is to determine the input-output transfer functions for each element. Noiseless computer models have been used for this task. Obtained response-period *vs.* stimulus-period curves are plotted in Fig. **1**, for both leader and the follower. From Fig. **1**, it is clear that the response period of the leader R1 is identical with the stimulus period of the follower S2. Also, the response period of the follower R2 is identical with the stimulus period of the leader S1. In Fig. **1** the curve marked »leader« presents R1 as a function of S1. Similarly, the curve marked »follower« presents R2 as a function of S2.

The leader curve has three distinguishable parts: alternation, partial delay, and solo overlap. Note the sharp quantum steps between these parts. The follower's curve is, in fact, the same shape, except for the fact that the partial delay and solo overlap parts are high up out of the frame of Fig. **1**. The two curves have only one common point, H; this is the stable operating point of the alternating calls. In a noiseless environment, the parameters of alternating calls would be exactly as dictated by the operating point H: S2 = R1 = 0.39 sec; S1 = R2 = 0.47 sec. The neighborhood of the point H is the attractor space of this chaotic duet. If for any reason the songs were to start with the parameters of point A, a drift towards the stable point H would occur in the following aspects: the leader sings at A (R1 = 0.67 sec). As R1 = S2, for S2 = 0.67 the follower's response is 0.31 (point B). As R2 = S1, for S1 = 0.31 leader's response is 0.46 (point C), and so forth. The sequence would drift through the path A, B, C, D, E, F, G, H. These eight chirps represent the transition. All subsequent chirps will have the parameters of the stable operating point H. Similarly, if the sequence begins at point J, it will drift through the path J, I, H, again ending up in the same operating point H.

An entirely different situation occurs if the sequence starts at point K (partial delay). From point K, it will drift into point L (alternation for the follower) and then to point M (solo overlap for the leader). The next step would lead to a very long response, R2, which is longer than the chirp period of the leader. As a result, in the next step the leader produces a solo chirp. The solo chirp period of the leader is 0.66 sec. That means that after point M the next leader's point will be A. The detailed sequence K, L, M, A is shown in Fig. **1**. From point A, the sequence drifts to the stable operating point H. Note that the stable operating point H is distant from the partial delay region of the follower, but very close to the partial delay region of the leader. As a result, noise or disturbance takes the sequence from point H to point K, producing partial delay, solo overlap, and solo parts in the leaders' chirps. Simultaneously, the follower is in the alternating mode of chirping.

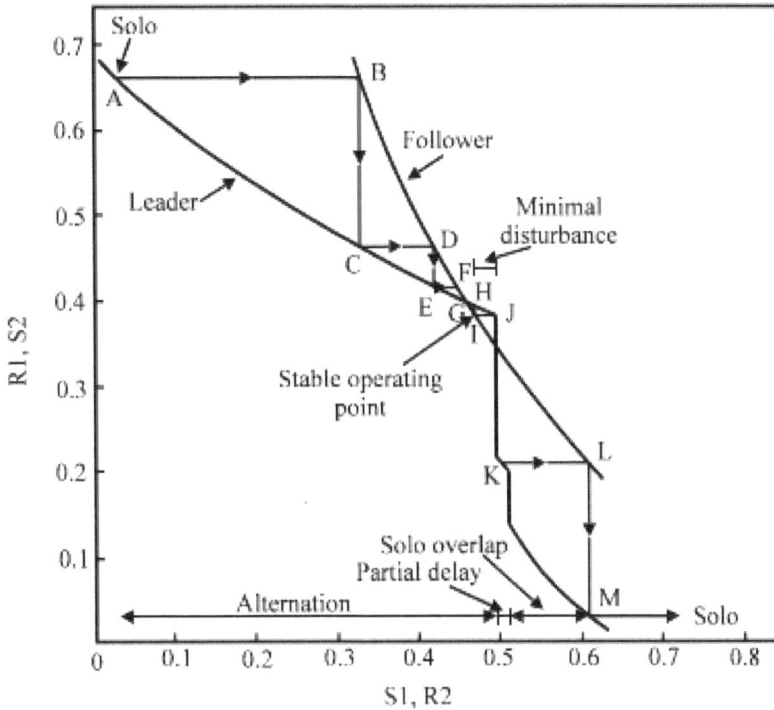

Figure 1: Response period-stimulus period curves for leader and follower. The two curves intersect at the stable operating point H.

Each katydid is considered as an element in a closed feedback loop and can be described through its response-period *vs.* stimulus-period curves. In an alternating mode, the two response curves intersect at a stable operating point H, which is near the partial delay region of the leader, but far away from the partial delay region of the follower. Because of disturbance or noise, the communication loop drifts out of the stable point, through the leader's solo chirps, and back to the stable point. In the aggressive mode, the two response curves are in a position such that the communication loop drifts constantly from solo chirps in the leader to solo chirps in the follower and *vice versa*. A disturbance moves the communication out of this pattern, which explains the numerous solos by both leader and follower in the aggressive mode. This theory has been used to design a computer model for alternating and aggressive communication. Computer-simulated chirping sequences are in excellent agreement with field-measured data see Fig. **2**.

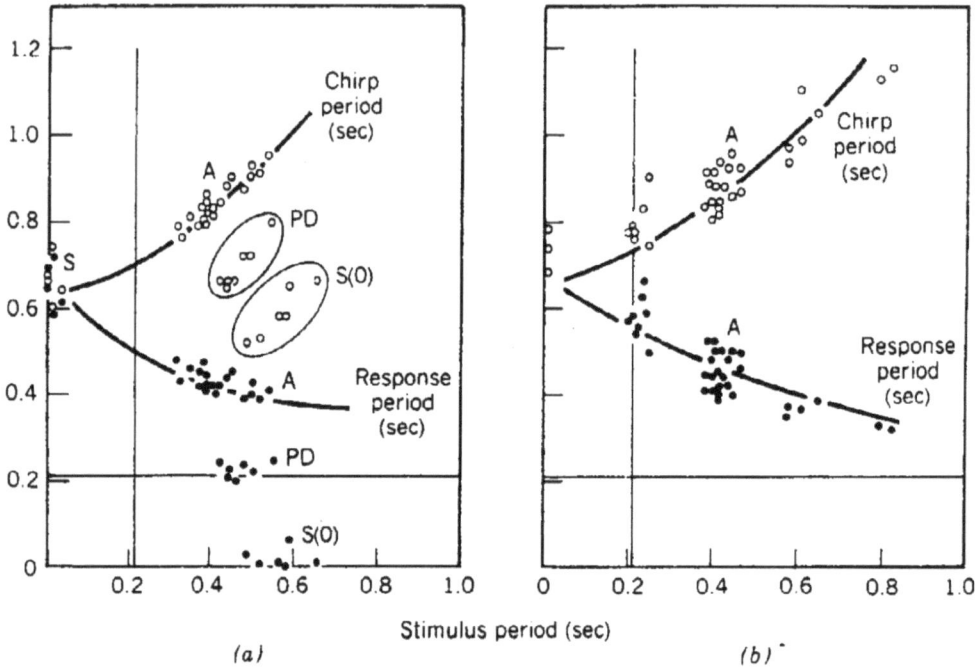

Figure 2: Computer-produced data simulating acoustical interaction in alternating calling. Marked areas are identical to those found in experimental data.

In the Universal Brain, the chaotic duets offer a dynamic storage. Now the leader and the follower of Fig. **1** represent mental knowledge and learning agents. Each agent has accumulated genetic and personal knowledge. This includes also its SR curve or band. When leader and follower agents enter into a chaotic duet, they rapidly converge into a joint conclusion, which is the point H. The point H is a symbol-signal association, that is a representative of one entire cluster or category. Hence, the self-organized chaotic duets perform data compression, clustering and discrete or quantum representation. The duet is a dynamic storage unit for the entire cluster, as well as for the point H. Every time the duet becomes active, it updates and refreshes its storage. Also, the low frequency patrolling brain activity refreshes the duet.

THE FIREFLY AGENTS: COURTING AND MIMICRY DUET

The Brain Windows [4, 5] present the base of the duet between fireflies. Upon receiving the stimulus interval I, the firefly responses with the latency L. The latency depends on the last stimulus interval I, but also on the past history of stimulation. Hence it is wrong to relate the response only to the last stimulus. These kinds of models are only approximations, neglecting the memories and the effects of the past history of stimulation. In the case of firefly Femme Fatales, FF, the past history contribution could be from zero to fifty percent of the contribution due to the last stimulus interval, and it cannot be neglected. The generation of the answering flash is controlled by the sequence of brain windows [4, 5]. The receive R-send S windows explain why a broad region has not been observed in measured latencies. This empty region coincides with the R windows during which the generation of the answering flash is not allowed.

The double-interval pattern is frequently observed in experimental data. It is composed of two intervals, I_1 and I_2. The range of the intervals depends on the species. In the case of Photinus macdermotti (courtship), and in Photinus versicolor (mimicry), the ranges are $1.1< I_1 <2.1$ and $2< I_2 <5$ sec. The FF readily responds to a stimulus I_1 in the middle of the range, but not so at the edges of the range. She first rejects a number of flashes and then she starts responding. Fig. **3** shows the communication pattern with the intervals 2.2 and 2.8, with each interval measured from the initial flash. The pattern is simulated on a computer. Fig. **3** displays 20 repetitions of the pattern 2.2, 2.8. In each repetition stimuli contribute to the memories, and in this way they modify the receive-send windows. The contributions to the memories are proportional to the values taken from the primary waveform, [4, 5]. Both values are negative and they push the memory into the negative region. In this way, S windows are narrowing and R windows are widening. After eight repetitions, the R2 window is wide enough to accept the stimulus interval I_1 and the FF responds with a flash. After twelve repetitions, the R3 window is wide enough to accept the stimulus interval I_1, and the FF responds with a flash.

We see in this experiment three modes of communication. In repetitions 0 through 8, the double interval pattern receives no response. In repetitions 8 through 12, the FF responds after the first interval $I_1 = 2.2$, but not after the second. This is the flash pattern of Photinus macdermotti males which induces mimicry responses from the FF. In repetitions 12 through 20, the FF responds to both intervals. This is double-interval communication with a double response, but it can also apply to flash patterns composed of a series of rhythmically repeated flashes.

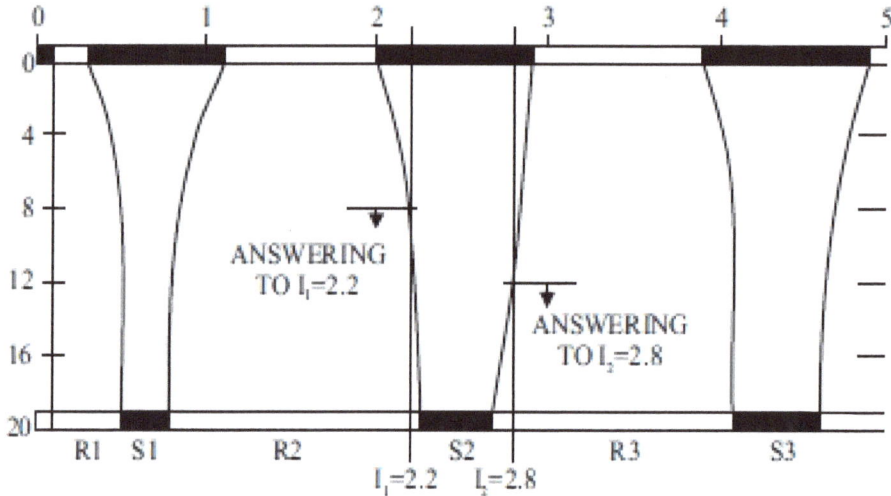

Figure 3: Dynamic adjustment of the receive-send window sequence. Computer simulation of an experiment K. Interval (I_1) was 2.2 sec, interval (I_2) was 2.8 sec. The firefly did not answer to the first eight pairs of intervals. After the eighth pair, she answered to the interval I_1. After the twelfth pair, she answered to both intervals I_1 and I_2.

Notice that the windows are quite "plastic" at the beginning of the sequence, and that they readily adjust. However, when the windows are pushed far away from the normal width, they resist further change. In double-interval patterns, experiments usually concentrate on the effects of the shorter interval. This model shows that both intervals carry the information. Both intervals also contribute to the response latency. In particular, a stable double-interval duet is the one, that does not modify the memory. A large number of experiments have been performed on Photuris FFs. Experiments are summarized in Fig. **3**. Each experiment presents a long repetition of double-interval patterns.

In Universal Brain, the courtship and mimicry duet offers the labeling or naming and context switching. The context has its discrete, symbolic, quantum representation as well as continuous, signal, cluster representation, as is shown in the Brain Windows, Fig. **3**. Many mental agents enter into duets. All of them have the same quantum context and label, but each one carries another part of continuous context.

THE BIRD AGENTS: PATTERN DUET

Study of bird songs provides much information about the sequential organization and control of a behavior which functions as communications. Here I present an account of song organization and duet in the white crested jay thrush. A bird song is expressed as a series of elements of varied frequency lying between 1.5 and 8 kHz. The individual elements of the song are called syllables. Syllables result from waveform analysis of acoustical records through continuous sampling and Furrier transformation. Four different syllables are found in the female song, coded F_1 to F_4, and twenty syllables are found in the male song, coded M_5 to M_{25}. For details see [3, 9]. A syllable can be recognized as a continuous trace on the sonogram which is separated from other traces of the same individual by 75 msec or more. Two adjacent syllables in the song form a pair, and three syllables form a triplet. One of the basic questions in sequential behavioral analysis is how strong the influence of a given syllable, pair, or triplet is on the element (syllable), which will appear N time-positions later in the sequence.

The analyzed record is composed of 141 duet songs and contains approximately 3000 syllables. By coding the female syllables with codes F_1 to F_4 and the male syllables with codes M_5 to M_{25}, a digital record has been produced as the input to the computer. By introducing the digital computer in bird communication study, it was possible to provide many classes of analysis with high statistical accuracy. Special attention is given to the study of motor patterns of each individual and to the study of message switching between individuals during duet. A computer program was written which superimposes the songs. Each song is split into the time intervals T1, T2,.., T50. One time interval belongs to one syllable. The program overlays the songs in such a way that the time interval T1 of all the songs is synchronized. The program then counts the frequency of occurrence of a syllable at a given time interval. To show the dependence on the preceding syllables, the overlaying technique produces branches whenever a new song differs from those songs already forming the overlying tree. For example, for

Song1: 1, 1, 2, 3, 4, 4

Song2: 1, 1, 3, 4, 4

The overlay will look as follows:

syllable 112344344

——————— _ $\rightarrow$ _ $\rightarrow$ _ $\rightarrow$ _ $\rightarrow$ _ $\rightarrow$ _ $\rightarrow$ _ $\rightarrow$ _ $\rightarrow$ _

frequency 221111111

Note that for time T1 and T2, both songs follow the same sequence, but after T2 the songs are different, producing two separate branches in the overlaying tree. As a result, the frequencies (lower number) for the first and second nodes are 2, whereas for higher nodes the frequencies are 1. The analysis starts for time interval T1 and proceeds until the end of a song is reached. For each time interval, the syllable of the song is compared with the tree structure for this time interval. An example of the tree produced using this technique is shown in Fig. **4**. The program allows up to five branches to go out from each node of the tree. The new syllable is treated as a descriptor for searching the tree.

Computer model of the brain associative memory is used to efficiently store and display hundreds of songs in the form of one single tree. The tree pattern is a new method to present both the brain communication process and behavioral control.

Since the songs are displayed in a sorted and comparative way, one can read from the tree the basic message units, decision-making points, variations of songs, frequencies, and probabilities of transitions. Each individual song can be recognized in the tree. The tree method presents the most efficient way to store hundreds of behavioral sequences in the brain. Next experiment is a male-female duet. Through inspection of the duet tree, it is found that the first message unit in most of the songs has a sequence of 22,1; 22,1; 22,1. At T = 6, major branching occurs. Large numbers of songs will continue with the pattern 22,1, but other new message units are also initiated. If the male has responded with 24, a new message unit starts, with the sequence 24,3; 24,3; 24. This is an obvious case of peripheral influence. It shows the interdependence of syllables produced by the male and the female. It was common practice in the past to analyze bird songs as a stationary

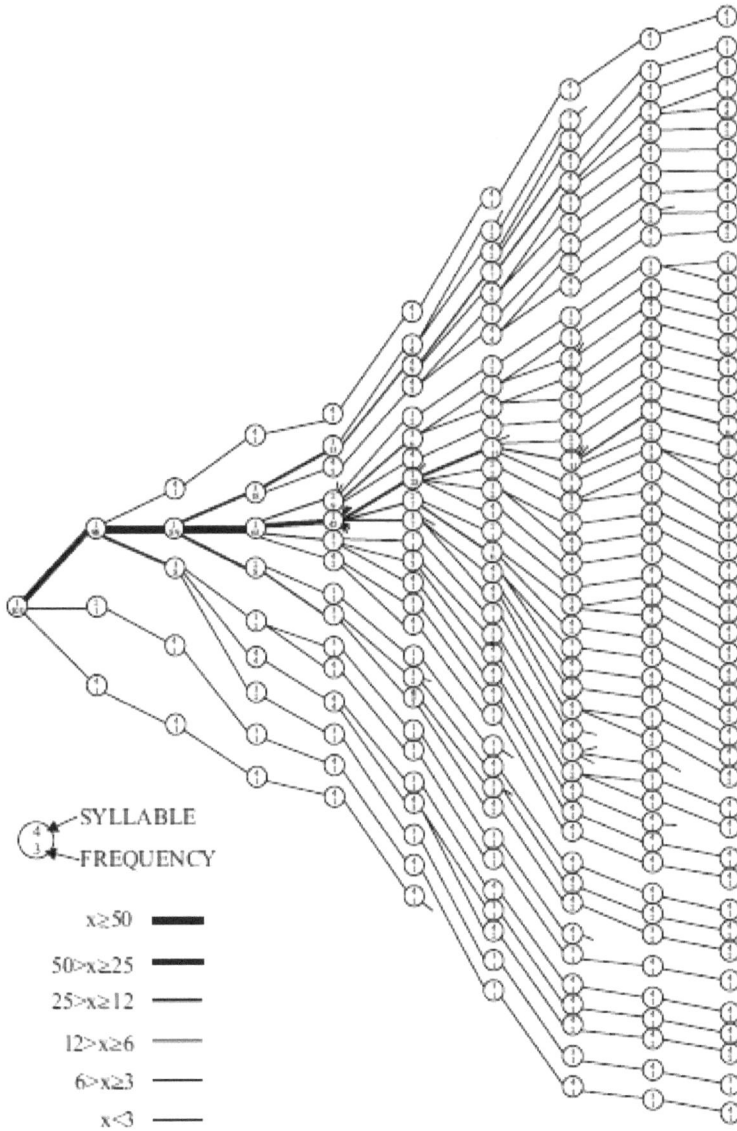

Figure 4: Brain Associative Memory tree. Tree stores only female portion of sequences beginning with 1. Tree contains 700 duets (frequencies are percentages). Tree is formed by the summation of common syllable types at each node in a time period. Reading the tree from left to right, 10 time periods are given, T=1 to 10. If a new syllable type is uttered, a branch is formed. Pins symbolize the termination of a sequence. Repetition of 1 gives a strong major pathway or branch.

sequence of events, assuming that the probabilities of different outcomes do not change with time. The present analysis clearly shows that duet songs are highly non stationary processes: the probabilities of outcomes are very much different at the beginning of the song from those in the middle or at the end of the song. In contrast to transition matrices, the tree method stores all observed duet sequences, preserving the relative time-dependent relationships between syllables. The analysis of bird songs based on associative trees, leads to the male M-female F model presented in Fig. **5**.

In the beginning of this study, the three patterns of syllables, M_{11}, M_{22}, and M_6, were observed and assigned discrete codes, 11, 22, 6. It turned out that the behavior of the female to these three types was indistinguishable. Moreover, the transitions from these to other male elements were identical. Finally, the linear interrelationships between M_6 and M_{22} suggested that both were members of a graded continuum.

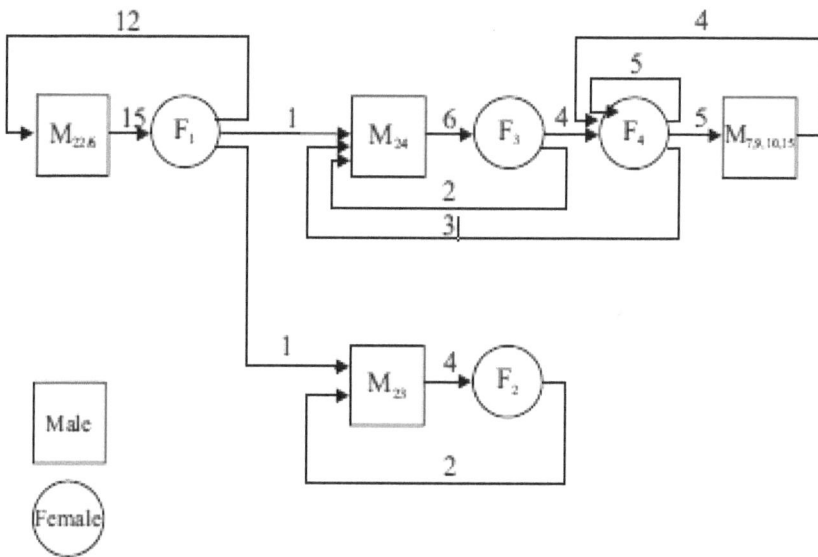

Figure 5: Pattern duet program. Diagrammatic representation of the structure of male (boxes) and female (circles) sequences, based on transitional data. Values shown above the lines are probabilities representing the utilization of sequence pathways.

Since the females apparently failed to discriminate between them, both are assigned to one pattern, $M_6 M_{22}$. M_{17} is also a member of this pattern, but because of its rarity it is not included in the pattern code. The code represents all patterns that belong to the quantum pattern space. These kind of duet performs a pattern recognition. It seeks to find regularities in the past experience and to compress them into generalization schemata. In Universal Brain, the quantum pattern duet offers even higher level of the discrete representation combined with continuous representation, Fig. **5**.

THE AGENT SPACE

The agent space is composed of many kinds of agents, with different levels of specialization. The agents support the elements of intelligence, as well as functions related to duet. So far I have observed three classes of duets: chaotic, courting/mimicry, and pattern. Clearly duet is open for further research. With the three duet classes it is possible to approximate a number of mental processes. Also these duets could be used to build intelligent systems. The Flow of Favorable Factors, FFF, through the Barrier is the generator of mental processes. FFF stimulates the agents to form the temporary network to do the task. Agents use quantum communication, such as duets, to synchronize and coordinate individual activities. Agents use the inherited knowledge and the knowledge acquired from their own experience. The agents are adaptive and they learn. The agent continuously interacts with FFF and it is ready to grab a task that it is set up for. The agents space is always in a self-organizing mode.

Here are important properties and advantages of the Universal Brain Network, UBN.

First, UBN allows arbitrary connections, which make the network more feasible by removing unnecessary constraints on network topology. The network architecture is general enough to take into account the characteristics of the targets. Second, the increased number of connections diminishes noise sensitivity and synchronization problems. Third, the additional connections may enable the network to converge faster. Fourth, the feedback (recurrent) connections are used to restore or deal with incomplete information. Fifth, the UBN is very flexible. Thus, it can be applied to complex problems including the natural language processing.

Here is an example. The Flow of Favorable Factors, FFF, through the Barrier, stimulates the flocks of agents A and B. Agent A and B broadcast the patterns PA and PB to the neighborhood. Through the chaotic attractions, A and B self-organize their duet, and finally they broadcast in the alternating mode. Agent C from the population, recognizes the pattern PA and responds with its pattern PC. Now A and C have established a new duet loop. A and C gradually narrow their receive and send windows, to become more selective. They exchange sequences of patterns. Finally, when both A and C are happy with what they receive, they start a joint action. In parallel, an agent D from the population, recognizes the pattern PB, and responds with its pattern PD, and in this way establishes another duet, BD, leading to another joint action. In the TISS, myriad of duet loops operate in this way.

Within fraction of a second, an avalanche of duets grows in a self-organized mode. A moment later, another avalanche grows, as a part of never ending self-organized process. This self-organized process narrowly follows the Flow of Favorable Factors, FFF, through the Barrier. The TISS is a parallel distributed system composed of autonomous intelligent agents. The TISS duets provide a way for self-organization of the system, for peaceful cooperation, negotiation and collective reasoning. In human mind, duets link one event to another and in this way they help building associations. Yet the TISS duets also provide a way for aggression, mimicry and wars between agents with different intentions or opinion.

Peace and war duets are present in all levels of mind and behavior processes. The results are mental processes, such as recognition, memory chunking, associations, reasoning, complex trains of thoughts, feelings, consciousness and perceptions.

CONCLUSIONS

The Brain-Mind tissue is the Time-Information-Space Set, TISS. TISS is composed of myriad of communicating agents. Frequent mode of communication is a duet. It carries messages both, between and within living organisms. In experimental data from katydid, firefly and bird duets, I have identified several processes; steps, Brain Windows, syllables as message quanta. I have observed three classes of duets (so far), that explain the Self Organization of the human brain as well as of the animal brains.

The chaotic duet is a dynamic structure, that uses non-linear response functions. The function may include the quantum steps. Exchange of chirps contracts with time and after several time steps, trajectories starting from all initial states become concentrated into a narrow attractor space, near the stable operating point. Evolution to attractor space from arbitrary initial states is a form of self-organizing behavior. It is possible that many duets in mental and behavioral spaces lie in the same self -organizing class. The goals are obvious: competing for the time and space resources of environment or of the brain and delivering the message. The case of katydids shows two solutions: alternation, where both the leader and the follower send their messages to the female population; aggression, where the leader has started an acoustic war, and eventually the acoustically defeated follower might leave the area. The stable operating point is H: S2=R1=0.39 sec; S1=R2=0.47 sec. This is an excellent example of the chaotic duet space that becomes self -organized very fast.

The courting/mimicry duet is based on symbol-signal processing. The receiver recognizes individual pattern as a symbol or label and relates it to the sender and to its intention. In this way the symbolic message informs the receiver. In the same time, a sequence of these symbols is connected to the additional message in the form of a signal, latency or song. Hence these duets are based on the symbol-signal processing.

In the nature the clean determinism between observation and causes is typically invalid. Hence the symbol-signal processing cannot operate on values that are certainly true or false. The symbol-signal duet is able to represent, evaluate and approximate information with some degree of fuzziness, uncertainty or incompleteness. Clearly, inexact inference is involved. Symbol-signal duet is fully capable to capture and to transmit the soft knowledge, that is typical in nature. It is capable of discovering the hidden information by observing sample behavior and comparing it with the past learned experience. Concrete example of learning is the firefly window narrowing for selective courting, and the window widening for aggressive mimicry. Through many duet loops the firefly learns about the partner, and adapts its answers and its behavior. This dynamics will result with a stable duet, if learning does not modify the memory any more. In the case of courtship and mimicry, the observed and theoretically confirmed ranges of intervals are $1.1 < I_1 < 2.1$ and $2 < I_2 < 5$ seconds.

The pattern duet is capable to capture a pattern through inexact inference. The bird songs are an example of inexact inference. The behavior of a female was indistinguishable to three types of male syllables, M_{11}, M_{22} and M_6. These male syllables, or symbols, or message quanta, are members of a graded continuum. A bird song is a good example of pattern learning: initially, almost random singing patterns, fall slowly into characteristic species song or into some modification thereof, depending on the auditory environment of the young bird. See pattern associations (Fig. **6**).

Universal Brain structure and Symbol-signal processing are the necessary conditions for selective attention that leads towards consciousness. Even at the level of insects or birds or neural vehicles, symbol-signal processing is responsible for a knowledge-learning traffic. In other words, the genetic, sensation and mental vehicles in all levels combine the born-with knowledge, with learning [6, 7].

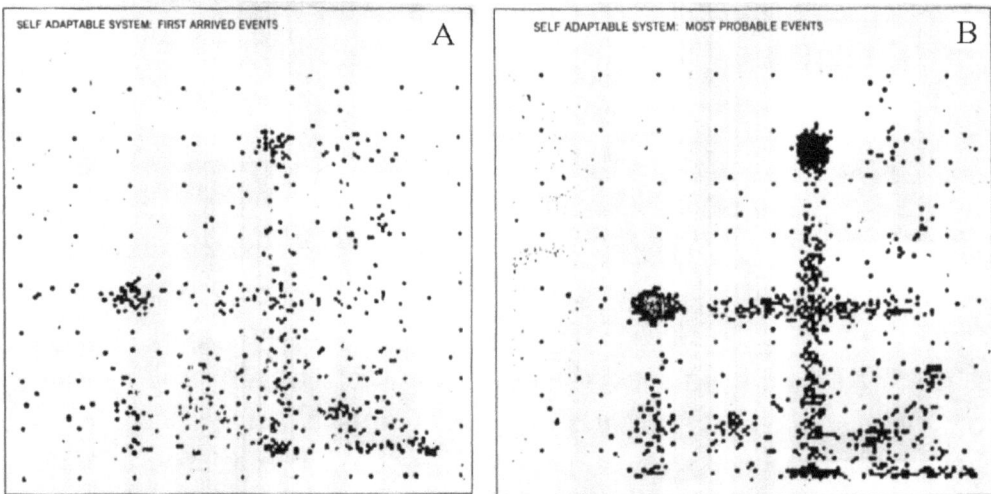

Figure 6: The human brain as a pattern association. The brain is exposed to a large sensory field, which might be mostly empty. In other words, many areas in the sensory field are of low activity: The questions are: How the brain assigns the available memory to highly active areas in the sensory field? How the brain makes the memory self-adaptation?. The brain uses two modes of operation: First arrived patterns and most the most probable patterns. A computer simulation of the pattern

associations is shown in Figs. **6A** and **6B**, which deal with measurements of two dimensional patterns. Input parameters I and J define the pattern. The content of the location presents the count: How many times a particular IJ combination has occurred during the experiment. The system first operates in the first arrived pattern mode. As the new IJ pattern comes from experiment, it takes the location from the memory. Next time when the same IJ pattern occurs, it only increases the count associated with that pattern. The result is presented in Fig. **6A**. Some memory spaces are associated to the highly active areas of sensory field, but some are associated with the areas of very low activity which might not be of interest for the brain. For this reason the brain divides all the contents of the memory by two. The spaces that have received only one count will be cleared to 0. By repeating this procedure several times the brain gives new chances to highly active patterns to associate themselves to the memory. The result is shown in Fig. **6B**. •In Fig. **6A** the patterns from hills and the low plane are stored in the memory. • In Fig. **6B** most patterns that come from hills (high activity) are stored in the memory. The low plane is discarded. This feature is the base of the learning and the self-adaptable brain associations. The IJ pattern is stored in the randomly defined memory space and not in IJ address(content addressable associations.)

A child learns the words, and after some time consciously understands the meaning of a spoken message, and yet it is unconscious of underlying grammar, syntax and of the linguistic symbolic links.

I conclude that duets support the Flow of Favorable Factors through the TISS Barrier [8]. The flow of vehicles carries distributed, discrete symbols, connected to the distributed continuous signals, through all layers of the mind barrier. The layers regulate the traffic through the Barrier: within the cell, within the neural structure, within the sensory and mental tracks. The layers are unconscious of the underlying traffic regulation. Yet each layer of the TISS Barrier recognizes the intention and the meaning of the messages within its duet domain. Duets are involved in the Universal Brain-Mind self -organization, that is in TISS. Duet transfer and response function are born with features. However the memories (parameters) are adaptive and they follow the history of stimulation. The TISS, the Universal Brain Theory, duets and symbol-signal processing will influence the brain research and the design of intelligent systems, networks and network's services. They also open the door for a new generation of intelligent society.

BRAIN NETWORK AGE

The technological ages of the human race include: hunting and gathering; agricultural age; industrial age; and information age.

Human race is now entering into a new age, that I call:

THE BRAIN NET AGE

It is based on the world wide recent discoveries, including: The Quantum Mind Theory [6], The Universal Brain Theory [7]; The Brain and Mind Tissue [8]; Self Organization of the Understanding, Consciousness, Emotions and Knowledge; BRAMA fractal protocol; brain windows; Time – Information – Space Set, TISS; internal brain agents and languages; Optimal Generalization, Concurrent Quantizing and Massively Parallel Associations.

BRAIN NET follows the human brain, but it offers much higher levels of speed, accuracy and complexity.

Hence the major future discoveries, designs and decisions will be dominated by BRAIN NET.

Already very young new fields have been created: 1. Universal Brain Networks smarter than humans; the first Cyborg robot uses the brain of the fish, eel, connected to the light sensors and wheels; 3. Brain- computer interfaces are able to extract recognizable images from neurons in the thalamus; 4. There are neural implants for Parkinson's disease and cochlear implants for deafness. From 2003 to 2010, BRAIN NET will grow into the dominant force in the world science, technology and business.

DISCLOSURE

"The content of this chapter has been previously published by *Periodicum Biologorum, Vol. 104, No. 3, 253-360, 2002".*

REFERENCES

[1] SHAW KC. Katydid Chirping. Behavior 1968;31: 203–259
[2] SOUCEK B. Model of alternating and aggressive communication with the example of Katydid chirping. J Theoretical Biology 1975;52:399–417
[3] SOUCEK B, VENCL F. Bird communication study using digital computer. J Theoretical Biology 1975; 49: 147–172
[4] SOUCEK B, CARLSON AD. Brain Windows in Firefly Communication. J Theoretical Biology 1986; 119: 47–65

[5]   SOUCEK B, CARLSON AD. Brain window language in Firefly. J Theoretical Biology 1987;125: 93–103

[6]   SOUCEK B. The Quantum Mind Theory. Period Biol1997;99: 1,3–18

[7]   SOUCEK B. Universal Brain Theory: The Self Organization of Understanding, Consciousness, Emotions, and Knowledge. Period biol2001;103: 219–228

[8]   SOUCEK B. The Brain and Mind Tissue, TISS: Node, Group, Flock and Pool. Period biologorum2002;104: 345–352

[9]   VENCL F, SOUCEK B. Structure and control of duet singing in the white-crested jay thrush. Behavior 1976;57: 20–33

Send Orders of Reprints at reprints@benthamscience.net

CHAPTER 10

Quantum Mind-Evoked Potential Link

Abstract:

Background and purpose: This work explains the link between Quantum Mind and the networks of oscillators in the brain. Through Primary Waveforms neural networks and brain component processes are linked to the mind and the behavioral integral processes.

Material and methods: Generation of Evoked Potentials through interaction of flocks of Primary Oscillators is explained. Computer simulated flock's responses are matched with experimental EP records, N400, triggered by verbal stimuli.

Results: Primary Waveforms have been recognized and extracted from EP records. Each Primary Waveform is directly related to the flock of Primary Oscillators in neural structure. EP record is related to a bundle of mental sequences, composed of overlapped Primary Waveforms. Critical parameter in Primary Waveforms is the amplitude of Sensation Elements. Dominant, quantum amplitudes lead to the clustering of Primary Waveforms.

Conclusions: Mental process is generated by the dynamics of flocks of agents or oscillators in neural structure and regulated by the BRAMA fractal protocol. Experimental data as well as the computer model point to the nested levels in the BRAMA. Each level is composed of about 7 nested waves. The resulting EP is not just a filtered sum of the activity of a large set of individual agents or oscillators. Instead the self-organization of agents space leads to dominant modes, binding the underlying oscillators. These dominant modes produce the dominant components, Primary Waveforms. Although Primary Waveforms are overlapped, it is possible to recognize them, in human and in rodent EP record.

Applications: New research and clinical methods, based on mind-brain links, through Primary Waveforms. Mind-body cross data banks and related drug testing. Direct mind-computer interfaces; mind reading machines; thinking machines.

Keywords: Mind, quantum mind, brain, mind-brain link, BRAMA protocol, evoked potential, neuron diagnoses, quantum mind theory, mind-computer interface, mind reading machines, primary oscillator, primary waveform, intelligent agent.

INTRODUCTION

Nervous systems are responsible for complex mental and behavioral capacities. Although neuroscience has advanced spectacularly, we still do not understand in satisfying detail the links between networks of neurons, mind and behavior. In other words, it is difficult to explain the mind level psychological phenomena in terms of brain level, neural network properties, short-term and long-term memories and memory capacities. For a long time, memories have been related to the oscillatory processes. The short -term memory has been explained by Hebb [1] as a post-stimulus sustained firing based on the reverberation of electrical activity in neuronal loops. More recent ideas [2,3,4-19] relate memories, awareness, perceptual information, high frequency brain oscillation in the beta-gamma range, and sequential 40 Hz waves. If seven 40 Hz cycles were nested together, the nesting oscillation would be in the alpha-theta range (5 to 12 Hz). Each cycle could be related to one item stored in the memory. This is in accordance with the Miller [8] short-term memory capacity: the magic number seven, plus or minus two. Sustained firing can be explained as a transient membrane after depolarization, that is refreshed on each cycle of a neural network oscillation [7]. The cycle could be related to the 38 ms reaction time observed in experiments with the short term memory [17].

In this work I explain the mind-brain link related to the Evoked Potentials, EP, triggered by verbal stimuli. N400 component, peaking around 400 ms post stimulus, appears to be an indicator of the semantic relationship between a word and the context in which it occurs [5, 18]. The N400 wave is completed in about 1.2 seconds. This corresponds to the frequency of about 0.8 Hz which is far away from the above alpha-theta range and from 40 Hz. In fact N400 timing is in the same range with the brain-window waveforms [10, 11] and with the Quantum Mind processes [12-15]. In the present study N400 component is explained as a reflection of the quantum processes [9] and of the Quantum Mind-brain link.

First, I identify EP's components and respective generator sources. I show that EP is generated by several flocks of agents defined by their Primary Oscillators, PO. I extend here the Quantum Mind theory to explain the interaction of the flocks of agents PO with the Flow of Favorable Factors, FFF, through the Quantum Mind barrier.

Second, I show that PO is controlled by the Sensation Element, SEL. SEL is formed through the interactions among flocks of agents, and through exchange of attributes. Hence SEL of one particular agent integrates attributes that arrive from other agents. The attributes include synaptic transmitter release; oscillator coupling; crosstalk; exchange of distinct phases; excitatory/inhibitory interactions.

Third I identify the quantum links stimulus-SEL-PO. These links are responsible for generation of the Primary Waveforms. Primary Waveform are not local primitives; rather they reflect holistic self-organization.

Fourth, I explain the forms of EP records as bundles of overlapped Primary Waveform. The obtained theoretical results are in excellent agreement with experimental EP records, triggered by verbal stimuli.

PRIMARY OSCILLATOR

In the Quantum Mind, the flocks of agents interact, without the leader or central control. Like in the school of fish, flock of birds or colony of ants, the behavior is built from the bottom-up. The result is a never ending chaotic self-organization, information compression and quantizing. Evoked Potential, EP is a visible manifestation of this dynamics of agents. The communication features of agent are controlled by an oscillator which defines the basic timing of behavior and communication. Hence, I call it the Primary Oscillator. The output of the Primary Oscillator is a Primary waveform, P(t), of a sinusoidal shape.

Upon receiving a stimulus, the agent modifies the operation of the Primary Waveform: constant period is changed into a waveform with a variable period (Figs. **1** and **2**). This modulation lasts for three or four cycles, after which time the period of oscillations is back to the original constant period. The variability of the cycles of the Primary Oscillator can be described with the phase-response curve (PRC). The PRC "Zeitgeberg" notation is used for biological clocks and their modulation. Each stimulus starts the phase-response curve and in this way modulates the oscillations of the oscillator. The oscillator's phase is presented in Fig. **3**. In Figs. **1**, **2** and **3**, abscissa is t/T1.

An alternative way to explain the modulation is to associate a memory to the Primary Oscillator. The memory accepts the stimulus and modulates the oscillations. However, the memory is not ideal and is slowly erased. Hence the modulator effect of the stimulus is strong immediately after the stimulation and slowly vanishes with time: the oscillations return to normal.

The modulated Primary waveform is shown in Figs. **1** and **2**. The Primary waveform is responsible for an inherent timing program that controls the communication and the behavior of the agents. The Primary waveform also controls the relationship between the stimulus and the response by narrowing and widening the receive and send windows. Hence the Primary waveform presents the basic, precise, and quantitative description of a part of the brain. I define the Primary waveform P(t) and its relation to the Evoked Potentials, EP, in the following way:

$$EP = \sum_i A_i \cdot P(t, T_i, D_i) \cdot G_i(t) \qquad (1)$$

$$G(t) = \begin{cases} 1 & \text{if } t < T_0 \\ 0 & \text{if } t \geq T_0 \end{cases} \qquad (2)$$

$$P(t) = \sin\left\{ 2\pi \left\{ \frac{t}{T1} + s \cdot F(t) \right\} \right\} \qquad (3)$$

$$F(t) = z \cdot e^{-g_1 \cdot (t-d)} + (1-z) \cdot e^{-g_2(t-d)} \qquad (4)$$

Ai = amplitude of the Primary Waveform

Ti = period of the Primary Waveform

τ_1 = co period of the Primary Waveform: Complete duration of the Primary Waveform

Di = Delay of the Primary Waveform relative to the stimulus

G(t) = a gate function, that defines how long after the stimulation the process is active

F(t) = a forgetting function. It is composed of two processes with time constant g1 and g2 and with the delay d. The parameter z defines the contributions of the two processes.

s = sum of linking attributes.

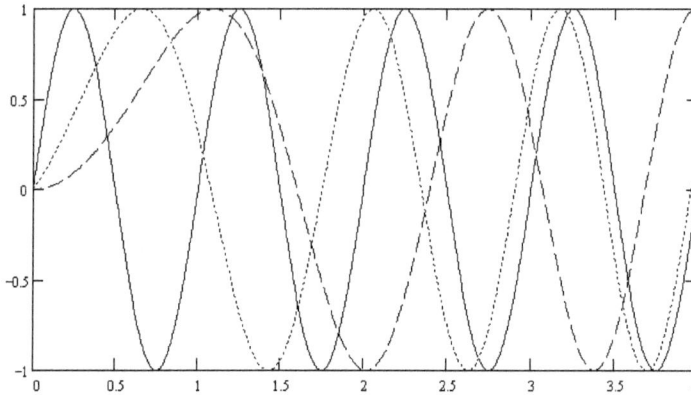

Figure 1: Primary Waveforms. Types $s = 2$; $s = 1$; $s = 0$.

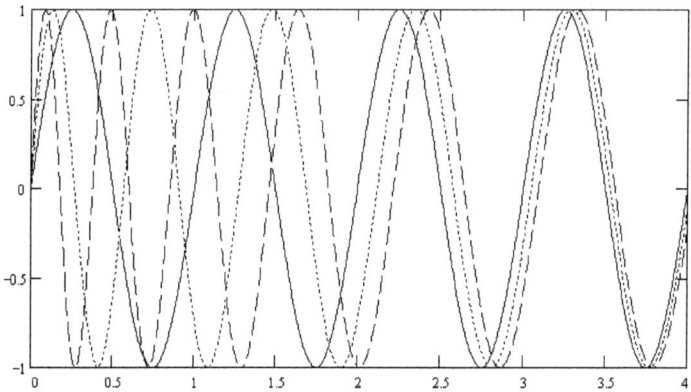

Figure 2: Primary Waveforms. Types $s = -2$; $s = -1$; $s = 0$.

Fig. **3** presents oscillators phase as a function of time, for the following values of s: -2, -1, 0, +1, +2

Fig. **1** presents P(t) for values of s: 0, 1, 2

P(t) for s = 0 is a non-modulated sin wave.

P(t) for s = 1 has longer initial cycles.

P(t) for s = 2 has much longer initial cycles.

Fig. **2** presents P(t) for values of s: 0, -1, -2.

P(t) for s =0 is a non-modulated sin wave.

P(t) for s = -1 has shorter initial cycles.

P(t) for s = -2 has much shorter initial cycles.

I will use Primary Waveforms to explain and to approximate brain sequences, including the Evoked Potentials. Primary Waveform is defined by a set of parameters from equations 1 to 4:

$$P(z, d, g_1, g_2, D, T_0, T_i, s)$$

Taking into account only most important parameters, Primary Waveform definition is reduced to:

$$P(g_1, T_i, s)$$

Crucial parameter in the Primary waveform is the sum s, of the Sensation Element Memory, SEL.

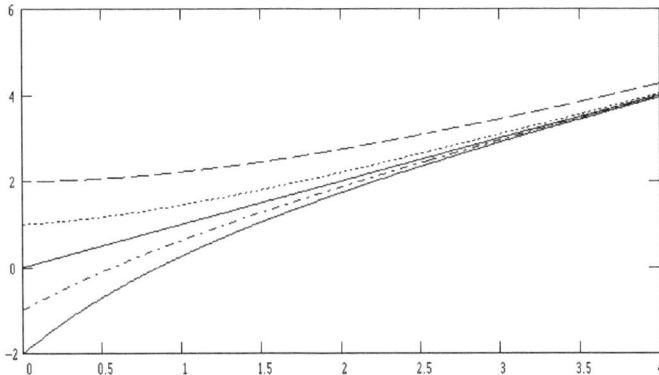

Figure 3: Phase of the oscillator for $s = 2$; $s = 1$; $s = 0$; $s = -1$; $s = -2$.

FLOCK OF PRIMARY WAVEFORMS

In the present study the evoked potential N400 will be explained through the attributes release during the verbal story that activates the associative chains and the associative search loops in the brain. The chains and loops involve the transmitter release, oscillator coupling, crosstalk, exchange of distinct phases, excitation and inhibition interactions. All these processes release the attributes that link the processes together. The linking attributes are accumulated into the sum s and stored in the Sensation Element memory, SEL. Hence the sum s is related to the past history of attribute releases.

- Continuous sum s defines a continuum composed of unlimited number of waveforms.

- Clustered sum s leads to the clustering of waveforms. The results are well defined waveforms types: 2, 1, 0, 1, -1, -2, *etc.* This case is presented in Figs. **1** to **4**.

- Quantum sum s leads to the complex probability distribution. This case is described in the Appendix and in Figs. **5** to **8**.

Primary waveforms of Fig. **1** are defined by the Sensation Element sum s: 0, 1, 2. These are Primary Waveforms type 0, 1, 2. Similarly Fig. **2** presents three waveforms defined by the sum s: 0, -1, -2. These are Primary Waveforms type 0, -1, -2. The gate function G(t) defines how long after stimulation the process is active.

Many Evoked Potentials records have been published so far. Take a typical EP record and cut it into short segments. In some cases, one segment will resemble one of the above Primary Waveforms. This kind of approximation concentrates on timing, rather than on amplitudes. Does the EP record composed of simple segments, becomes a sequence of Primary Waveforms?

Most EP segments will ask for more elaborate approximation, that involves two or several Primary Waveforms. In this case the waveforms collaborate in parallel or serially, to approximate the segment. For example the sum of three waveforms, properly shifted and scaled presents a good approximation of many complex EP segments. This includes EP triggered by verbal stimuli, containing so called N400 component. The closer in meaning the word is to expected sentence ending, the smaller the N400 wave. The sum of only three Primary Waveforms approximates the N400 wave: one waveform type-3, one waveform type -1, and one waveform type 0. The resulting EP is presented in Fig. **4**, and it is in excellent agreement with the experimental EP, measured in [5]. More examples of EP approximations using Primary Waveforms are presented in [15].

The inherent feature of the EP record in Fig. **4** is: the Primary waveform is distributed across the entire EP record. Cutting such EP record into segments would result in a loss of essential parts of Primary waveform. For this reason the entire record is approximated with overlapped Primary Waveforms.

What are the relations between Primary Waveforms and neural network structures and processes? For a long time talking, language, thinking and abstract capacities were attributed to Broca's and Wernicke's areas in frontal region of the left side of cortex. Today neurology focuses also on other cortical and subcortical areas to support the language and talking, which are strictly related to thinking as well as to the memory. Positron-emission tomography and functional magnetic resonance imaging show that the most complex aspects of behavior are not regulated in a single part of the brain, but are based on a distributed support. For all these reasons, I consider the mind as a distributed, quantum, dynamic space of agents and oscillators. The oscillators are controlled by sensory elements, that integrate synaptic transmitter release, oscillator coupling, crosstalk, exchange of distinct phases, excitatory and inhibitory interactions.

EVOKED POTENTIALS RELATED TO UNDERSTANDING

In the Quantum Mind dynamic space, flocks of agents generate flocks of concurrent sequences, composed of Primary Waveforms. The agents and the sequences interact, through chaotic self-organization. The sequences communication is orthogonal to their flow, using the brain window language. The result is a never ending data-compression and quantizing regulated by the Flow of Favorable Factors, FFF, through the Quantum Mind Barrier. A bundle of sequences serve to memorize an experience, which by itself is a sequence of events. The brain uses dominant events of experience sequence to index or to label the sequence. Some of these events may be part of another experience sequence. This is the base for multiple labeling, and hence for associations. The brain solves a new problem by comparing it to the right experience sequence stored in the memory.

In Semantic Priming [5, 17] experiments N400, a person is able to finish sentences, because he/she believes to know what words are coming next. Such expectations are based on associations among parts that come from several sequences of past experience. Evoked Potential, EP, is electrical activity of the brain recorded by the macro-electrode. It is generally believed, that the activity of single neuron is not more discernible in EP record.

Is this true also for individual brain sequences? Could we relate, say, N400 record to individual brain sequences and to the mind, sensation and perception processes?

Evoked Potential is generated by the dynamics of flocks of agents or oscillators. The resulting EP is not just a filtered sum of the activity of a large set of individual agents or oscillators. Instead, the agents space is determined by just a few dominant modes, binding the underlying agents. These dominant modes produce the dominant components in the recorded EP. In case of, say, N400 record, I identify three dominant components in EP. See Table **1**. In terms of Primary Waveforms these are: type -3; type -1; type 0. I relate these Primary Waveforms to the process of perception. The brain is making hypotheses about the world, and it changes them when unexpected occurrences contradict these working models. The resulting adaptation or understanding is a locking procedure between dominant components: the selective attention; the unexpected hypotheses and the sensory data stream. These dominant components are partially visible in EP as the dominant Primary Waveforms. See Table **1** and also Fig. **4**.

Table 1: Semantic Priming and Evoked Potentials

Sentence Ending	A_1	s_1	A_2	s_2	A_m	s_m	$(A_2-A_1)/A_1$
Unrelated	1	-3	1	-1	0.1	0	0
Related	1	-3	1.3	-1	0.1	0	0.3
Best Word	1	-3	2.5	-1	0.1	0	1.5

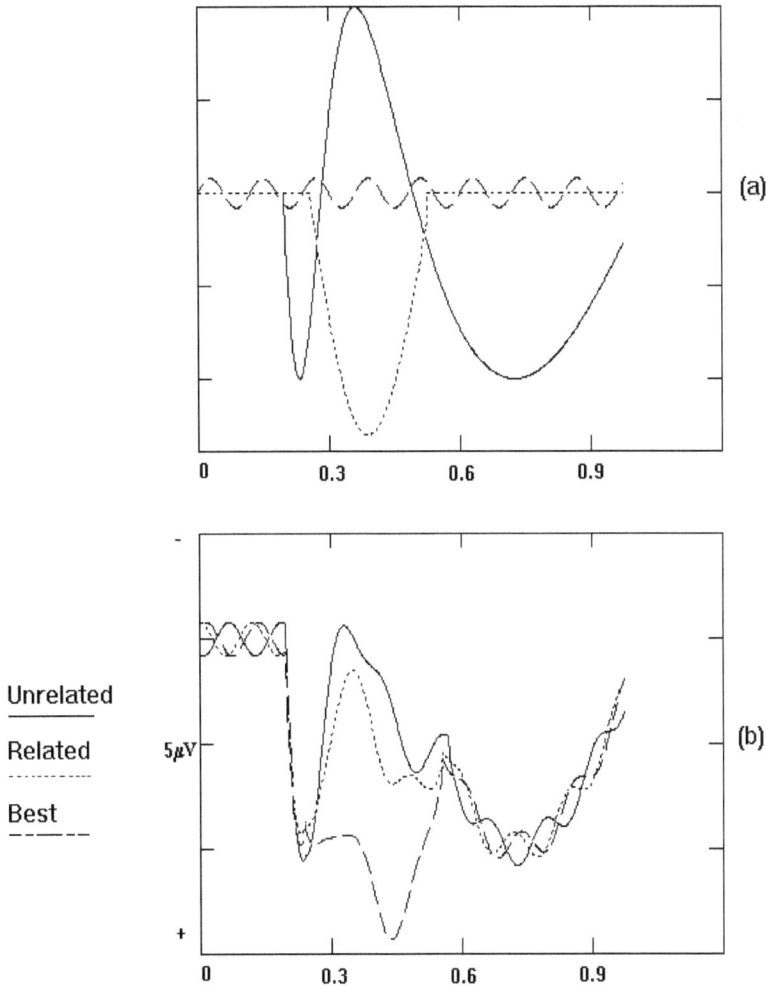

Figure 4: Evoked Potential triggered by a verbal stimulus, a) component Primary waveforms b) top to bottom: EP for unrelated; related; best sentence ending.

I conclude: Looking down, A_1, A_2 and A_3 of Table **1** indicate intensities of three dominant flocks of Primary Oscillators and of Primary Waveforms. Looking up, $(A_2-A_1)/A_1$ indicates the degree of semantic priming in sentence ending. In other words:

- flock of oscillators type (A_1, s_1) is related to the Sensory data stream. Its Co period τ_1 is about 1225 ms.

- flock of oscillators type (A_2, s_2) is related to the mental process of making hypotheses and to expectation $\tau_1 = \tau_2$.

- flock of oscillators type (A_m, s_m) is related to the selective attention, or semantic consciousness. It oscillates with the Co period τ_m of about 175 ms. Hence semantic consciousness frequency is about 5.7 Hz.

BRAMA NESTING AND UNDERSTANDING

The flocks of oscillators cooperate in the following way.

- flock (A_1, s_1) keeps the sensory data in the short-term memory for overall understanding.

- flock (A_2, s_2) searches for associations with the experience sequences stored in the long-term memory.

- flock (A_m, s_m) is a muster of the associative search.

In the sensory stream, data are coded in a dispersed form. The brain performs data compression and quantizing. In this way compact chunks are formed. Through associations, one item of the chunk recalls the other items of the same chunk. Also, multidimensional associations are formed, with overlaps between the categories.

The co period τ_1 is a sequence of seven co periods τ_m. Now I break each τ_m in a sequence of seven τ_a; and each τ_a in a sequence of seven τ_b. I noticed that $\tau_a = 25$ ms. Hence co period τ_a corresponds to 40 Hz wave, observed in experiments with the short term memory [7]. I also noticed the co periods τ_b in the Brain Steam Auditory Potential, BSAEPs. In [15], I have decomposed BSAEP into seven primary waveforms with the co periods τ_b of about 1 to 3.6 ms. Note: seven τ_b nested within τ_a.

The resulting 7x7x7 sequence forms the BRAMA fractal protocol:

BRA: BRAND THE FEATURES. Each τ_b is responsible for one information element.

AMA: AMASS THE CHUNKS. Each τ_a is responsible for one chunk and for associations within this chunk, in the short-term memory.

MA: MASTER THE ASSOCIATIONS. Finally, τ_m is responsible for a class of associations with chunks that come from the long-term memory.

BRAMA: UNDERSTANDING. Finally τ_l is responsible for a high dimensional overall associations between chunks.

The whole process exhibits the self-similarity between the macro and the micro sub processes. Co periods τ_m are nested within τ_l. Co periods τ_a are nested within τ_m. Co periods τ_b are nested within τ_a.

The folds and branches crisscross the brain surface and fill three-dimensional space, like the surface of a sponge. The brain's structural irregularity seems the same on macro and on micro scale, revealing undulations within undulations, branches within branches. For example, Purkinje network branching is self-similar on smaller and smaller scale. The nature of this branching is fractal.

Brain fractal structure and self-similarity between large scale and small scale, provide the key to the nonlinear dynamics of flocks of oscillators. Based on the above self-similarity, I explain the structure of the flocks in terms of recursion and nesting.

Recursive nested flocks are capable of generating deterministic non periodic chaotic process of great complexity, and rich of information. This chaos is a template for a class of stimulation sequences. The flock stores only a set of features related to the class. The chaotic process itself is not stored; it is generated when the flock receives the stimulus: resulting bundle of sequences presents an experience, which by itself is a sequence of events.

The mental process of understanding operates in the following way: the stimulation pattern passes through a classification, clustering, quantizing and the pattern flock is triggered: it generates a complex pattern chaos, a representative of a stimulus pattern. The stored experience is triggered and it generates a complex class chaos, a representative of the whole class. Class and pattern chaotic processes are constantly matched, and a degree of similarity is established.

Extracted class and pattern features update the memories of respective flocks of oscillators. If the pattern has been received before, updating has a small effect.

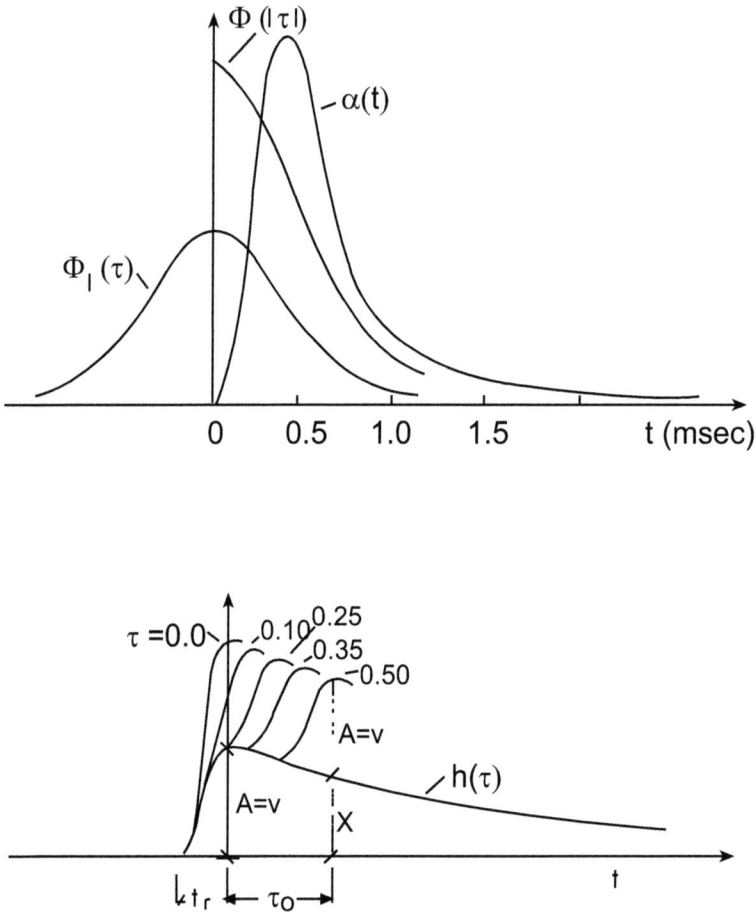

Figure 5: Upper: the distribution of $\alpha(t), \Phi(|\tau|), \Phi_1(\tau)$. Constant delay of ~0.5 msec for release rate is not shown because it does not influence the distribution. Lower: building Sensation amplitudes from two attributes with relative delays from 0 to 0.5

A bunch of $7 \cdot 7 \cdot 7$ sequences operate in parallel. Flocks of neural agents chaotically interact, converging to the common attractors. The evoked potential is a reflection of the above parallel, sequential, chaotic, associative activity. The relation $r = (A_2 - A_1)/A_1$ indicates the intensity of this activity.

- Unrelated event finds only a low-dimensional associations, t.e. itself. Hence the activity is weak, r = 0;

- Related event finds more associations. Medium activity, r = 0.3;

- Best event comes close to a complete, high dimensional associations. Strong Activity, r = 1,5.

The parallel sequences communicate with the association maps and with each other through the windows, using the Quantum Mind barrier traffic procedure. The Quantum Mind barrier with its windows could be considered an intelligent agents structure. It has inherited from the parents some predefined operations and knowledge. In the same time it is able to learn, to adapt, to carry a message or a content between agents, to identify and to switch the context. In other words, the Quantum Mind barrier supports the knowledge-learning features.

The adaptive co periods that come out of equation 3, depend on τ_1, s and F(t). One could read these co periods from Figs. **1** and **2**. The process of learning, as well as the adaptive co periods are parts of a never ending, chaotic Quantum Mind self-organization. The Continuous, Quantizing, Discrete processes, CQD, are crucial for the Quantum Mind self-organization. Adaptive, Discrete windows interact with the association maps through a release of Continuous as well as of Quantum attributes.

RESULTS AND CONCLUSIONS

The process of verbal understanding is built from the bottom-up, and yet it is regulated by the Quantum Mind Barrier and by BRAMA protocol. By comparing the experimental results with the computer model, this work points to the nested levels in BRAMA:

- co period τ_1 with about 7 nested waves of co period τ_m

- co period τ_m with about 7 nested waves of co period τ_a

- co period τ_a with about 7 nested waves of co period τ_b

The above time levels disinhibit the structure of windows in the Quantum Mind Barrier. Why the structure in all levels is based on the 7 information windows?

The answer is the Quantum Information Processing. The quantizing performs grouping, clustering, or round off of the continuous signal into the groups, clusters or classes. According to the Quantum Mind Theory, the quantizing reduces the system complexity. In random data processing, time averaging, correlations, event-train and neural spike processing, the quantizing step should be such that the bell-shaped signal's distribution is measured in at least eight steps. Quantizing into more than eight steps would increase the complexity, without improving the result.

This quantizing step explains why the short-term memory capacity is 7 chunks; why the sensitivity of human perception is 1/7, leading to the seven basic colors, seven basic tones, *etc.*

This quantizing step also explains why there are seven information windows in each level of the BRAMA protocol.

At the core of mind and brain is the quantum information.

DISCUSSION

An accurate understanding of the mechanics of the individual neurons and their interactions may be achieved, but that will reveal little about how brain processes information. The way out is to recognize a specific group of processes, and to extract the fundamental, common features. This work extracts the Primary Waveforms; and the flocks of Primary Oscillators. Presenting EP with the Primary Waveforms, establishes two missing links:

EP and Up: To the Mind and Behavioral Integral Processes

From Primary Waveforms up, to the flock of waveforms, experience sequences, chains of thoughts. The macro-level Primary Oscillators explains macro level records, such as EP and macro-level psychological phenomena.

EP and Down: To Neural Networks, to Structures, Features and Processes

From Primary Waveforms down, to the Brain Window logic and languages, receive and send windows, context switching. From Primary Waveforms, related to the micro-level, embedded Primary Oscillators to micro-level communication and neural network processes.

In conclusion, Primary Waveforms relate in a new way the neural network and brain features and processes to mind and behavior integral processes. Primary Waveforms will have direct impact on research, neurological diagnoses and testing.

The brain breeds the whole group of oscillator structures, that produce the same EP. The structures within the group are not necessarily similar. Some of these structures are quite different from the rest of the group. Multiplicity of structures suggest that two segments of EP records might look alike, and yet they might be reflections of two different internal structures. However these two different internal structures can support the same mental process, realized in two different ways. Multiplicity of structures comes as a result of genetic factors, as well as acquired experience. Because EP, and related mental process, can be the outcome of more than one structure, it cannot be linked with any one structure, but rather with the group of structures.

The mental process can be the outcome of more than one dynamic organization. Stimulus X leads to the dynamic organization X. Yet, next time stimulus X will lead to another dynamic organization Y. This is due to the highly sensitive nonlinear dynamics of flocks of oscillators. Just a slight variation in conditions will generate sequence Y, rather than X. Competing flocks of oscillators specialize on stimulus pattern. Every time a stimulus pattern is presented, a self-organization process increases the specificity with which an oscillator reacts to patterns. Finally, the system settles to a state, where one mode dominates. This mode is related to the perception pattern class. Hence sequences X, Y, *etc.*, might converge to the same dominant mode of oscillations. The dominant mode reflects the extent to which stimulus and hypotheses are related, rather than to the specific response to the stimulus. EP record is a visible manifestation of the above process.

Holistic mental self-organization, behind EP record, cannot be completely reduced to localized, logical primitives. Primary waveforms are not localized, primitive elements. Rather they reflect the dynamics of distributed information compression and of nonlinear, chaotic interaction within the Quantum Mind space. Primary waveforms have been used here to correlate EP records with the mind and brain processes. Computer generated EP records, based on Primary waveforms of Table **1**, are presented in Fig. **4**. They are in excellent agreement with EP records measured in [5]: for unrelated, related and the best stimulus word.

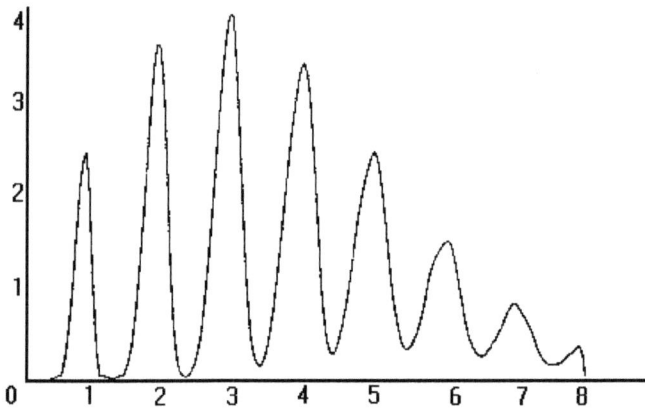

Figure 6: The distribution function f(s) for v = 1, σ =0.1, m = 4, no latency fluctuation.

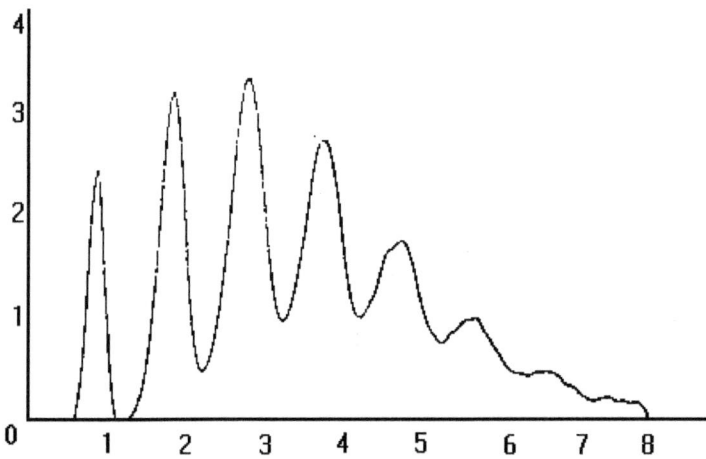

Figure 7: The distribution function *f(s)* for *v* = 1, σ =0.1, *m* = 4, $\alpha(t)$ and *h(t)* as in Fig. **5**.

APPENDIX: QUANTUM PROCESS OF ATTRIBUTE RELEASE

Sensation Element, SEL, integrates the attributes released by the stimulus. I assume that attributes are released in packets of an approximately constant size, that the packets are released in an all-or-none fashion, and that the total amount of attributes released must be some integral multiple of the least unit. Furthermore, release of packets is not a deterministic phenomenon, but rather is probabilistic; thus the number of packets released by a stimulus varies in a random fashion from stimulus to stimulus and, in some instances, attributes release fails to occur.

Suppose that a large population of excitable units is available, each unit capable of responding to a stimulus by producing a unit attribute, or quantum. Suppose further, that even in the absence of a stimulus, there is small probability of spontaneous response from any given unit. Then the number of quanta which make up the SEL should fluctuate in a manner described by Poisson's law. If the mean quantum content m is known, the theoretical distribution of the SEL amplitudes can be calculated from the mean v and variance of the spontaneous amplitude distribution. Such calculation is based on the assumption that the quantum release is instantaneous and coincident and that the spontaneous attributes amplitude distribution is Gaussian.

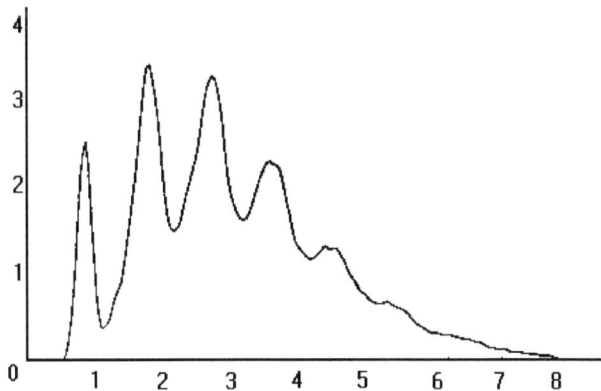

Figure 8: The distribution function f(s) for v = 1, σ =0.1, m = 4, $\alpha(t)$ as in Fig. **5**, h(t) 50% faster fall time.

In fact the quantum release is not instantaneous, but rather fluctuates in a random way; attribute amplitude distributions can be skewed rather than Gaussian. I develop here a general theory taking into account random fluctuation of release times, skewed distribution of attributes, and influence of pulse shapes of attributes as in [9]. The attributes include transmitter release; oscillator coupling; crosstalk; exchange of distinct phases; excitation/inhibition interactions.

In the absence of stimulation, attributes packets are released at random intervals with a low probability. The number of units released by a stimulus follow a Poisson distribution. After stimulation the release rate $\alpha(t)$ rapidly increases to a high value and then returns to the resting level. The time course of $\alpha(t)$ is shown in Fig. **5**. The same unit potentials of, say, 0.25 msec rise time and 0.5 mv size can appear as early as 0.5 msec and as late as 2.6 msec after the arrival of the stimulus. This indicates that the stimulus is followed by a period of a few milliseconds during which the probability of quantum release is increased as shown in Fig. **5**. The latency fluctuations can, therefore, be explained as a statistical consequence of the quantum mechanism of attributes release.

My goal is to obtain an expression for amplitude distribution $f(s)$ of SEL's. The amplitudes of SEL, are composed of a sum of attributes whose amplitudes we shall denote by A. Attribute amplitudes are randomly distributed with distribution function $P(A)$. The number of attribute units composing a SEL is Poisson distributed. Hence, the probability distribution of the SEL's amplitude s, which is composed of $1,2,3,..,k$ attributes, will be:

$$f(s) = \frac{e^{-m}}{0!} \cdot g_0(s) + \frac{e^{-m}}{1!} \cdot m^1 \cdot g_1(s) + ... + \frac{e^{-m}}{k!} \cdot m^k \cdot g_k(s) \qquad (5)$$

I have inserted into the Poisson distribution the functions $g_0(s)$. $g_k(s)$ which will be used to describe different ways of summation of the attributes into SEL. The results are presented in Figs. **6** to **8**. Amplitude s is normalized to s/v.

The first term of equation (5) describes the number of failures to responses. For such cases $s=0$, hence

$$g_0(s) = \delta(s) \qquad (6)$$

The function $\delta(s)$ is used to denote that the function is different from zero only in one point, in this case for $s=0$.

The second term describes the cases when SEL response is composed of only one attribute, hence s and A will have the same probability distribution function.

$$g_1(s) = P(A) \cdot \delta(s) = P(s) \tag{7}$$

The third term describes the cases when SEL response is composed of two attributes added to each other, Fig. **4** lower part. One attribute is added with a full amplitude, A, the other one with fractional amplitude x because of the delay between them. Fraction x has a distribution function $g(x)$ which will be derived later. As $s=A+x$, its distribution function $g_2(s)$ can be obtained according to the theorem for the sum of two independent stochastic processes.

The sum will have the value s, if one variable has the value A, and the other one the value $x=s-A$. The probability of having the above combination is

$$P(A) \cdot g(x) = P(A) \cdot g(s - A) \tag{8}$$

As A can have any value between $-\infty$ and $+\infty$ there will be a large number of combinations, forming the value s. Probabilities of all those combinations, when integrated, form the probability of s:

$$g_2(s) = \int_{-\infty}^{+\infty} P(A) \cdot g(s - A) dA \tag{9}$$

The integral of this kind is known as a convolution,

$$g_2(s) = P^+(A) * g(x)$$

In a similar way, one can conclude:

$$g_3(s) = P(A) * g(x) * g(x),$$

$$g_k(s) = P(A) * g(x) * . * g(x) = g_k(s) * g(x)$$

I use experimental data available in the area of quantum transmitter release. The latency fluctuation $\alpha(t)$ is shown in Fig. **5**. The $\alpha(t)$ curve is composed on the basis of experimental data from the measurement of the time course of acetylcholine in a frog muscle. Constant delay of ~0.5 msec for release rate $\alpha(t)$ is not shown because it does not influence the process. The pulse shape h(t) of attributes, has exponential form. Its amplitude, rise time, and half-fall time depend on the distance from the stimulus focus, on the temperature, *etc.* In mammalian muscle, the rise time and the half-fall time are about one-half and one-third, respectively, of the corresponding values for the frog attributes.

Attributes amplitude distribution function P(A) can be represented with the Gaussian distribution, having the mean value ~0.5 mv, and coefficient of variation (*i.e.* standard deviation divided by the mean), between 0.1 and 0.2. The value depend largely on the experimental conditions and the noise level in the system. In this analysis, I take the value 0.1.

Using equations 5 and 9 I can describe different models for building SEL from attributes. I start with the simplest model and gradually take more and more parameters into account going toward more realistic models. On the basis of this theory, a computer program for calculation of SEL's distribution function f(s) has been written. The program reads experimental data describing $\alpha(t)$, h(t), P(A) and m and plots the functions f(s). The program can be used to describe different models for building SEL's from attributes.

(a)   Arbitrary Distribution of attributes and immediate **response**. For this case we have $x=A$ and

$$g_1(s)=P(s)$$

$$g(x)=P(x)$$

because each attribute is added with a full amplitude. Hence

$$g_k(s)=P(A)*P(x)*. *P(x) \tag{10}$$

This expression is valid regardless of the form of *P(A)* which can be normal or skewed. For normal distribution we have:

$$g_1(s) = normal(v,\sigma)$$

$$g(s) = normal(v, \sigma)$$

The convolution of the normal distribution (v, σ) by itself produces again normal distribution $(2v, \sqrt{2}\sigma)$. After k convolutions, we have:

$$g_k(s) = normal(kv, \sqrt{k}\sigma)$$

according to the law for addition of normal random variables. Hence

$$f(s) = \frac{e^{-m}}{0!} \cdot \delta(s) + ... + \frac{e^{-m}}{k!} \cdot m^k \cdot normal(kv, \sqrt{k}\sigma) \tag{11}$$

The distribution is shown in Fig. **6**.

(b)   Random times, constant amplitude v of attributes. Suppose that attributes have a constant amplitude $A=v$ but their time of arrival is governed by the variable rate $\alpha(t)$, as shown in Fig. **5**. Let attributes have pulse shapes given by

$$x = v * h(t) \tag{12}$$

Suppose that SEL is composed of two attributes with times of arrival t_1 and t_2. The peak amplitude s of SEL will then be

$$s = v + x$$

That mean one of the attributes is added with a full amplitude v, the other with the fraction x, which is a function of delay:

$$\tau = t_1 {}_- t_2$$

As we are measuring maximum amplitude at $t=t_r$, it follows

$$x = v\, h(t_r + t_1 - t_2) = v\, h(t_r + \tau) \tag{13}$$

The probability distribution of t_1 and t_2 are equal and given by the distribution $\alpha(t)$. Hence $\tau = t_1 {}_- t_2$ presents the sum of two random variables. In the same way as in the case of equation (9), the distribution $\Phi_1(\tau)$ of the sum is expressed by the convolution

$$\Phi_1(\tau) = \alpha(t) * \alpha(-\tau) \tag{14}$$

It is not important which attribute is regarded as first. Hence, we can conclude that $\Phi_1(\tau) = \Phi_1(-\tau)$ and take into account the distribution for $|\tau|$

$$\Phi(|\tau|) = 2 \cdot \alpha(\tau) * \alpha(-\tau) \tag{15}$$

The distributions $\alpha(t), \Phi(|\tau|), \Phi_1(\tau)$ and summation of two or more attributes are illustrated in Fig. **5**.

The distribution of the fraction x, used in addition, can be calculated from equations (13) and (15). We have random variable τ, with the distribution $\Phi(\tau)$. This variable is transformed into the variable x = x(t), equation (13), whose distribution $\rho(x)$ we want to calculate. The distribution $\rho(x)$ will be function of $\Phi(\tau)$ and x(t); it can be obtained according to the theorem for transformation of the random variable

$$\rho(x) = \frac{\Phi|\tau_a|}{|h'(\tau_a)|} + ... + \frac{\Phi|\tau_s|}{|h'(\tau_s)|} \tag{16}$$

where $\tau_a ... \tau_s$ are root of equation (13). For the pulse shape, h(t), of attributes, as shown in Fig. **4**, there will always be only one root τ_a for a given fraction, x. We now have

$$g_1(s) = P(s) = \delta(s - v)$$
$$g(x) = \rho(x)$$
$$g_2(s) = \delta(s - v) * \rho(x) \tag{17}$$
$$g_k(s) = \delta(s - v) * \rho(x) \cdot ... \cdot \rho(x)$$

From Fig. **5** we can conclude that the most probable fraction, x, will be v and that the probability distribution, $\rho(x)$, will exponentially decrease as x tends to 0.

(c) Random times, random amplitudes of attributes. We come now to complete model in which both times of arrivals and amplitudes of attributes are random variables with distribution function $\Phi(\tau)$ and P(A). The difference from the previous case is that the fraction x is now a function of P(A). Knowing $\rho(x)$ for $A = v =$ constant, one can calculate the distribution g(x) for the case when A is a random variable. If $A =$ constant $= 1$, the distribution of the fraction x will be $\rho(x)$, equation (16). If amplitude is A instead of 1, the distribution will have the same shape but the scale will be multiplied by A. Hence it will be

$$\frac{1}{A} \cdot \rho\left(\frac{x}{A}\right)$$

As A can have value between $+\infty$ and $-\infty$ there will be a large number of cases producing the value x. All these cases, multiplied by the probability for a given A, and integrated, will form the probability for

$$g(x) = \int_A P(A) \cdot \rho\left(\frac{x}{A}\right) \cdot \frac{1}{A} dA \tag{18}$$

We now have

$g_1(s) = P(s)$

$g_2(s) = P(A) * g(x) \tag{19}$

$g_3(s) = P(A) * g(x) *. * g(x)$

If attributes have pulse shapes as shown in Fig. **5**, and if P(A) is normal distribution, the g(x) will be of similar shape as $\rho(x)$ but with rounded ends around v, where v is the mean value of attributes amplitudes. This case is illustrated in Figs. **7** and **8**.

DISCLOSURE

"The content of this chapter has been previously published by *Periodicum Biologorum, Vol. 100, No. 2, 129 - 140,1998*".

REFERENCES

[1] Hebb DO. The Organization of Behavior. Wiley New York 1949.

[2] Kihlstrom J F. The Continuum of Consciousness. Consciousness & Cognition 1993; 334-354.

[3] Knowlton BJ, Square LR. The Learning of Natural Categories: Parallel Memory Systems for Item Memory and Category-Level Knowledge. Science 1993;262, 1747-1749.

[4] Koch C, Davis JL, Eds. Some Further Ideas, Regarding the Neuronal Bases of Awareness in Large Scale Neuronal Theories of the Brain. MIT Press Cambridge MA 1994.

[5] Kutas M, Hillyard SA. Brain Potentials During Reading Reflect Word Expectancy and Semantic Associations. Nature 1984; 307, 161-163.

[6] Kutas M, Iragui V, Hillyard SA. Effects of Aging on Event Related Potentials (ERPs), in a Visual Detection Task. EEG Clinic Neurophysiology 1994; 92, 126-129.

[7] Lisman JE, Idiart AP. Storage of 7 ± 2 Short-Term Memories in Oscillatory Sub-cycles. Science 1995; 267, 1512-1515.

[8] Miller GA. The Magic Number Seven, Plus or Minus Two. Psychology Rev 1956; 63, 81-97.

[9] Souček B. Influence of the Latency Fluctuations and the Quantum Process of Transmitter Release on the End-Plate Potentials' Amplitude Distribution. Biophysical Journal 1971; 11, 127-139.

[10] Souček B, Carlson AD. Brain Windows in Firefly Communication. Journal of Theoretical Biology 1986;119, 47-65.

[11] Souček B, Carlson AD. Brain Windows Language in Fireflies. Journal of Theoretical Biology 1987; 125, 93-103.

[12] Souček B. The Quantum Mind. Period Biologorum1996;98, 1, 67-76.

[13] Souček B. The Quantum Mind Theory. Period Biologorum1997; 99, 1, 3-18.

[14] Souček B. Quantum Mind Networks. FESB Split;ISBN: 953-6114.20-8.1997.

[15] Souček B, Abbattista F, Bellifemine F, Dalbis D. Quantum Mind Breeder. Period Biologorum 1998; 100, 2, 211-217.

[16] Squire LR, Knowlton B, Mussen G. The Structure and Organization of Memory. Ann Rev Psychol 1993; 44, 453-495.

[17] Sternberg S. High Speed Scanning in Human Memory. Science 1973;153, 652.

[18] Stuss DT, Sarazin F, Leech E, Picton TW. In Brain Information: Event related Potentials. Monogr. (eds. Karreer R.; Cohen J. and Tueting P.), New York Accademy of Sciences 1982.

[19] The BRAMA names have been inspired by my children, Branko, Amalia and Marina.

INDEX

A

Abstractions, 157

Agent, 3, 166

Alpha theta range, 185

AMA amass the chunk, 140

Anesthesis, 3

Association, 157

Attribute release, 201

B

Bank, 3, 16

Base, 3, 16, 29, 47, 74

BILO, 135

Biology, 3, 74, 142

Bird, 135, 165

Body, 3

Brain, 3, 16, 29, 47, 74

Brain agent universe, 134, 165

Brain barrier, 166

Brain internal language BILO, 135

Brain event train, 3, 29, 74

Brain mind signs, 96

Brain mind tissue, node, group, flock, pool, 133, 147, 159

Brain network, computing, cooperation, 133, 134, 147

Brain windows, 136

BRAMA, 133, 194

BRAMA principle, 133

BRA brand the features, 140

BRAMA protocol, 133

BRAMA waves, 140

Brain network age, 182

Business, 3, 46

Learning, 3, 96, 163
Life, 3, 16
LIFEBIZ, 3, 16
LIFEBIZ laws, 3
LIFEBIZ Manifesto, 3
Long term memory, 157
Lower pons, 141

M

Market, 3, 16
Master the associations, 140
Mental process, 199
Message quantum, 139, 165
Mid upper pons, 141
Mimicry, 3, 16
Mind, 3, 16, 184
Mind computer interface, 184
Mind reading machine, 184
Mind tissue, 3
Money, 3, 16

N

Neural diagnosis, 184
Neural net, 3, 16, 199
Nodes and groups, 149
Normal distribution, 204, 205

O

Operation, 3
Organization, 3
Overlapp, 184

P

Packaging, 29, 158

www.ingramcontent.com/pod-product-compliance
Lightning Source LLC
Chambersburg PA
CBHW050840220326
41598CB00006B/410